DESIGN, BUILD & SCALE

The Roadmap to Success for Product Manager

By

Shady Ramadan

ISBN: 978-0-6459291-3-3

DEDICATION

To my wife and children

In this special moment, I want to say thank you. Thank you for being the light in my life, the ones who stand by me, and the reason I keep dreaming.

My wife, you've been right there with me through every up and down, encouraging me, believing in me when I doubted myself, and you were there for me when I needed it most. Your love has been my strength, and your faith in me has made me reach further than I ever imagined.

And to my kids, you've been part of this journey from the start. Your questions, your laughter, and your belief in me have added so much happiness and motivation to my days. You make everything I do feel even more worthwhile.

This book is for you, my family. You're my support, and my everything. Without you, none of this would be real.

Thank you for being my biggest fans and my home.

With all my love,

Shady Ramadan

ACKNOWLEDGMENT

As I reflect on the journey that led to this book, my heart overflows with gratitude for the incredible people who have been part of my path. My venture in business wasn't straightforward—starting in the energetic yet traditional field of sales and marketing, quickly transitioning into the digital marketing era leading me to finally dive into the innovative new world of product management.

The field of product management was an unexpected challenge, pushing me into an intense process of discovery. I absorbed every resource I could — from books to videos, articles, and podcasts —driven by a passion to excel in what quickly became my true calling.

A heartfelt thank you to my colleagues and managers. Your challenges, inspiration, and high expectations have provided invaluable lessons that have shaped my growth both personally and professionally. Our debates and discussions have been vital, enriching my journey in ways I cannot fully express.

This journey of learning extends to everyone I've collaborated with across sales, finance, customer service, marketing, and the executive team. Your insights have been a fountain of knowledge, shaping my perspective and approach. Thank you for sharing your time and wisdom so generously.

A special shout-out to my daughter, Rawan, and my sons, Abdelrahman, and Ahmed. Rawan, your drawings in this book carry your unique signature, adding a deeply personal touch to these pages. Abdelrahman, our discussions and your careful review of the drafts have been incredibly valuable. Ahmed, your passion and encouragement to press forward have been truly remarkable.

And to you, the reader, I extend my deepest gratitude. Your engagement with this book represents both an honor and a profound responsibility. It is my sincere hope that the insights and experiences shared within these pages not only inspire you but also empower you to reach new heights in the ever-evolving and dynamic world of product management.

With all my gratitude,

Shady Ramadan

ABOUT THE AUTHOR

Shady Ramadan stands out as a professional in product management, renowned for his strategic foresight and ground breaking approach across diverse sectors including pharmaceutical, digital health, retail, FMCG, automotive, eCommerce, and Fintech. With a rich career spanning over two decades, Shady has become known with leading digital transformations, pioneering product innovations, and building effective scaling strategies. His deep industry insight and extensive experience have solidified his reputation as a leader capable of navigating complex market dynamics.

Driven by a natural curiosity and a strong passion for digital transformation, Shady's path led him from sales and marketing to the forefront of product innovation. His leadership roles at Aster DM Healthcare and Majid Al Futtaim - Carrefour in Dubai, UAE, underscore his expertise at building products from inception to market success. Notably, amongst these are his efforts concluded in the launch of the UAE's premier healthcare super app and a significant uplift in Carrefour's customer experience and online expansion.

Shady's expertise extends beyond product management; he has also excelled in key marketing leadership roles. His dedication to customer engagement and a nuanced understanding of the customer journey have enriched his product management approach, enabling deeper customer connections and adding substantial value.

Shady's academic credentials include an MBA in Marketing from The University of Leicester, complemented by specialized certifications in AI and Machine Learning in Healthcare from Stanford University, Scrum Master certification, and a series of professional development courses in analytics, consumer experience design, and leadership.

This comprehensive background has given Shady the unique capability to tackle the specific challenges of each industry he ventures into, applying his product management skills to drive innovation and adaptability. Throughout his career, he has led product teams to launch numerous digital initiatives, clearly impacting company growth and enhancing market presence.

At the heart of Shady's work is a deep-seated commitment to delivering outstanding customer experiences. His talent for transforming abstract concepts into concrete products that resonate with customers and drive business growth is unparalleled.

PREFACE

Welcome to the dynamic world of product management – a field where constant evolution mirrors the ever-changing landscape of business, technology, and market needs. In this fast-paced journey, staying a step ahead isn't just about keeping up; it's about being agile, adopting innovative thinking, and deeply understanding the digital transformation that's reshaping our world.

Through my years of leading and coaching product teams, I've seen a pattern of misconceptions about what it truly means to be a Product Manager. For some, it's seen as a marketing role; for others, it's about collaborating with the engineering team to build the product. In truth, the role encapsulates a larger landscape. It's a multifaceted role that binds these elements and more, creating a unique blend of skills and responsibilities. This confusion isn't limited to the outside world; it is often strongly prevalent within our own organizations, even among us, the Product Managers. Have you ever found yourself wondering about the fine line between your role and that of a project or program manager? Exactly!!!You're not alone.

Think of product management as the driving force in today's race for innovation. As a Product Manager, you're leading ventures from the spark of an idea to their emergence as market disruptors across diverse industries. You are the voice of the customer, the strategist crafting the vision, and the lifeblood of your business's success.

In my interactions with Product Managers, from those taking their first steps to seasoned professionals, one challenge stands out: balancing the deep passion for creating groundbreaking products with the grim realities of tight deadlines and demanding requirements. Ever found yourself so wrapped up in release cycles that you missed out on crucial opportunities? Let's change that story. The role of a Product Manager is definitely challenging, but equally rewarding.

So, why this book, and why now? The idea for this book sparked over four years ago from a simple question: "Do we need another book on product management?" While many excellent books exist, from which I have learned a lot, I always felt something was missing. A different kind of book is needed, not just another manual; it should provide a fresh perspective for everyone stepping into this field or looking to level up their skills.

With over a decade of experience in delivering professional training, coaching, and mentoring, I envisioned a book that bridges theory with real-world experiences. A guide that not only walks you through concepts but also ties them into actual case studies and provides actionable steps. Think of it as your playbook for translating ideas into real-world success.

'Design, Build & Scale: The Roadmap to Success for Product Managers' is designed to be your comprehensive guide through the evolving story of product management. We'll dive into the latest trends, technologies, and best practices, all tailored to foster your growth and success in this field.

Together, we'll cover everything essential for a successful product journey – from shaping a compelling vision and developing a robust strategy to understanding customer needs and fostering effective team collaboration. We'll also venture into the worlds of Big Data, AI, and Digital Health, equipping you with strategies to navigate these thrilling areas.

Whether you are just starting or seeking to enhance your skills, this book will be your companion on the journey towards mastery and success. Let's embark on this path of discovery and innovation, unlocking your potential to build products that not only meet but exceed the rapidly evolving market's expectations. Are you ready to take the first step?

INTRODUCTION

Reflect on the last two decades, and you'll notice a profound transformation that's raced across our world, driven not just by rapid technological advancements but by the creation of groundbreaking products. Consider the impact of the iPhone, Facebook, Airbnb, or Uber. These innovations have done more than change the market; they've revolutionized how we communicate, travel, socialize, and conduct our daily lives.

At the heart of this revolution is product management. It's the discipline that, when mastered, turns innovative ideas into products that redefine market expectations. It combines strategic foresight, customer empathy, and a nuanced understanding of the interchange between technology, market needs, and user experience.

Let's begin by understanding what we mean by a 'product.' It's more than just a tangible item or a service; it's a solution to a problem, a means to fulfill a need, be it active or passive. Whether it's a smartphone or an online service, the ultimate goal is to create value for the customer. In the digital age, this often focuses on digital products like software, mobile apps, and e-books, which are known for their global reach, scalability, and personalized experiences.

So, what is product management? Think of it as the captain of a ship, steering an idea from conception to market launch. It's an art and a science, involving market research, vision development, team collaboration, and execution. Product management addresses the 'why,' 'what,' and 'when' of a product—identifying market and customer needs ('why'), defining the product that meets these needs ('what'), and strategizing its development and launch ('when').

The role of a Product Manager is different within organizations, driven by one key concern: 'How can our product effectively solve customer problems?' This perspective is crucial for a product's success, aiming not just to meet customer needs but to enrich their lives with innovative and practical solutions.

Martin Eriksson, a leading figure in product leadership, describes product management as the intersection of business, user experience, and technology. This concisely captures the essence of the role: aligning product development with business goals, prioritizing user experience, and leveraging technology to add continuous value.

Take Netflix as an example. Its growth to a leading streaming platform was a thoughtful mastery of these elements: aligning its business strategy to stand out in the streaming market, prioritizing a user-friendly experience, and using advanced technology for personalized, seamless viewing experiences.

Who is a Product Manager, then? It's challenging to pin down a single definition. Product Managers are strategists, empathetic leaders, researchers, data analysts, team facilitators, and decision-makers. They bridge business objectives with customer needs, ensuring products not only solve core problems but also add significant value.

To fully appreciate the role, understanding its evolution offers deeper insights. Did you know the concept of a Product Manager dates back to the 1930s? The role has evolved significantly since then, reflecting changes in markets, technology, and business strategies. Let's explore this evolution and understand how Product Managers have become integral to success in today's fast-paced, innovation-driven world.

The Evolution of Product Management

Today, product management is central in steering the lifecycle and success of products. Yet, its evolution is far from a linear path, shaped by rapid technological changes and shifts in the industry landscape. Let's revisit a key moment that set the stage for the birth of the Product Manager role.

In 1931, amidst the Great Depression, Neil H. McElroy at Procter & Gamble wrote a revolutionary memo. He identified a significant gap in the company's product development strategy, advocating for the creation of 'brand men'—individuals wholly dedicated to a product's development, marketing, and financial success. This idea of holistic product ownership was revolutionary, laying the basis for the modern Product Manager role.

McElroy's vision didn't just transform Procter & Gamble. It also influenced David Packard and Bill Hewlett of Hewlett-Packard (HP), whom McElroy mentored at Stanford University. They adopted this holistic approach at HP, reinforcing it as a cornerstone of the company's success.

The journey of product management also saw significant advancements outside the United States. In post-war Japan, companies like Toyota were redefining product management in manufacturing. Toyota's Just-in-Time (JIT) methodology and the Kanban system minimized costs and maximized efficiency, influencing global manufacturing principles and workflow management across industries.

By the 1970s, with the tech industry's rise, the agile methodology began to replace traditional manufacturing approaches, inspiring the Product Manager's role. The 1980s saw this role becoming a core in profit-driven businesses. The Agile Manifesto's release in 2001 was another landmark, challenging norms and setting the stage for modern product management practices.

In the last two decades, the introduction of digital products, AI, and big data has once again reshaped the Product Manager's role. Today, Product Managers navigate a complex landscape, balancing technological innovations with customer needs and business goals. They lead cross-functional teams, turning ideas into products that resonate in our rapidly changing global market.

This ongoing transformation highlights product management's critical role in current business. As we explore deeper, we'll discover how these historical milestones have shaped current practices, preparing Product Managers to tackle the challenges of a digitally interconnected world.

ABOUT THIS BOOK

'Design, Build & Scale: The Roadmap to Success for Product Managers' is more than just a book—it's your comprehensive playbook for mastering product management. Our journey through these pages is structured into three pivotal stages of the product development lifecycle: Design, Build, and Scale. Each stage is crafted to guide you through the key phases of bringing a product from concept to market leader.

Design: Dive into the creative side of product management. You'll learn the art of ideation, how to write a compelling product vision, conduct impactful user research, and adopt innovative product discovery practices. We'll navigate the process of designing intuitive user experiences and validate your Product-Market Fit with Minimum Viable Product (MVP) for market success, setting a solid foundation for your product journey.

Build: Step into the Agile world, where flexibility and efficiency rule. This section explains Agile development practices, offering insights into effective team collaboration, product development, backlog management, and prioritization techniques. You'll gain the skills to smoothly transition your MVP into a fully-fledged market offering, ready for user adoption.

Scale: Focus on elevating your product's reach and impact. Explore strategies for adapting your product over its lifecycle, understand the complexities of crossing the chasm between early adopters and the mass market, and master the art Product-Led Growth (PLG) strategies, showcasing how to leverage PLG as a cornerstone for scaling in today's competitive landscape.

That's not all though, we have included a dedicated chapter on the crucial role of data analysis in product management. From gathering and analyzing data to visualizing insights and making data-driven decisions, this chapter will enhance your skills in leveraging customer insights for strategic advantage.

Additionally, two specialized chapters tackle the challenges and opportunities of managing products in the new era of Big Data, AI, and digital health. These chapters equip you with the knowledge and skills to navigate the complexities of today's tech-driven market.

The book's modular format allows you to dive into the sections most relevant to your current challenges or interests. The key to getting the most out of this book is implementation. With each chapter, pause at the step-by-step guides, review the examples, apply them to your own product context, and seek feedback to refine your approach. This cycle—from theory to practice, to real-world application—completes your training in product management.

Are you ready to start on this transformative journey? Turn the page, and let's dive into mastering the art and science of product management together!

CHAPTER 1
BUILDING THE VISION OF YOUR PRODUCT

"Start with the end in mind." This powerful advice from Steven Covey's "The 7 Habits of Highly Effective People" resonates deeply with the essence of product management. Every groundbreaking product starts with a simple idea—a vision that acts as your North Star, drawing the path from concept to market reality.

A well-defined, vision is essential for crafting a product that not only meets user needs but also shapes a unique position in the market and achieves your business goals. In fact, McKinsey & Company found that companies driven by an inspiring product vision are twice as likely to achieve above-average revenue growth compared to those without one.

Icons like Steve Jobs and Henry Ford didn't just dream big; they had visions that fundamentally transformed their respective industries. Jobs envisioned "a computer for the rest of us," guiding Apple's product design and market strategy to unparalleled heights. Ford's Model T went beyond being just another car; it revolutionized mobility for the average person through innovative manufacturing and distribution methods.

In this chapter, let's dive into the art of dreaming big and the science of strategic planning. We'll start by defining a product vision and revealing its critical role. Next, we'll break down the elements of crafting a compelling vision and how to articulate it in a way that not only aligns your team but also energizes them.

The connection between product strategy and vision is well defined. We'll outline practical steps for crafting a product strategy that complements your vision and strengthens it, supported by real-life examples of how visionary strategies have driven companies to success.

Envisioning and communicating a grand vision comes with its obstacles. We'll tackle common challenges and equip you with strategies to overcome them, ensuring your vision is not only compelling but also realistic and clearly understood by all stakeholders.

Ready to shape a vision that drives your product forward? Let's embark on this journey to turn your dream into a strategy that unveils successful products.

Shaping Your Product Vision

What is a Product Vision and Why Does it Matter?

A product vision paints the ultimate goal of your product. It captures the essence of your product's purpose and outlines the long-term impact you aim to have on customers and society. A product vision should not list features or set revenue goals. Instead, it's about answering, "What change do we want to bring about?" This vision serves as a north star, guiding your product from its initial concept, through development, to its launch and subsequent growth phases.

Why is a compelling vision so crucial? It guides your product team and the entire organization, aligning efforts across engineering, design, marketing, sales, and more towards a shared goal. It energizes and inspires everyone involved, from stakeholders to customers, serving as a supporting point to overcome challenges and strive for excellence. Moreover, it ensures the product remains on course, adapting and evolving in the right direction over time.

Consider Airbnb's vision: 'To create a world where anyone can belong anywhere.' This vision goes beyond providing a place to stay. It focuses on fostering a sense of belonging and cultural exchange. It has shaped everything from their core product design to their community initiatives and feature developments, like local tours, enhancing users' involvements of belonging.

You might question, "How does a vision relate to revenue?" After all, businesses ultimately aim for financial returns. While true, a product vision prioritizes solving a significant problem or fulfilling a vital need in a novel way. This emphasis on value creation is what drives user adoption, loyalty, and ultimately, sustainable revenue growth. Revenue and ROI are critical and are the results of a well-articulated and executed vision.

Let's explore how to craft this vision and bring your ambitious goals to life, ensuring your product not only succeeds but leaves a lasting impact.

Align Your Vision with Your Company's Goals

Let's start with aligning your unique product vision with the broader goals of your company. Think of your product not as a solo adventure but as a piece of the overall business puzzle. This alignment is key—it's what makes sure everyone's moving in the same direction, towards a shared goal.

Now, achieving alignment between your product vision and the company's goals might not be straightforward, but trust me, it's a journey worth focusing on. When your vision and the company's objectives move in harmony, it's like magic. Everyone's efforts magnify, pushing towards common goals. This ensures your product plays a significant role in the company's story of success.

So, how do you get there? Start with a deep understanding of your company's strategy and ambitions. As you're crafting your product vision, keep those company goals at the forefront of your mind. Challenge yourself with the question, "How can my product strengthen the company's success?" Once you've got that vision refined, don't keep it for yourself. Share it within your organization. Seek out feedback, initiate conversations, and engage in discussions that matter. It's all about making sure everyone's visions are aligned.

Remember, aligning your vision with the company's goals isn't just about ensuring your product fits; it's about making sure it succeeds, contributing significantly to the journey towards collective success.

Crafting Your Product Vision

Crafting your product vision is a blend of art and strategy, demanding a deep dive into understanding your customers, market trends, the competitive landscape, and technological advancements. Here's how to navigate this exciting process:

Dive Deep into Customer Insights: Start with getting to know your customers inside out. What do they struggle with? What do they wish for? How can your product be the solution they've been looking for?

Analyze the Market: Next, take a broad look at the market landscape. What's trending? Who are you up against? What technological advancements could influence your product's development? What opportunities are untapped? How is the market expected to evolve?

Dream Big About the Future: Now, let your imagination fly. Think about the lasting impact your product will have. How will it improve your customers' lives? What mark will it leave on your industry? How does it fit with the way the market is evolving?

Craft a Product Vision Statement That Inspires: Combine your insights and aspirations to create a concise and powerful vision statement. This should capture the essence of what you're setting out to achieve in a few compelling sentences.

Refining Your Product Vision Statement

> As you shape your product vision statement, there are key characteristics to think about. These elements ensure your vision is not just a statement but a guide to your team and your product.

Set Stretch Goals: Your vision should stretch the imagination and capabilities of your team, aligning with the broader strategic objectives for the next three to five years. Aim for goals that push the boundaries but remain achievable. This balance encourages your team to reach higher while keeping the vision grounded and attainable.

Bring Emotional Investment: Your vision should inspire your team, fostering a deep connection with the product's purpose, making everyone feel personally invested in the journey and success. When your team believes in the product's purpose, their dedication and passion will naturally increase.

Review and Adapt: The only constant in business is change. Regularly revisit your vision to ensure it remains relevant and resonates with evolving market dynamics and consumer needs. This agility allows your vision to be a living part of your product strategy, adaptable and responsive to the outside world.

Crafting a compelling vision is just the beginning; the real challenge lies in bringing this vision to life through strategic actions and continuous adaptation. Let's examine how a well-defined vision can not only inspire but also transform an industry, using Tesla and Spotify as examples.

Tesla: Tesla's vision, "To accelerate the world's transition to sustainable energy," illustrates the power of a vision that extends beyond product features—it's about leading a global shift. This ambitious vision encompasses creating a sustainable energy ecosystem, showcasing how visionary goals can drive significant environmental and social impacts. Tesla's commitment to this vision has pushed the development of innovative, eco-friendly products, expanding its reach by introducing more affordable models and advancing battery technology for longer travel ranges.

Spotify: Consider how Spotify transformed music consumption. Its vision of making music accessible and on-demand for everyone catalyzed a revolution in music streaming, reshaping the industry. Spotify's focus on user experience, personalization, and content expansion exemplifies how a clear, compelling vision can lead to continuous innovation and market leadership.

These examples highlight the transformative power of a well-crafted product vision. Whether you're driving towards a sustainable future like Tesla or changing the way the world experiences music with Spotify, your vision is the cornerstone of innovation and success. Let it be your guide as you navigate the challenges and opportunities ahead, inspiring your team and captivating your audience.

Differentiating Between Product Vision and Product Goals

Understanding the distinction between your product vision and product goals is like knowing the difference between your dream destination and the milestones along the journey. While both are essential, they serve unique roles in the roadmap to success.

Product vision expresses the aspiration, painting a broad picture of your aims. On the other hand, you will define and measure product goals as the steps you take to navigate towards the product vision. They are the specific, achievable objectives that shape the way, making the vision achievable, one milestone at a time.

The key elements for setting product goals:

Vision Alignment: Every goal should reflect and push you towards your vision, acting as a tangible extension of that big dream.

Focus on the 'What': Define the success milestones but leave the 'how' open-ended, giving your team the space to innovate and find the best path forward.

Data-Informed Decisions: Ground your goals in data and insights. The stronger your data foundation, the more targeted and effective your goals.

Collaborative Creation: Set your goals with input from your team and stakeholders. This collective effort ensures your goals are both ambitious and supported in reality.

Measurability Matters: Anchor each goal with clear Key Performance Indicators (KPIs) to track progress and adapt strategies as needed.

Motivate and Challenge: Craft goals that initiate your team's passion and push their limits. Strike a balance—too hard to achieve might discourage, too easy could lead to underperformance and boredom. Aim for that sweet spot where goals are stimulating yet achievable.

With your vision and goals set, the journey doesn't end there; it's time to chart the path with a robust product strategy. This strategy acts as your map, detailing the routes and tactics to turn your vision into reality.

In the next section, we'll dive into leveraging your product vision to craft a powerful product strategy. We're about to translate dreams into action, mapping a way that leads from vision to market triumph. Ready to take that leap from envisioning to executing? Let's journey on, turning your visionary goals into a concrete success story.

The Art of Product Strategy

In the world of business, strategy is your blueprint, guiding each choice/decision and action towards the company's long-term aspirations. As a Product Manager, your day is full of ideas and suggestions from all stakeholders. Your challenge is how to keep focus on the core problem your product aims to solve. While no ideas are inherently good or bad and gathering customer feedback and stakeholder input is crucial, you need a robust filter to select through the noise. This filter is your product strategy.

What is a Product Strategy, and Why is it Valuable?

A product strategy is your roadmap for achieving your product vision. It outlines key goals and milestones and includes decisions on target markets, value propositions, essential features, and unique selling points.

At its core, product strategy is about making informed decisions. It's choosing where to compete by identifying target markets and customer needs and determining how to stand out through differentiation and superior value. It ensures your product aligns with your company's business strategy and meets customer needs. The value of a product strategy lies in:

Clarity: It clarifies your objectives and how to achieve them, setting clear expectations and reducing ambiguity.

Alignment: It ensures that everyone, from leadership to the development team, is aligned towards a common goal and direction.

Focus: It helps prioritize efforts and resources, guiding your decision-making process, and allowing you to bypass initiatives that don't match your strategic goals.

Physical vs. Digital Product Strategy

Though the core principles of product strategy apply to both physical and digital products, their execution varies. Physical products often emphasize design, manufacturing, distribution, and retail presence. Digital products, meanwhile, focus on technology development, user experience, scalability, and digital marketing strategies.

Regardless of the type, the ultimate aim remains the same: to deliver a product that adds value to customers and achieves business goals. For example:

Apple's iPhone: Apple's strategy with the iPhone is to offer a high-quality, user-friendly product that integrates hardware, software, and services seamlessly. This approach involves careful design, advanced technology, a robust ecosystem, and powerful branding. The result? A solid product experience that commands a premium price.

Netflix: Netflix's digital strategy aims to provide a personalized, convenient, and affordable streaming experience. Their strategy spans strategic content acquisitions, leveraging advanced technology for personalized recommendations, and employing competitive pricing models. Netflix's approach has established it as a frontrunner in the streaming industry.

Understanding and applying the right product strategy marks the difference between a product that succeeds and one that merely survives. As you move forward, keep your strategy aligned with your vision, adaptable to change, and always focused on delivering value to your customers.

Exploring Product Strategy Types

Your product strategy serves as the compass guiding you through the product development journey, ensuring alignment with market needs and organizational objectives. Let's explore various strategies, each offering different advantages and posing unique challenges, to illustrate different pathways to success for your product.

"Focus" Strategy: Mastering the Niche

The focus, or niche strategy, focuses on a specific market segment. While small companies with limited resources often adopt this approach to compete effectively, larger corporations also use it to capture overlooked or underserved segments, uncovering new growth ways in specialized markets.

Success in a focus strategy depends on a deep understanding of your target segment's unique needs, preferences, and pain points. Customizing your product to meet these specific requirements allows you to differentiate in the market—whether through a standout feature, superior service, or an innovative user experience.

Take Spotify, for example it caters to music enthusiasts, offering curated playlists, personalized recommendations, and a vast library that appeals to diverse musical tastes and genres. This targeted strategy not only positions Spotify as a leader in its industry but also optimizes resource allocation, enabling the development of features and services that resonate deeply with its core audience.

To effectively execute a focus strategy, start by identifying a customer segment with unmet needs. This initial step is crucial as it sets the direction for your tailored efforts. Dive deep into comprehensive market research and actively engage with potential customers to understand their preferences and pain points. Utilize data to capture and analyze the unique attributes and behaviors of this group. With these insights, you can then tailor your product development, marketing strategies, and customer support to meet these specific needs precisely.

A focus strategy transforms your product into a vital part of your customers' life by providing solutions unavailable elsewhere. Done right, it ensures your resources are used carefully, maximizing the return on investment.

"Cost Leadership" Strategy: Excellence in Efficiency

The Cost leadership strategy is about offering products or services at prices lower than those of competitors, prioritizing value over being the cheapest option. For Product Managers, the goal is to deliver high-quality offerings at competitive prices.

Achieving cost leadership requires careful management of development and operational expenses. This might involve streamlining product features to those that deliver core value, optimizing processes to save time and enhance productivity, and leveraging external resources for cost-effective solutions.

Google Drive demonstrates cost leadership by offering secure, accessible storage solutions at competitive prices. With 15 GB of free storage—exceeding what many competitors offer—and reasonably priced paid plans providing more storage for less, Google Drive stands out. It reinforces its value proposition through seamless integration with other Google services, enhancing user experience.

In competitive markets where price is a decisive factor, the cost leadership strategy can significantly expand your customer base and increase market share. However, it requires a delicate balance between reducing costs and maintaining the quality and satisfaction that your customers expect.

"Differentiation" Strategy: Stand Out Uniquely

When the marketplace is crowded with similar offerings, a differentiation strategy can be a game changer. This approach focuses on giving your product unique qualities that set it apart from the competition. The goal? Not just to attract customers, but to create lasting loyalty and drive revenue growth.

To successfully implement a differentiation strategy, start with thorough market research to identify unmet needs or desires within the market. Understanding these gaps is essential for positioning your product uniquely.

Next, clearly define what sets your product apart, whether it's an innovative feature, cutting-edge technology, or an unparalleled customer experience. Each of these elements can serve as a key differentiator that distinguishes your product from the competition. Finally, craft a brand identity that reflects your product's uniqueness. This branding should influence how customers perceive and connect with your product, embedding your product's distinctive qualities in the minds of your target audience.

Consider Slack as a prime example. Amidst the crowded messaging apps, Slack stands out with its intuitive design, seamless integrations, and focus on enhancing team collaboration, making it a go-to for businesses worldwide.

"Innovation" Strategy: Leading the Future

At the frontline of product strategies lies the Innovation strategy. This approach is defined by a bold commitment to meet customer needs in revolutionary ways. It calls for creativity, a willingness to take risks, and a drive to disrupt the status quo. Whether introducing novel technologies, exploring fresh business models, or venturing into uncharted market segments, the Innovation strategy is about leading change.

To foster an innovation strategy effectively, begin by encouraging out-of-the-box thinking to uncover unique solutions to customer challenges. This approach helps in generating novel ideas that can significantly impact the market. It's crucial to align these innovations with genuine customer needs, which requires conducting rigorous market research to understand and validate these needs accurately. Additionally, cultivate a culture of innovation within your team or organization where new ideas are not just welcomed but celebrated. This involves promoting diversity of thought, which enriches the creative process and leads to more innovative outcomes.

Airbnb is a prime example of innovation in action, reimagining the traditional hospitality model by connecting travelers with local hosts. This disruptive concept has not only reshaped the lodging industry but also created a new market category.

An Innovation strategy sets companies at the forefront of their fields. It blends creativity with strategic risk-taking, all aimed at designing products that redefine markets and enrich customer experiences. For Product Managers, this means advocating for innovation, staying ahead of market trends, and maintaining agility in product development.

Strategizing for Success

Choosing the right product strategy is crucial. Whether you're focusing on a niche market, adopting cost leadership, differentiating your product, or leading with innovation, each strategy brings its own benefits and challenges. The key to success lies in applying these strategies thoughtfully, tailored to your market's specifics and your product's unique demands.

Remember, strategies can be mixed and matched. For example, a cost leadership strategy might pair with differentiation to deliver value-priced products that still capture attention; Or, an innovation strategy could complement a focus strategy, targeting a niche with a revolutionary offering.

The goal is to deeply understand your customer's needs and craft a strategy that not only aligns with these insights but also supports your primary business objectives. It's about finding the perfect balance—matching your product's unique value with market opportunities and customer expectations.

As we progress, we'll explore actionable steps and considerations to develop a strategy that not only aligns with your market but also positions your product for sustained success.

Crafting an Effective Strategy: Step-by-Step Guide

Creating a strong product strategy can sometimes feel like climbing a mountain even for the most experienced Product Managers. It requires a profound understanding of your target market, deep insights into what your customers really need, a detailed analysis of your competition, and an honest evaluation of your organization's resources. To create a strategy that leads to success, you'll need to blend creativity with analytical thinking and a dose of strategic foresight. Though no single formula guarantees success, there are essential steps every Product Manager can follow to chart a clear course.

Step 1: Dive into the Market

The journey to a successful product strategy starts with engaging yourself in the target market. Understanding the complexities of the market is critical for spotting both, opportunities for innovation and potential threats. Begin by assessing the market size, exploring demographic details, studying customer behavior, and conducting a comprehensive analysis of your competitors, including their offerings and pricing strategies. Pay close attention to market and technology trends and consider how regulatory and economic factors could impact your market.

For instance, if you're launching an online grocery store, start by sizing up the market. Look into the number of online grocery shoppers, their spending habits, and demographics. Examine what other online grocery stores are doing in terms of operations, product range, and pricing strategies. Consider whether trends like healthier eating or a shift towards plant-based diets could open-up opportunities for new product lines or services. Reflect on technology trends, such as the increasing use of AI to enhance online shopping experiences and evaluate how they might influence your strategy.

Step 2: Define Your Target Audience

At the heart of any successful product strategy is a crystal-clear definition of your target audience. Trying to appeal to everyone is a common trap; aiming for universal appeal can dilute your product's effectiveness. Instead, focus on a specific user segment to achieve better results.

To accurately define your target audience, explore both, demographic data (age, income, education) and psychographic factors (values, interests, lifestyles). Employ market surveys, customer interviews, and focus groups to tailor your product to the specific needs of your audience.

If your online grocery store is targeting segments like 'busy working parents' or 'elderly individuals seeking to avoid crowded places,' get to know these groups closely. What does a typical day look like for them? What challenges do they encounter in their grocery shopping? How can your product ease these specific pain points?

Step 3: Identify the Problem

Identifying the core problem that your product aims to solve is pivotal. This step extends beyond mere recognition to a deep, empathetic understanding of the issue. Consider the nature of the problem: Is it ongoing or sporadic? How does it impact your target audience? Are there existing solutions, and if so, why do they miss the mark?

With a clear understanding of the problem, assess its significance. Is the issue significant enough to warrant a solution? Sometimes, what seems like a problem to you may not be perceived as such by your target audience, or they might have adapted to it to the extent that it no longer bothers them. Evaluate the problem's scale, severity, frequency, and the number of people it affects to determine its priority.

In the context of your online grocery store, the problem might be "the difficulty of shopping for groceries due to time constraints or the desire to avoid crowded places." Validate this problem by engaging with potential customers — busy parents or elderly individuals — to confirm whether they view it as a significant issue and are in search of convenient shopping alternatives.

Step 4: Craft Your Value Proposition

Articulating your value proposition is the next crucial step. This involves more than listing features or benefits; it's about creating a compelling story that showcases the unique advantages your product offers to your target audience, connecting on both a practical and emotional level.

Begin by listing all the key features and benefits of your product. For each feature, pinpoint the specific benefit it delivers. Ensure these benefits directly tackle the needs and solve the problems of your target audience, as identified in the previous steps. Also, highlight how your product surpasses the competition.

Then, refine this information into a concise, powerful statement that captures the unique value of your product. This statement should answer three critical questions: What does your product do? Who is it for? Why is it better than the alternatives?

Your value proposition should clearly articulate what sets your product apart, whether it's through innovation, quality, or customer service, and weave this into a story that resonates with your audience.

For example, the value proposition for your online grocery store could be: "Rediscover the joy of grocery shopping with [Your Store Name]. Designed for busy professionals and seniors, we bring fresh, quality groceries right to your doorstep. Our intuitive platform, personalized selections, and swift delivery promise a shopping experience that's not just convenient but tailored to your safety and lifestyle needs."

Remember, your value proposition is not set in stone. It should evolve with your product updates, market trends, and changing customer needs. Continually refine it based on feedback and new insights to ensure that your product strategy remains dynamic and relevant.

Step 5: Define Success Metrics

Defining success metrics is an essential step in any product strategy. These metrics serve as concrete, measurable indicators of your progress toward achieving your strategic goals. Importantly, these metrics should directly relate to the value proposition and goals established earlier.

Success metrics should cover both quantitative and qualitative data to offer a comprehensive view of your product's performance. Include metrics like Average Revenue Per User (ARPU) and Customer Lifetime Value (CLTV) if boosting revenue is a goal. But remember, these metrics are not static; they should adapt as your product and the market landscape evolves.

Identifying and refining these metrics is an ongoing process that demands continuous monitoring and adjustment. It's a balancing act between measurable outcomes and indicators that genuinely reflect your product's success.

Step 6: Stay Focused

The final, yet equally crucial, step is maintaining focus throughout the development of your product strategy. It's tempting to get carried away by the attraction of new features or the latest technological innovations. However, it's vital to remember that adding more features doesn't automatically translate to increased value and can lead to unnecessary complexity.

To keep your product strategy on track, regularly revisit your original product vision, value proposition, and customer needs. Make strategic choices about which features to develop and where to allocate your resources. Avoid falling into the trap of 'feature creep' — the tendency to continuously add features, which can lead to a product that's overcomplicated and drifts away from its core value proposition.

Flexibility is key in maintaining focus. As market conditions and customer preferences change, be ready to adjust your strategy. However, ensure these adjustments are consistent with your overall product vision and genuinely enhance value for your customers.

In essence, crafting your product strategy is a vital step toward success, laying a solid foundation based on thorough market understanding, clear customer insights, and a focused approach to solving real problems. Keep these steps in mind as you navigate the complexities of product development and market positioning, ensuring your strategy is not only well-informed but poised for long-term success.

Case Study – The Fitbit Success Story

Fitbit's rise to becoming a leader in the fitness wearable sector is a testament to the power of a meticulously crafted product strategy that emphasizes deep market insights and a commitment to user-centric design.

Market Research and Understanding the Target Audience

Fitbit's strategic journey began with an exhaustive dive into market research, utilizing surveys, focus groups, and data analytics to tap into the health-conscious consumer's evolving needs and preferences. By conducting a thorough competitive analysis, Fitbit pinpointed market gaps, especially what was lacking in existing fitness wearables.

Identifying its target demographic extended beyond just catering to active individuals; Fitbit aimed to appeal to anyone aspiring to a healthier lifestyle. This broadened perspective allowed Fitbit to tap into a universal desire for an accessible, engaging means of tracking health and activity.

Problem-Solving with a Compelling Value Proposition

At the heart of Fitbit's strategy was the ambition to address significant health management obstacles, such as sustaining motivation and monitoring various health metrics. Fitbit envisioned a device that would serve as an all-inclusive health companion. Their value proposition was compelling: Fitbit devices were not just about tracking; they offered personalized insights, goal setting, and a sense of community to foster motivation and user engagement.

Innovation and Adaptability: Staying Ahead of the Curve

Innovation is the cornerstone of Fitbit's enduring strategy. The brand consistently enhances its devices with the latest sensor technology and broadens the array of health metrics tracked. Integration with leading third-party apps ensures that Fitbit devices remain relevant and provide a cohesive user experience.

Fitbit's ability to adapt is showcased in its response to emerging health trends and technological advancements, broadening its product range to address a wider spectrum of health concerns, including stress management and sleep quality.

Measuring Success Through Comprehensive Metrics

Fitbit's evaluation of success covers device sales, levels of user engagement, customer satisfaction scores, and specific health metrics such as daily steps and sleep quality. These diverse metrics provide a comprehensive snapshot of their success, guiding strategic decisions and product evolution.

Fitbit has strengthened its position as a pioneer in the digital health and fitness landscape through a combination of user-centric design, ongoing innovation, and responsive adaptability. Its unwavering focus on understanding and addressing genuine user needs, coupled with an agility in product development, underscores the importance of a strategic, informed approach in achieving market leadership and enduring success.

As demonstrated by Fitbit's rigorous approach to product strategy and performance measurement, setting clear objectives and robust tracking mechanisms are vital for any technology-driven company. The next crucial step is finding an effective method for executing and measuring these strategies to ensure alignment and drive success. Here, Objectives and Key Results (OKRs) emerge as a powerful tool, especially within the tech industry, to translate product visions and strategies into actionable, quantifiable goals.

Objectives and Key Results (OKRs)

Larry Page, Co-founder of Google, once highlighted the transformative power of OKRs: "OKRs have helped lead us to 10x growth, many times over. They've helped make our crazily bold mission of 'organizing the world's information' perhaps even achievable. They've kept me and the rest of the company on time and on track when it mattered the most." This endorsement underlines the OKR framework's potential to streamline strategy execution within your organization.

OKRs break down into two fundamental components:

Objectives: Define what you aim to achieve. They should be significant, concrete, and action based.

Key Results: Outline the means of achieving your objectives through specific, time-bound, and measurable actions. Key results should be quantifiable and tightly linked to the objective, ensuring they are measurable with a clear definition of success.

This duo creates a roadmap for turning your product vision and strategic planning into reality, driving focused efforts towards shared objectives.

How OKRs Drive Strategy Execution

OKRs link specific objectives (the 'what') with measurable key results (the 'how'), offering clear directives for every team member. This method excels at simplifying complex strategies into attainable tasks. For example, if your strategy aims at market expansion, an OKR could set the objective to penetrate two new international markets, with key results focusing on establishing key local partnerships and hitting defined user growth targets.

Objectives	Objective 1	Objective 2	Objective 3
Key Activities	Description Description Description	Description Description Description	Description Description Description
Results	SCORE	SCORE	SCORE

Hierarchical Structure and Alignment

OKRs are adaptable across different organizational levels, ensuring that everyone's efforts contribute effectively to the broader vision:

At the Leadership Level, OKRs set wide-reaching objectives in line with strategic priorities.

The Department/Team Level tailors specific objectives to support these broader goals, customized to each team's function.

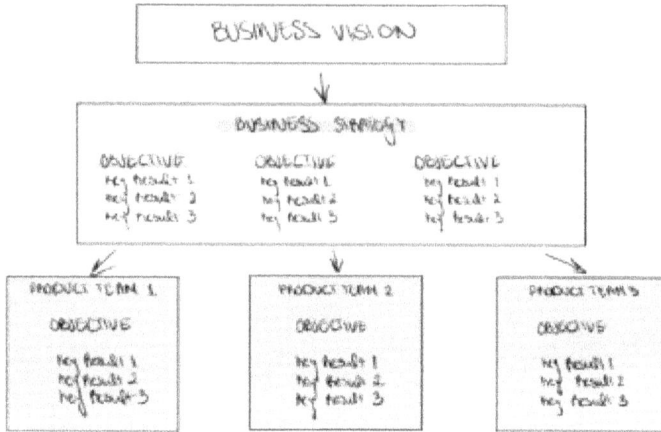

The Individual Level focuses on practical goals in harmony with team objectives, specific to individual roles.

The beauty of OKRs lies in their alignment and transparency. With objectives cascading from the top down, each layer of the organization sees how their contributions fit into the wider goals, enhancing collaboration and shared responsibility.

The measurable nature of OKRs provides a clear snapshot of performance against established goals. Regularly reviewing OKRs allows teams to track progress and identify discrepancies between expected and actual outcomes. This feedback allows teams to make strategic adjustments, either tweaking key results or revising objectives to maintain alignment with the product vision and market realities.

Example of an OKR

Imagine a SaaS team aiming to boost user engagement. Their objective could be to enhance engagement metrics, with key results including a 20% increase in weekly active users, a 10% reduction in churn, and an improved Net Promoter Score.

Should weekly active users not rise as anticipated, it signals a need to reevaluate engagement strategies or improve product features. A failure to reduce churn as expected may call for examining customer experiences or rethinking the value proposition.

Addressing Implementation Challenges

While implementing OKRs, challenges such as maintaining alignment across levels and setting realistic targets may arise. It's vital to setting OKRs that push the team beyond their comfort zone yet remain achievable and foster open communication for continuous review and adaptation.

Consider integrating (OKRs) seamlessly into your company's operational rhythm and culture. Leadership plays a pivotal role here, not only by passionately committing to the OKR framework themselves but also by exemplifying this commitment through their actions and decisions. By doing so, leaders can foster a culture that values accountability and continuous improvement.

It's about showing, not just telling, your team that OKRs are more than a box-ticking exercise—they're a strategic compass guiding every project, decision, and daily task. Encourage your leaders to champion OKRs, celebrate milestones reached through this approach, and openly discuss learnings from missed objectives.

In essence, OKRs are a dynamic framework that can significantly enhance your product strategy's direction and adaptability. They provide a structured yet flexible approach, ensuring every team member's work aligns with the organization's overarching vision, driving collective progress towards the product's success. It is also an excellent tool for analyzing self-achievement by measuring objectives achieved which helps build personal confidence and helps identify areas to boost capability at a personal level.

Articulating the Product Strategy

Ensuring everyone understands and believes in your product strategy is crucial—it might even be the most critical skill you need to master. Here's how to communicate effectively to all stakeholders involved in your product's journey.

Key Elements for Successful Articulation

Highlight the Benefits: Start by explaining how your strategy meets customer needs and emphasizes your unique value proposition. Use storytelling to bring these benefits to life, focusing on how you solve customer pain points.

Show Alignment with Business Goals: Demonstrate how your product strategy aligns with the wider business objectives. Use solid examples and data to make your case persuasive and credible.

Address Stakeholder Concerns: Be prepared to answer stakeholder questions. Show empathy and be open to feedback, making sure everyone feels their input is valued in shaping the strategy.

Tailoring Communication for Different Stakeholders

Effective strategy communication varies across stakeholders. Here's how to adjust your approach:

For the Product Team: Involve them early, clarifying goals and the roadmap. Their feedback is crucial to ensure alignment with team objectives.

For Executives: Highlight the strategy's business value and market potential, focusing on key metrics and milestones.

For Investors: Stress the market opportunities and competitive advantages, being transparent about revenue projections and risks. Highlight the product's growth potential and your plan for profitability.

For Customers: Use language that centers on the customer to explain the product's benefits and features. Gathering their feedback is key to refining your message.

Choosing the Right Communication Channels:

The success of your product strategy communication hinges on selecting channels that cater to the specific needs and preferences of your stakeholders. Here's how to ensure your message is both heard and understood:

Interactive Meetings: Make the most of interactive meetings, whether they're in-person or virtual, to foster real-time engagement. These sessions are perfect for diving deep into discussions, sparking creative brainstorming, and gathering immediate feedback. To maximize their effectiveness, ensure each meeting has a focused agenda, invites diverse stakeholder input, and concludes with clear summaries and actionable next steps.

Comprehensive Documentation: Utilize detailed documentation, such as strategy reports, product roadmaps, and white papers, as key reference materials for ongoing consultation. Platforms like Google Docs or Microsoft Teams are ideal for collaborative document management, making it easy to share updates and keep everyone on the same page with the latest strategy insights.

Visual Aids: Visual aids, including charts, infographics, and process diagrams, are invaluable for simplifying complex aspects of your strategy. These tools transform dense information into digestible, engaging content. Leverage design platforms such as Canva to craft eye-catching visuals and consider establishing standard templates to maintain consistency in your communications.

Online Collaboration Tools: In today's increasingly remote and hybrid work environments, online collaboration tools are indispensable for sustaining seamless communication. Platforms like Slack, Asana, or Trello, with their shared workspaces, instant messaging, and task management features, play a crucial role in keeping your teams synchronized and up-to-date on strategy developments.

Remember, the goal is to keep everyone aligned and informed, fostering a shared understanding and commitment to the strategic vision and its execution.

Overcoming Communication Challenges

Effectively sharing your product strategy means being prepared to tackle several potential hurdles:

Tackling Language Barriers: Language should never be a barrier to understanding. Aim for simplicity and clarity, steering clear of industry jargon. When technical terms are essential, accompany them with straightforward explanations or analogies. Visual aids, such as infographics and diagrams, can bridge comprehension gaps, making complex ideas accessible to all. Consider holding sessions to walk stakeholders through more complicated concepts, enhancing their grasp of the strategy.

Aligning Diverse Priorities: Conflicting priorities can mix-up strategic focus. Align your product strategy with the broader business goals to ensure consistency across departments. Facilitate workshops where teams can reconcile their priorities with the strategy's objectives, promoting a unified direction. Support your strategic decisions with data and analytics, demonstrating their alignment with the company's overarching ambitions.

Embracing Change: Change often meets resistance. To ease this, include stakeholders in developing your strategy, fostering a sense of joint ownership, and minimizing pushback. Understand their reservations and counter them with examples of successful change, underscoring the strategy's benefits and its positive impacts. This not only alleviates concerns but also boosts support for the strategy.

Cultivating a Feedback-Rich Environment: Feedback is the lifeblood of strategy refinement. Establish regular channels for feedback, actively encouraging stakeholder engagement. Show them their insights are valued and instrumental in fine-tuning the strategy. Embrace active listening and ensure feedback translates into meaningful adjustments or clarifications, keeping the strategy dynamic and relevant.

Leveraging the Power of Storytelling

Storytelling isn't just for tales; it's a critical tool for communicating complex product strategies in an engaging, memorable way.

Begin by setting the scene—identify the problem your product addresses. Delve into the customer pain points, exploring how these issues weave into their daily experiences. Introduce relevant characters that embody your audience, adding depth and emotion to your story. Highlight their struggles, focusing on the emotional journey—frustration, aspiration, and need.

Introduce your product as the narrative's hero. Show how its features and benefits directly tackle the identified challenges, enriching your story with data and statistics for credibility. Utilize metaphors, analogies, and vivid descriptions to make your tale engaging and relatable.

Engage your audience in the story. Pose questions, create scenarios, or prompt personal reflections on how the product might transform their lives. This involvement deepens the narrative's impact, fostering a personal connection with your strategy.

For example, if promoting a fitness app, share Ali's story—a character grappling with fitness consistency. Explore Ali's emotional journey and how your app introduces a turning point. Highlight key features, like personalized plans, and illustrate their transformative effect on Ali's fitness journey, culminating in a healthier, more confident lifestyle.

End with a vision of success. Show how your strategy's fruition benefits not just Ali but the broader community, leaving your audience inspired and committed to the product strategy.

Incorporating storytelling into your strategic communication not only conveys your vision effectively but also ensures it resonates deeply with stakeholders, leaving a lasting mark on your audience. The art of storytelling lies in its flexibility, clarity, and the empathetic connection it fosters, making your product strategy not just understood but felt.

Chapter Summary and Reflections

This chapter took you on a deep dive into creating and sharing a compelling product vision, a cornerstone in guiding your product to success. We've discussed the importance of a vision that looks to the future and sparks inspiration while aligning closely with your company's broader goals. Achieving this synergy demands a profound understanding of customer needs, market dynamics, and competitive positioning.

Our journey covered essential steps for creating and conveying a robust product strategy. Starting with a solid market understanding, we focused on pinpointing your target audience, identifying the core problem your product addresses, and crafting a value proposition that distinguishes your product. We discussed the significance of setting clear success metrics, fostering a user-centered design culture, and the necessity of refining your strategy based on feedback.

A key highlight was the exploration of Objectives and Key Results (OKRs). We delved into how OKRs are essential in driving your product strategy, ensuring alignment with your vision, and serving as measurable indicators of your progress. They're vital for synchronizing team efforts and focusing on what truly matters.

The chapter also emphasized the crucial role of effective communication in strategy execution. Articulating your strategy involves more than laying out plans; it's about engaging diverse stakeholders, gaining their support, and using storytelling to forge a deep emotional bond with your vision.

In wrapping up, reflecting on these insights encourages us to see product strategy not just as a set of tasks but as a dynamic, ongoing process. It's about understanding where you are, envisioning where you want to be, and mapping out the path to get there. As we move forward, remember that a well-crafted product strategy is your blueprint for success—a document that lives, breathes, and evolves with your product.

Reflections for Product Managers

As Product Managers, continuously refining your approach to both, crafting your product strategy, and effectively communicating it is essential. Here are key reflections to guide you towards greater product success:

Harness the Power of Vision: Begin with crafting a compelling product vision. This vision serves as your guiding star, aligning and inspiring your team and stakeholders. It provides direction and purpose, grounding all strategic decisions and initiatives.

Establish Clear, Focused Goals: Set SMART (Specific, Measurable, Achievable, Relevant, Time-bound) goals that not only resonate with clarity and feasibility but also drive your product vision forward. These goals act as concrete milestones, directing your team's efforts and providing a measure of success.

Emphasize User-Centricity: Place the user at the core of every strategic decision. Ground your strategy in a deep understanding of user needs, behaviors, and challenges. This focus ensures that your product genuinely connects with and fulfills the expectations of your target audience.

Implement and Adjust OKRs: Adopt Objectives and Key Results (OKRs) or similar frameworks to break down your vision and strategy into actionable, measurable objectives. Regularly review and refine these OKRs to ensure they remain aligned with your strategic goals, tracking progress and maintaining focus.

Master Communication: Crafting a remarkable product strategy is just the beginning. The ability to communicate this strategy effectively to a variety of stakeholders is equally crucial. Adapt your communication approach to meet the needs of different audiences, employing storytelling to create a compelling and relatable narrative.

Welcome Feedback: Cultivate a culture that embraces feedback, recognizing it as a vital component of strategic refinement and iterative improvement. Encourage feedback from both your team and users, viewing it as an opportunity for learning and growth.

Looking Ahead

You've now set the foundation for success. The next phase is investigating into product discovery, where we'll explore user research, prototyping, and idea validation techniques to make informed, data-driven decisions in your product development journey.

The world of product strategy is ever-evolving. Staying adaptable, receptive to feedback, and ready for change is key. As we venture into product discovery, you'll gain further insights and tools to refine your strategy, ensuring it stays robust, centered on the user, and true to your overarching vision.

CHAPTER 2
THE ART OF PRODUCT DISCOVERY

Every standout product you encounter isn't a product of chance but the result of careful research, strategic foresight, and committed execution by skilled Product Managers. This path to success always starts with an essential phase: product discovery.

At the heart of product discovery lies the crucial task of deeply understanding customer needs and challenges. This phase is dedicated to uncovering these needs, generating a range of ideas, and rigorously validating them to identify solutions that truly hold the potential to succeed in the market. Given the unique nature of each product journey, the product discovery process requires a customized, agile approach that goes well beyond just idea generation.

This dynamic process covers continual exploration and direct engagement with customers, allowing for real-time feedback and adjustments. It also involves proactive risk management, where potential pitfalls are anticipated and strategically addressed. Through this comprehensive approach, you ensure that your development efforts are aligned not just with current market demands but are also resilient to future challenges and changes.

The advice to "engage more with your customers" is not just a saying in product management—it's the core of your role. While listening to your customers and understanding their problems is vital, the true challenge is in discovering the optimal solution for their problems. The product discovery stage harnesses your skills in user research, ideation, product design, user experience, and prototyping to pinpoint the perfect Product-Market Fit.

It's critical to acknowledge that product discovery isn't a one-off event but a recurring, continuous process. The most successful product teams integrate this process into their daily routines, always on the lookout for deeper customer insights, identifying gaps in their offerings, and motivated to deliver solutions that exceed customer expectations. Adopting a mindset of constant curiosity and flexibility is fundamental, allowing for ongoing strategy refinement based on fresh market insights and user feedback.

This chapter aims to navigate you through the key principles and methodologies of effective product discovery. We'll cover the scope of this process, from conducting exhaustive user research and finding fundamental customer issues to crafting compelling customer journeys and studying different discovery models that lead to optimal Product-Market Fit. By mastering these approaches, you'll unlock critical insights, enabling you to develop product concepts that resonate deeply with your target audience.

Let's begin this journey by diving deep into the product discovery process, marking your first significant milestone towards building a product that truly stands out.

The Product Discovery Process

The product discovery process is central to product management. It captures the essence of creating products that truly resonate with users. This critical process provides teams with a structured framework to dive deep into understanding customer needs and pain points. It's the cornerstone for identifying viable product concepts, validating ideas, and refining them into solutions that hold real value for users. Failing to accurately define your target audience's needs can result in costly mistakes, from investing in features that users don't want to launching products that ultimately fail. Unfortunately, even seasoned Product Managers in large corporations can fall into this trap. Recall the story of Amazon's Fire Phone?

Launched in 2014 with high expectations, the Fire Phone quickly became a market failure. The misalignment with customer needs was obvious. Amazon focused on sophisticated technical features like the 3D display and dynamic perspective technology, failing to assess whether these innovations solved any actual customer problems.

The Fire Phone's flagship feature, its integration with the Amazon store for direct purchases, didn't address a significant customer need. Most users already had devices capable of online shopping, making the Fire Phone's unique selling proposition redundant. Moreover, its steep price didn't help, especially without offering clear benefits over competitors.

This example highlights a vital insight for Product Managers: aligning product features with the company's business model doesn't guarantee they meet customer needs. The priority should always be on creating features that genuinely address specific customer problems and pain points, rather than on integrating technologies or capabilities that suit the company's strengths.

The lesson is clear: your primary goal is to develop products that solve particular issues or fulfill unique needs for your target audience. Adding features or technologies without considering their utility to the customer can lead to wasted resources and block your product's success and adoption. This realization marks the beginning of our discovery journey: understanding the customer's problem.

Understanding the Customer's Problem

As you start your journey on the development of a new product, understanding the complex dance between two critical dimensions—the problem space and the solution space—is crucial for your product's success. This journey kicks off with a deep dive into the problem space, where you uncover customers' needs, challenges, and desires.

The heart of why customers turn to any product or service is rooted in their intrinsic motivations. People don't use products for the sake of usage; there's always a deeper need, challenge, or problem driving their engagement. Pinpointing and fully understanding this underlying issue is your first task. As a Product Manager, your role swings between uncovering the customer's problem in the problem space and navigating towards crafting its solution in the solution space—a cycle essential for product success.

Your primary mission within the problem space is to gain a comprehensive understanding of what your customers are facing. Your aim is to uncover the core problems that matter most to them. It's critical to differentiate between those that are truly impactful and those that are just superficial. Focusing on minor problems could lead to creating solutions that don't resound or significantly improve your customers' lives which leads to less engagement with your product. Think about in-depth user interviews, user testing, and a variety of research methods to explore your customers' mindset, behaviors, motivations, and needs.

Invest sufficient time in the problem space. The success of your product centers on accurately identifying and validating the essential problems. With a solid understanding of these issues, you transition into the solution space. Here, your creativity is unleashed as you brainstorm, prototype, and test various solutions, ensuring they meet your customers' needs and expectations.

Navigating the product discovery journey is a continuous process, synchronizing between understanding the problem and developing the solution. Maintaining this delicate balance is critical for developing a product that not only meets customer needs but also adds significant value to your business. Mastering the dynamics of both the problem and solution spaces is what transforms products from merely existing to making a profound and lasting impact.

The Space Pen Story: A Lesson in Understanding the Problem Space

The story of the Space Pen, frequently mentioned in product discovery discussions, serves as a compelling example of the importance of thoroughly understanding the problem space before leaping into solutions. A popular story goes that NASA, faced with the challenge of writing in space where traditional pens wouldn't work due to zero gravity, spent millions developing a pen that could write under these conditions. Meanwhile, the Russians apparently used a simpler, more cost-effective solution: pencils.

This tale, while engaging, isn't entirely true. Both American and Russian astronauts initially used pencils in space. The Space Pen was actually developed by inventor Paul Fisher and later adopted by NASA. Despite the factual inaccuracies, the myth offers a valuable lesson for product discovery: the danger of rushing to solutions without fully understanding the real problem. It suggests that a narrow problem definition, such as "creating a pen that works in zero gravity," could blind one to simpler, more elegant solutions.

As you venture into product development, it's easy to fall into the common pitfall of quickly jumping at solutions, particularly those that seem innovative or cutting-edge. This eagerness can lead to assumptions or decisions based on incomplete feedback. However, exploring the problem space in detail opens the door to a wider array of creative, more effective solutions.

Crafting a Clear Problem Statement: Step-by-Step Guide

At the core of every successful product is a precisely defined problem statement, deeply rooted in an exhaustive understanding of user needs. Here's how to craft one:

Start with Market Research: Initiate your assessment with an in-depth look at your customers—their challenges, behaviors, and how they navigate their world. Ensure your research is driven by relevant questions and a clear objective.

Identify Customer Needs: Analyze your research findings to spot common themes and challenges faced by your target audience. Understanding these needs is crucial in pinpointing the main problem areas your product should address.

Prioritize Customer Needs: Rank these needs by importance and the impact solving them would have. This prioritization guides your development focus, ensuring the most critical issues are tackled first.

Craft the Problem Statement: Formulate your insights into a concise statement that captures your users' core challenges and their desired outcomes. This statement should reflect the needs of your target audience, their key challenges, and what success looks like to them.

Consider the Nike+ running app. Through extensive user research, Nike identified key needs among runners: tracking progress, setting goals, and connecting with a community. The company might articulate a problem statement for the Nike+ app: "Runners seek a tailored experience that allows them to track progress, set new goals, and find community support."

Before moving forward, take a moment to reflect on your users' challenges. Dive deep to uncover the primary issue they're facing and craft a problem statement that captures this challenge. With a clearly defined problem statement and a comprehensive understanding of your customers' needs, you've laid a solid foundation in your product discovery journey. However, this is just the beginning. Your research will likely reveal multiple customer segments, each with unique needs and behaviors. The next step is to develop detailed user personas to deepen your grasp of your users and foster empathy.

Creating User Persona

User personas are fictional, yet realistic representations of your key customer segments, derived from user research and market analysis. They bring to life the attributes, behaviors, and motivations of different user groups, making them indispensable in shaping your product's story and direction.

Personas promote empathy, offering your team vivid insights into users, their requirements, and what drives them. They ensure user needs remain central to decisions regarding product features, design, and overall strategy, providing a common language for your team and stakeholders.

Here's How to Build Impactful User Personas:

Gather User Data: Start by gathering rich details about your users, covering demographics, behaviors, needs, motivations, and frustrations. The more nuanced the data, the more lifelike your personas.

Analyze for Patterns: Dive into the data to spot trends, like similar behaviors, shared challenges, or common goals. These patterns form the backbone of your user personas.

Segment Your Users: Break down your users into distinct groups based on these identified patterns. Each group should reflect a different user type, showcasing unique traits and needs.

Craft Each Persona: Develop a detailed profile for each segment, including demographic info, behaviors, needs, and other relevant characteristics. Give each persona a name and face to humanize them.

Narrate Their Stories: For each persona, craft a story that represents a day in their life, focusing on the obstacles they face, their emotions, how they interact with different products, and their decision-making process.

Create User Scenarios: Form scenarios that illustrate how each persona might come across and use your product. These scenarios offer insights into the diverse ways your product might be utilized.

Prioritize Your Personas: Understand that not all personas can be equally central to your product's success. Decide which personas are most vital based on business objectives, market potential, or specific user needs to direct your product development.

Iterate and Share: Continually refine your personas with new insights, sharing updates with your team and stakeholders. Personas should evolve as your understanding of your users deepens.

Bottom of Form

To emphasize the value of user personas in product development, let's consider three distinct users of the Nike+ App:

"Marathon Adam" - The Serious Runner

Adam, a mid-30s software engineer, is a passionate marathon runner. He is obsessive about improving his performance and achieving new personal bests. Adam looks for advanced analytics, personalized training programs, and expert guidance. He values detailed performance metrics and well-structured training plans. Being tech-savvy, Adam frequently uses various apps and devices to track and analyze his running performance.

"Jogging Mona" - The Casual Runner

Mona, a late-20s teacher, enjoys running for leisure and stress relief. Her daily runs in the park are more about enjoyment than competition. She prioritizes simplicity, convenience, and social aspects in a running app. Mona appreciates an intuitive user interface, easy integration with wearable devices, and the ability to share her runs on social media.

"Fitness Maryam" - The Fitness Enthusiast

Maryam, an early-40s health coach, indulges in various activities like running, yoga, and cycling for overall fitness. She values insights that help improve her health and wellness. Maryam looks for features that track cross-activity performance and offer holistic health recommendations. A tech enthusiast, she utilizes a range of apps and devices to monitor her fitness journey.

By defining personas like Adam, Mona, and Maryam, you cater to a broad spectrum of user needs. These personas guide your product development, ensuring every decision resonates with your customers.

In summary, the product discovery phase is about precisely pinpointing the problems your customers face. Through detailed research, crafting a sharp problem statement becomes possible, steering you towards effective solutions. This journey encompasses a deep dive into both the problem and solution spaces, from defining the issue, understanding user needs, to developing personas for various customer segments. Moreover, constructing scenarios that show how your product addresses different needs is crucial. While demanding, this rigorous process leads to a product that not only aligns with your target audience but also fulfills their unique requirements.

The Customer Journey Map

In your journey as a Product Manager, recognizing your customers' challenges is just the beginning. Equally important is charting their entire journey from the moment they face a problem to when they embrace a solution, including how they discover and interact with your product. This is where the customer journey map becomes your essential compass, lighting the way through the landscape of what your customers seek, dream of, and struggle with.

Imagine the customer journey map not simply as a tool, but as your trusted guide, revealing the full story of your customers' journey. This story begins with the initial search for solutions, leads to the discovery of your product, and evolves into a relationship where they become loyal users. It captures every touchpoint, from their digital footprints to their direct interactions with customer service, offering a panoramic view of their experiences. Carefully mapping these experiences helps you validate your product idea, elevate the customer experience, and tackle challenges head-on.

Whether you're in the beginning of the discovery phase, figuring out how your product fits into your customers' search for solutions, or fine-tuning the customer experience based on how they currently engage with your product, the customer journey map is invaluable. Look at how Airbnb used it to refine their service. By charting the customer journey across key touchpoints — from exploring listings to booking and communicating with hosts — Airbnb identified critical service pain points. They simplified the search experience, enhanced filtering options, and clarified pricing, making the journey more intuitive and transparent for users.

The customer journey map identifies areas of friction and uncovers opportunities for improvement. Creating an impactful map involves gathering rich data and listening closely to customers. Commitment to ongoing refinement ensures every step of the customer journey is seamless and satisfying.

Building a Customer Journey Map

Developing a customer journey map is a multifaceted process that blends creativity, analytical insight, and strategic planning. It's about telling the detailed story of your customers' interactions with your product or service across different touchpoints. Here's how to create a meaningful customer journey map:

Start with Your Personas: Use the user personas you've developed as your foundation. These personas represent the varied motivations and objectives of your user base and are key to customizing the journey map to their needs.

Outline the Customer Journey Stages: Break the customer journey into different stages, typically including awareness, consideration, purchase, usage, support, and advocacy. Adapt these stages to reflect your product's unique journey.

Collect Customer Insights: At each stage, gather data and insights. Probe into customers' needs, desires, and how you can effectively engage them at each point in their journey.

Identify Touchpoints: Determine where customers searching for solutions, or interact with your product—be it through your website, app, social media, customer service, or in-store experiences. Document these touchpoints and investigate the customer experience at each juncture.

Visualize the Journey: Represent the journey visually, using flowcharts or timelines to map out stages, touchpoints, customer actions, and decision points. This visual tool helps link everything together, providing a clear overview of the journey.

Spot Pain Points and Opportunities: Analyze the map to pinpoint friction areas and potential enhancements. Focus on moments where customers disengage or encounter obstacles, viewing these as chances to improve the overall experience.

Prioritize Improvement Areas: After identifying key improvement areas, rank them based on their potential impact on the customer experience and your business goals. Concentrate on initiatives that promise the most significant benefits within your strategic and resource constraints.

This methodical approach equips you with a detailed customer journey map, serving as a strategic asset in delivering a product that meets your audience's needs and ensures a smooth, engaging experience. Next, we'll explore how to integrate emotions into the journey map with the Emotional Map, adding a layer of depth to our understanding of the customer experience.

Emotional Mapping: Adding a Human Dimension to Customer Journeys

While customer journey maps are invaluable for plotting out the interactions and touchpoints customers have searching for solution and engaging with your product, they often overlook a crucial aspect: the customer's emotional journey. Emotional mapping fills this gap, adding a vital layer of empathy to the customer experience.

Emotional mapping charts the range of emotions customers experience throughout their journey, from initial excitement and anticipation to potential frustration and disappointment. This method extends beyond simple satisfaction metrics, exploring the emotional triggers behind customer behaviors.

Here's how emotional mapping enriches your customer journey map:

Captures Emotional States: It acknowledges and records the emotions customers experience while engaging with your product. This offers deeper insights into the customer experience, highlighting areas for enhancement that might otherwise be missed.

Identifies Emotional Highs and Lows: Emotional mapping reveals where emotions fluctuate, pinpointing moments of delight and dissatisfaction. These points of dissatisfaction are crucial; they represent key opportunities for product development focus.

Facilitates Empathetic Design: With a clear understanding of what triggers various emotional responses, products can be designed to better meet users' emotional needs, significantly improving the user experience.

Informed Strategic Decision-Making: Merging emotional insights with the customer journey map leads to more informed, empathetic decisions, emphasizing the user's emotional well-being. This approach deepens the emotional connection between your product and its users, enhancing satisfaction and building loyalty.

Emotional mapping is not just an add-on to the customer journey map but an essential element for understanding the full customer experience. By weaving emotions into the product discovery process, you improve your business outcomes and affirm your dedication to a customer-centric approach.

Building an Emotional Map: A Step-by-Step Guide

Incorporating an emotional layer into your customer journey map adds steps to the discovery process but yields invaluable insights. Here's how to craft an emotional map:

Set Emotional Objectives: Define the target emotions for key touchpoints in your customer journey map. Aim for excitement during discovery, trust at payment, or satisfaction during use, aligning these emotions with your brand values and customer expectations.

Conduct Emotional Research: Focus on uncovering your customers' emotional landscape during research. Utilize open-ended questions to delve into their emotional states, triggers, and feelings at each journey stage. Questions like "How do you feel?" can uncover happiness levels or frustrations, providing essential insights.

Analyze Emotional Insights: Examine the data to identify patterns, trends, and moments of significant emotional impact. Pay special attention to recurring emotions or emotional peaks that notably influence the customer experience.

Visualize the Emotional Journey: Create a visual representation that integrates the emotional journey with the customer journey map. This could be a detailed diagram or infographic, illustrating the range of emotions felt at each stage.

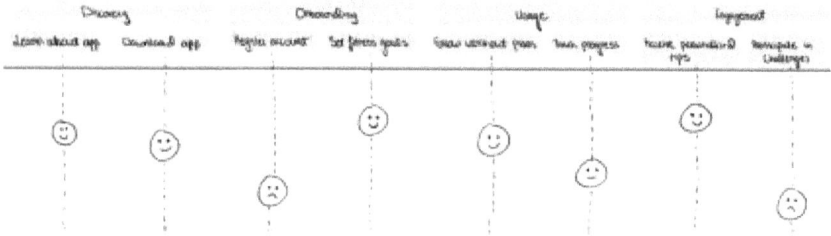

Remember, crafting an emotional map complements your customer journey mapping efforts. This holistic view is crucial for pinpointing where you can amplify positive emotions or mitigate negative ones, leading to deeper customer engagement and more impactful experiences.

As we wrap up our exploration of the product discovery process, keep in mind that this phase lays the groundwork for successful products. It's where you achieve a thorough understanding of your customers, their needs, and the value your product can bring. However, truly knowing your customers is just the start. The next critical step is addressing their problems in a way that's both commercially viable and scalable.

This transitions into our next phase: examining various discovery models that offer structured approaches for effective product discovery. In the following sections, we'll dive into these models, discussing their principles, phases, and how they can be practically applied to fuel your product discovery journey.

Product Discovery Models

In the complex journey of product discovery, structured frameworks can guide you through problem-solving and innovation phases effectively. Models like the Double Diamond and Design Thinking provide a systematic approach to transitioning from problem identification to solution implementation. These models start with broad research and idea generation, then narrow down to specific, actionable outcomes. By systematically uncovering customer needs, brainstorming creative solutions, and iterating based on feedback, these models play a crucial role in aligning products with customer expectations, enhancing the chance of achieving Product-Market Fit and ensuring long-term success.

Double Diamond Model

The Double Diamond Model, introduced by the British Design Council, visualizes the process of divergent and convergent thinking in problem-solving. It encourages teams to expand their perspective in the early stages of product discovery, then refine their focus as they move towards developing and delivering solutions. The model's two diamonds represent the phases of Research (Discover and Define) and Design (Develop and Deliver), detailed as follows:

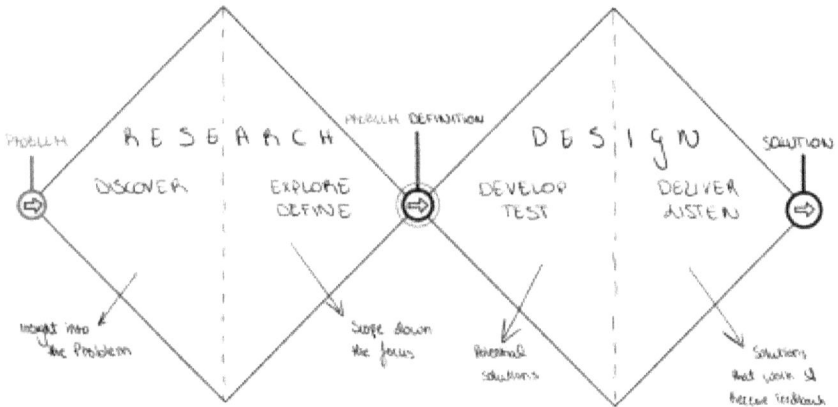

Discover: The journey begins with understanding the problem space through divergent thinking. This phase is about gathering a broad spectrum of insights on customer needs and challenges, employing techniques such as market research, customer interviews, and empathy maps to gain a deep understanding of the target user group.

Define: The process then narrows down to pinpoint the specific challenge to address. Insights from the Discover phase are combined to create a clear problem statement, articulating the core issue the product seeks to solve.

Develop: Here, the focus widens again, encouraging exploration of various solutions to the defined problem. This stage involves selecting promising ideas, prototyping, and transforming conceptual ideas into tangible solutions.

Deliver: In the final convergent phase, teams refine the chosen solution, readying it for launch. Activities include solution testing, feedback gathering, iterating, and optimizing the product's UI and UX for the best possible user experience.

The Double Diamond Model underscores the iterative nature of product discovery, emphasizing continuous exploration, experimentation, and refinement.

Design Thinking Model

Design Thinking offers a holistic model for product discovery, centered around empathy, experimentation, and iterative design. Originating from the design discipline, this human-centered approach has gained traction across industries for its effectiveness in driving innovation.

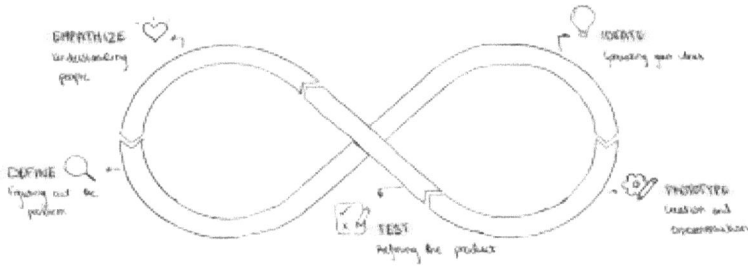

At its core, Design Thinking revolves around the principle that an immersive user understanding, and empathy are the keys to creating solutions that truly resonate. It encompasses five stages, each vital to crafting solutions focused on user needs:

Empathize: Gain a profound understanding of your users through interviews, observations, and research. This stage is crucial for gathering insights into user needs, desires, and the context of their challenges.

Define: Armed with user insights, the next step is to define the specific problem your product will tackle. This involves framing the issue from the user's perspective and crafting a problem statement that reflects their needs and challenges.

Ideate: Creativity takes center stage in the ideation phase. Here, you brainstorm a wide array of possible solutions, fostering a culture of open-mindedness and exploration to extract the most practical and innovative options.

Prototype: Moving ideas into prototypes, ranging from simple to interactive models, is crucial. Prototyping brings your concepts to life, allowing for visualization, testing, and further refinement.

Test: The testing stage involves user feedback on prototypes, offering insights into what works well and what needs improvement. Based on this feedback, solutions are iterated and refined until they effectively meet user needs.

Design Thinking is an iterative, user-centric process. By empathizing with users, defining their needs clearly, generating innovative solutions, creating prototypes, and conducting rigorous testing, you ensure your product is not only valuable but deeply relevant to your target audience.

User Research: Uncovering Customer Needs

User research stands as a cornerstone of the product discovery process, integral across all discovery models. It involves identifying your target audience, collecting diverse data, analyzing this information, and harnessing these insights to inform your product development. The core challenge in user research is pinpointing the actual needs of your customers, distinguishing between genuine requirements and misleading feedback. Conducting customer interviews is a crucial method for achieving this clarity.

To conduct effective customer interviews, the key is to formulate questions that prompt honest and valuable feedback. Inspired by the principles from Rob Fitzpatrick's "The Mom Test," it's obvious the importance of framing questions that avoid generic, often misleadingly positive feedback when asking close associates like friends and family. The aim is to ask open-ended questions that probe into the users' real-life experiences and feelings, steering clear of guiding them towards any predetermined concepts about the product.

Inquiring about the customer's challenges, their current solutions, their satisfaction levels with those solutions, and what they feel is lacking in the market today are pivotal. Steer clear of direct inquiries about the product itself; questions like "Do you like this product?" or "Would you use this product, and how often?" tend to yield artificially positive responses. The focus should remain on deeply understanding the user's problem, asking about the issue without mentioning your product or proposed solution, avoiding any bias that might validate your hypothesis prematurely.

This approach is fundamental to your product's success. By delving into the user's problems and refraining from steering the conversation towards your solution, you avoid the trap of confirmation bias and gather insights that truly reflect your customers' needs and pain points. This careful approach to user research is what paves the way for developing a product that not only addresses real customer problems but also stands a significant chance of success in the market.

The Value of In-Person Research

Despite the wealth of digital data available and the ability to track customer behavior online, the importance of in-person research and direct customer interaction remains paramount. In-person research brings a unique depth to understanding your users, offering insights that digital methods alone cannot capture. Why in-person research is valuable?

Depth of Conversation: Direct interviews facilitate nuanced discussions, allowing users to share their experiences, perceptions, and ideas more freely. This can lead to unexpected insights and uncover ideal user needs.

Non-Verbal Cues: Observing users' body language, facial expressions, and emotional reactions often provides deeper insights into their experiences than verbal feedback alone. Watching users interact with your product in real time can highlight immediate pain points and usability issues, guiding swift enhancements.

Flexibility: Face-to-face interactions offer the opportunity to delve deeper with follow-up questions, explore responses in greater detail, and cover new topics as they arise, resulting in a richer understanding of the user experience.

Complementing In-Person Research with Digital Tools:

While in-person research is irreplaceable, digital tools offer valuable support across various stages of the product discovery process. Here are some tools that can enhance your user research:

User Testing: This platform offers real-time feedback from your target audience, enabling remote usability testing where users interact with your product and share their immediate thoughts. It helps identify usability issues and inform product decisions.

Sprig (formerly known as User Leap): Sprig gathers insights through micro-surveys within your product, providing AI-enabled analysis and sentiment assessment for actionable feedback on user experiences.

User Zoom: Supporting a range of research methodologies, User Zoom provides both quantitative and qualitative data, aiding in a deeper understanding of user behaviors and attitudes.

UserVoice: Focused on feedback management, UserVoice helps prioritize feedback and integrates with tools like Jira and Salesforce, aligning product enhancements with user expectations.

In summary, Digital tools should be seen as supplements to, rather than replacements for, direct user interaction. A balanced approach that combines both in-person and digital methods can provide comprehensive insights essential for informed product decisions.

As we move from thorough research and exploration towards building your initial product version, the focus shifts to achieving 'Product-Market Fit' — ensuring that your product meets market demands. The forthcoming section will delve into the significance of Product-Market Fit and strategies to attain it, leveraging the insights gathered through the product discovery phase.

Product-Market Fit: The Key to Sustainable Success

In the world of product development, the harsh reality is that customers aren't inherently concerned with your product, your company, or your brand. Their primary focus is on finding solutions to their problems. The true measure of success is achieving a seamless Product-Market Fit. Your product should not only address a need but also deeply resonate with your target audience. It's about creating something your customers want and value profoundly. Reaching Product-Market Fit transcends a mere milestone; it is an essential phase in your product's lifecycle, challenging yet crucial for lasting success and growth.

Product-Market Fit Pyramid: Understanding the Five Layers

The Product-Market Fit Pyramid presents a structured framework to evaluate your product's alignment with market needs. It lays out a step-by-step approach to ensure your product meets and exceeds market demands and customer expectations.

This model unfolds across five layers, each foundational to achieving Product-Market harmony:

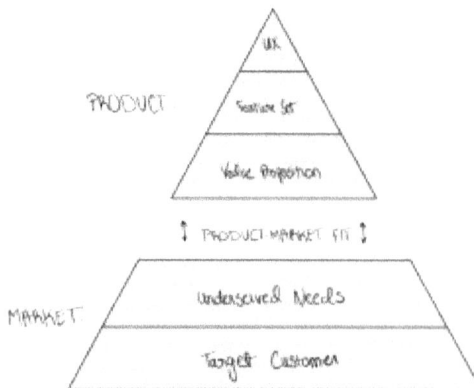

Identity Your Target Market: Start by immersing yourself in the lives of your potential customers. Understand their daily challenges, desires, and the segments they belong to. Creating comprehensive customer profiles at this initial stage is critical for guiding all future decisions.

Identifying Specific Needs: The next layer demands a focus on the specific needs that unveil market opportunities. Before jumping into solution mode, analyze these needs in-depth, considering the shortcomings of existing market solutions. This analysis is vital for gathering insights that shape your approach.

Value Proposition: Ascending to the third layer, it's time to highlight your product's value proposition. Outline the unique blend of features, benefits, and advantages your product brings to solve your targeted customers' specific problems. Clearly articulating your product's value is fundamental.

Feature Set: Explore the specifics of your product's features. With a clear vision and value proposition as your guides, evaluate how each feature addresses customer problems and where your product stands out against competitors.

User Experience (UX): At the pyramid's peak lies the user experience. This layer is dedicated to the interaction between your customers and your product. Crafting an intuitive, engaging, and enjoyable UX is essential for fostering product adoption and ensuring user satisfaction. A deeper dive into UX considerations will follow in this chapter.

Putting It All Together

The essence of the Product-Market Fit Pyramid is to analyze how well the top three layers—value proposition, feature set, and UX—meet the specific needs identified at the base. Confirming this alignment is a significant step towards your product's success.

Various methods exist to test this fit, from research and prototype testing to the invaluable concept of the Minimum Viable Product (MVP), which we'll dive into later. For now, recognize the MVP as a strategy to test your product's fundamental features against the market's needs, offering a measure of its potential and directing further development.

Product-Market Fit Case Study: Spotify

To clarify the concept of Product-Market Fit and the practical application of the Product-Market Fit Pyramid model, let's examine Spotify as a case study:

Identify Target Market: Spotify focused on music enthusiasts who were dissatisfied with the current options, such as purchasing tracks, dealing with piracy, or continuing ad-interrupted radio streams. Through market research, Spotify gained insights into this audience's behaviors, preferences, and frustrations.

Pinpointing Specific Needs: Spotify identified essential needs within this market segment, including the desire for access to an extensive music library, effortless music discovery, personalized listening experiences, and an ad-free premium option.

Value Proposition: Spotify positioned itself as a revolutionary music consumption platform, offering unlimited access to a vast library of music, personalized playlists, and new music discovery features, all within a single platform.

Feature Set: Aligned with its value proposition, Spotify introduced features like an expansive music library, mood-based and curated playlists, personalized "Discover Weekly" playlists, social sharing capabilities, offline listening for premium subscribers, and a choice between a free, ad-supported tier and an ad-free premium subscription.

User Experience (UX): Spotify focused on creating a seamless and intuitive user interface that featured quick download times and smooth transitions between tracks, significantly enhancing user satisfaction.

Putting It All Together: Spotify's dominance in the music streaming market is a testament to its successful alignment with market needs. By redefining the music listening experience and addressing specific user problems,

Spotify's alignment of its value proposition, feature set, and UX with market demands has established it as a frontrunner in the music streaming space.

In summary, navigating through the product discovery process is foundational to creating a product that truly resonates with your target market. The journey, encompassing a deep understanding of the core problem, crafting comprehensive customer journey maps, integrating emotional dimensions, and developing detailed user personas, collectively steers the design of a product that deeply connects with your audience.

While addressing these components individually is feasible, adopting a holistic and structured approach to product discovery is far more beneficial. This strategy ensures a full understanding of both market and user needs, leading to a more focused and impactful product strategy.

As we move beyond the basics of product discovery, it's crucial to acknowledge that the journey doesn't end with merely understanding customer needs and devising solutions. The user experience (UX) and user interface (UI) significantly influence how users interact with and perceive your product. As our exploration of Product-Market Fit and discovery models have shown, exceptional UX is vital in driving product success.

The upcoming section delves into the world of user experience, discussing the essentials of good UX, the pivotal role of Product Managers in shaping it, and how effectively designed UX can surpass user expectations. This exploration aims to illustrate how an accurately crafted user experience enhances user satisfaction, fosters deeper engagement, and ultimately secures your product's market victory.

User Experience (UX) and User Interface (UI): The Heart of Product Design

Have you ever encountered a product that either captivated you with its flawless execution or left you frustrated by its awkward and unintuitive design? The line between a product delighting or frustrating its users often hinges on the quality of its User Experience (UX).

Steve Jobs summarized this sentiment by stating, "Most people make the mistake of thinking design is what it looks like. People think it's this veneer – that the designers are handed this box and told, 'Make it look good!' That's not what we think design is. It's not just what it looks like and feels like. Design is how it works." So, what exactly are UX and UI, and why do they matter so much?

User Experience (UX): Beyond Aesthetics

UX surpasses the mere look of a product. It covers the whole of a user's interaction with the product, from usability to the ease of completing tasks and the emotional resonance it causes. UX design is inherently multidisciplinary, weaving together interaction design, information architecture, visual design, usability, and human-computer interaction. The ultimate aim of UX is to optimize the product for an effortless, effective, and enjoyable journey for the user.

User Interface (UI): The Visual Component

UI, on the other hand, zeroes in on the product's visual and interactive elements—think screens, buttons, menus. It's about defining the typography, color schemes, layout, and animations that users engage with. UI design's mission is to craft interfaces that are not just visually appealing but also intuitive and favorable to a good user experience, thereby enhancing the UX.

The Interaction between UX and UI

While UX and UI serve different purposes, they are inseparably linked components of product design. UX design adopts a holistic stance, interaction design, usability, and function to create a comprehensive user experience. UI design, conversely, focuses on the concrete, tangible aspects of the product's interface.

Exceptional products that resonate with users are born from the harmonious collaboration of UX and UI. UX provides the foundation with strategic, evidence-based insights, while UI translates these strategic visions into tangible, engaging design elements. Together, they constitute the essence of a product's design, vital for its success and user satisfaction.

The Product Manager's Role in UX Design

As a Product Manager, you might find yourself questioning the extent of your involvement in UX design, traditionally seen as the domain of specialized UX professionals. However, your role is central in shaping a product that is not only functional but also provides a seamless and enjoyable user experience. You are the custodian of the product's vision and its user experience, acting as the crucial link between the UX team's design initiatives and the overarching product strategy.

Your position as a Product Manager places you as the customer's advocate, emphasizing the importance of a design that centers around user needs. Your task involves weaving UX considerations into every aspect of the product, from individual features to broader strategic goals. The insights, user stories, and feedback you provide are instrumental in guiding the UX team's design direction.

An understanding of UX principles not only strengthens your collaboration with the design team but also ensures a unified approach to product development. While the focus on functionality and feature enhancement is vital, overlooking the significance of UX refinements can lead to missed opportunities for elevating the user experience.

Monitoring user interactions with your product is a continuous responsibility. Identifying usability issues, collecting user feedback, and employing A/B testing are key strategies in pinpointing areas for improvement. When users encounter difficulties, it's crucial to collaborate closely with the UX team to create effective solutions, addressing concerns related to usability, accessibility, consistency, and error management.

A successful Product Manager views UX design as an integral component of the product development process. This perspective prioritizes the creation of intuitive and engaging user experiences. Maintaining an ongoing partnership with the UX team is essential, ensuring the product not only functions optimally but also align with and surpasses user expectations.

In essence, your role as a Product Manager involves a comprehensive understanding of both strategic and user experience considerations. By fostering a strong collaboration with the UX team and advocating for a user-focused design approach, you contribute to the development of a product that truly resonates with users and stands out in the market.

Principles of Effective UX Design

For Product Managers, the journey towards creating an exceptional user experience (UX) exceeds aesthetic design—it's a comprehensive process involving research, testing, and a deep understanding of user needs. Here are the foundational principles that guide effective UX design:

Simplicity: The essence of UX design lies in simplicity. An interface that's easy to navigate minimizes cognitive load, enabling users to interact with your product smoothly. Aim to streamline complex functionalities and remove unnecessary elements, enhancing overall clarity.

Usability: Usability ensures your product is intuitive and user-friendly. Tracking metrics such as task success rate and error rate can measure usability, ensuring users accomplish their goals with minimal friction.

User Onboarding: The onboarding process often forms users' first impressions. A seamless onboarding experience familiarizes users with your product's core functionalities. Utilize tools like tooltips, walkthroughs, and progressive disclosure to welcome users effectively. Remember, onboarding is crucial not only at product launch but also when introducing new features.

Information Architecture: A well-organized information architecture facilitates easy content discovery, allowing users to find what they need effortlessly. Employ methods like card sorting and tree testing to validate your content structure, ensuring it's accessible and navigable.

Consistency: Consistency in UX design fosters a sense of familiarity and predictability. Developing a design system with reusable components promotes standardized design patterns and visual cues, ensuring uniformity across your product.

Visual Design: Visual design plays a pivotal role in enhancing usability. A consistent color scheme, alongside effective typography and spacing, not only beautifies your product but also improves readability and interaction.

Interaction Design: Interaction design focuses on crafting seamless user-product interactions. Anticipating user actions and designing intuitive flows, such as the "pull to refresh" gesture, can significantly elevate the user experience.

Performance and Speed: In the digital age, responsiveness is critical. Collaborating with the engineering team to optimize performance ensures your product reacts quickly to user inputs, providing a swift and satisfying experience.

Error Handling: Effective error management can mitigate user frustration. Provide clear, constructive error messages that guide users towards resolving issues, enhancing the overall experience.

Contextual Relevance: Customizing experiences to fit user context adds significant value. Leverage analytics and machine learning to personalize interactions, making them more relevant and engaging. Context-specific features, like location-based recommendations or timely notifications, can enhance user engagement.

Incorporating these UX design principles leads to a product that doesn't just fulfill functional needs but also delights users. As we delve deeper into the product development process, our next focus is on prototyping. This crucial phase allows us to bring design concepts to life, enabling iterative testing and refinement with our target audience, moving us closer to achieving the ideal product vision.

Building a Prototype

Prototyping is a key stage in the product development process, offering a unique opportunity to test ideas, engage users early, examine user interactions, and spot potential issues prior to embarking on full-scale development. It represents the initial tangible version of your product concept, integrating interactive elements and the intended user experience to ensure alignment among stakeholders and developers.

Building Prototype: A Step-by-Step Guide

Define the Objectives: Initiate the process by pinpointing exactly what you intend to achieve with your prototype. Identify the specific features, functionalities, or user experiences you wish to explore or validate.

Gather Requirements: Compile essential information about the required features, functionalities, and user flows. Collaborate with designers, the business team, and potential users to gain a well-rounded perspective on what the prototype needs to include.

Choose Your Tools: Select prototyping tools that best suit your project's needs and your team's skill set. Whether it's simple paper sketches or sophisticated software like InVision, or Figma, the right tool will facilitate the prototyping process effectively.

Develop the Prototype: Build your prototype with a focus on key user flows and interactions. The fidelity of your prototype can vary, but it should offer enough detail to enable meaningful user testing. Consider creating several versions for A/B testing or to evaluate different design approaches.

Test and Iterate: Engage target users in testing your prototype, paying close attention to how they interact with it and seeking their feedback. Ask targeted questions that align with your prototyping objectives, examining not just usability but the relevance and effectiveness of the proposed features. Iterate on the prototype based on this insightful feedback.

Prototyping is essential for resource management, mitigating the risk associated with developing features that may not meet user needs or show viability. By introducing users to the prototype early, you can validate assumptions and refine the user experience based on direct feedback, significantly enhancing the product's usability and appeal. Moreover, prototyping fosters clear communication and collaboration across different teams, ensuring a consistent approach to the product's development and execution.

Digital Tools for Prototyping

The digital landscape offers many prototyping tools, each with distinct features tailored to strengthen the creative process.

Sketch: Well-known for its user-friendly design interface, Sketch is a prime choice for creating interactive prototypes. It facilitates the crafting of user interfaces and the development of click-through prototypes, invaluable for outlining user journeys and supporting design decisions at the outset. With vector editing ability and a robust plugin ecosystem, Sketch adds a layer of flexibility to the design workflow.

Figma: Figma excels with its collaborative, cloud-based approach to design and prototyping. It supports simultaneous collaboration, allowing team members to contribute to a design in real time. This tool excels in generating interactive prototypes and designing interfaces while simplifying the feedback loop. Figma's cloud foundation eliminates software installation hassles and version discrepancies, fostering a transparent and immediate collaborative environment.

InVision: InVision offers a holistic solution for crafting high-fidelity prototypes and facilitating team collaboration. It enables the creation of dynamic prototypes that mimic real-world interactions through hotspots, transitions, and animations. The platform's collaboration features make feedback gathering and design iteration straightforward. Its seamless integration with other design tools, such as Sketch, streamlines the transition from design to development.

Balsamiq: Balsamiq prioritizes simplicity and rapidity, making it an excellent tool for low-fidelity wireframes. It's designed to foster quick ideation and conceptualization, helping Product Managers to convey their visions effectively. The tool's sketch-like aesthetics encourage early-stage feedback and discussions, focusing on functionality and user interaction rather than design intricacy. This emphasis on swift prototyping and iterative design in the initial stages of product development makes Balsamiq a potent tool for shaping product concepts.

Each tool presents unique functionalities and workflows, enabling Product Managers to select the most fitting option based on the project's specific requirements and team dynamics. These digital prototyping tools are critical in bringing product ideas to life, ensuring that they resonate with user needs and expectations, thereby enhancing the overall design and development process.

A/B Testing in Product Development

A/B testing, or split testing, plays a pivotal role in the product development landscape, offering a robust framework for making data-driven decisions and validating hypotheses. This method involves segmenting users into groups to test different versions of a product or feature, thereby generating actionable insights on the impact of specific variations on crucial metrics such as user behavior, conversion rates, and overall engagement.

Key Principles of A/B Testing

Define Clear Metrics: The first step in A/B testing is to identify and set clear, measurable metrics for evaluation. These metrics should remain consistent throughout the testing process to ensure the results are focused and actionable.

Embrace as a Continuous Practice: A/B testing should not be seen as a one-off exercise but as an integral, ongoing part of the product development cycle. Every piece of user feedback or data point can be a trigger for further testing, often uncovering unexpected insights that challenge initial assumptions.

Cultivate a Culture of Experimentation: Encouraging an environment where experimentation is valued is crucial. Promote the testing of new ideas and hypotheses within your team, ensuring that resources and support are readily available for such initiatives.

Prioritize Data Over Opinions: While intuition and experience are important, they should not conceal the practical evidence and insights gained from user feedback. A/B testing offers an objective foundation for decision-making, helping to reduce bias and reliance on subjective judgments.

Adopting A/B testing is coherent to including a mindset of continuous inquiry, validation, and iteration, guided by objective data. This mindset ensures that product decisions are firmly anchored in actual user behaviors and preferences, facilitating a more targeted and user-centric approach to product development.

Keep in mind, A/B testing is more than just a technique; it's a critical strategy for refining and optimizing your product based on solid data. By systematically applying A/B testing, you ensure your product evolves in a direction that genuinely resonates with your users, ultimately leading to a more successful and engaging product experience.

Conducting Effective A/B Testing

To ensure that A/B testing is both reliable and yields meaningful insights, a structured approach is essential. Here's a roadmap for conducting A/B tests that can lead to successful outcomes:

Identify the Testing Goal: Start with a clear definition of what you aim to achieve with the A/B test. This could range from boosting user engagement, enhancing conversion rates, to evaluating the performance of a new feature.

Formulate a Hypothesis: Craft a hypothesis based on your goal. For instance, to increase sign-ups, you might hypothesize, "Changing the sign-up button from blue to green will increase user registrations."

Select the Variables: Identify the specific variable you wish to test. Remember, in A/B testing, you should only alter one variable at a time (like button color, page layout, or call-to-action phrasing) to accurately measure its effect.

Create the Variants: Develop two versions for testing: Version A (the control) and Version B (the variant), with only the chosen variable differing between them.

Segment Your Audience: Divide your audience into two similar groups randomly. Each group will experience one of the two product versions.

Run the Test: Launch both versions to your segmented audience for a period that's not only sufficient to collect meaningful data but also concise enough to prevent external factors from influencing the results.

Analyze the Data: After completing the test, analyze the results to see which version met your goal more effectively. Utilize analytical tools to track and understand user behavior.

Draw Conclusions: Determine if your hypothesis stands. If the variant proved more effective, consider implementing the change. If not, delve into the reasons and learn from the outcome.

Report and Iterate: Share your findings with your team and stakeholders. Every test, regardless of its outcome, provides valuable insights. Use this knowledge to refine your approach or to plan further tests.

Implement and Monitor: If you decide to roll out the successful variant, keep monitoring the relevant metric to ensure the change continues to yield positive results over time.

Integrating A/B Testing Throughout the Product Lifecycle

A/B testing offers value in both, the prototyping phase and after the product has been launched. Here's how you can effectively integrate A/B testing throughout different stages of your product's lifecycle:

During Prototyping

Objective: Evaluate design decisions, UI elements, and user interactions.

Benefits: Early identification of usability issues, facilitating adjustments before product finalization.

Application: Compare design layouts, navigation flows, or content structures to arrive at informed design choices.

After Product Launch

Objective: Validate real-world changes through immediate user feedback.

Tools and Techniques: Use analytics to segment users and test features or updates, keeping an eye on key performance indicators.

Adaptability: Quickly respond to user needs, market trends, or competitive pressures, optimizing for retention, engagement, or revenue.

By incorporating A/B testing at every stage, from early prototypes to post-launch adjustments, you ensure continuous refinement and optimization of your product based on real user feedback and data. This diligent approach is crucial for developing a product that not only meets user needs but also stands out in the competitive market.

Chapter Summary and Reflections

In our detailed exploration of product discovery within the expansive field of product management, we've underscored the critical importance of adopting a user-centered approach to build products that truly resonate with users. This chapter has illuminated product discovery as the foundational phase of the product development lifecycle, essential for ideation, understanding user needs, and conceptualizing solutions that meaningfully connect with users.

Key Insights and Learnings

Crafting a Precise Problem Statement: Initiating our journey with the creation of a clear problem statement proved foundational. This crucial step deepens our understanding of user needs and challenges, paving the way for innovative solutions.

Developing User Personas: We emphasized the creation of user personas, which serve as detailed, fictional representations of our target audience. These personas guide our design decisions, ensuring our solutions are finely tuned to meet user expectations.

Mapping the Customer Journey and Emotions: The techniques of customer journey mapping and emotional mapping emerged as invaluable tools. They provide a comprehensive view of user interactions and emotional experiences with our products, identifying opportunities for enhancing the user experience and addressing pain points.

Structured Product Discovery Approaches: We delved into systematic methods like the double diamond model and design thinking. These frameworks guide us through identifying problems, ideating, prototyping, and testing, ensuring a thorough and effective product discovery process.

Achieving Product-Market Fit: The concept of Product-Market Fit was highlighted for its significance in aligning our products with market needs. Through the Product-Market Fit pyramid model, we examined strategies for identifying market needs and aligning our product's features and value proposition.

The Integral Roles of UX and UI: The discussion extended to the crucial roles of UX and UI in product discovery. UX design focuses on creating seamless user experiences, while UI design enhances the product with appealing visual elements. Together, they are paramount in delivering a product that captivates and satisfies users.

The Importance of Prototyping: Prototyping was underscored as a vital stage, enabling the visualization, testing of product ideas, and gathering early user feedback to refine our approach before extensive development efforts.

Leveraging A/B Testing: Lastly, A/B testing was presented as an essential mechanism for hypothesis validation and product optimization, driven by data and user feedback to compare different product features effectively.

Reflection for Product Managers:

As we wrap up this comprehensive exploration of product discovery, it's essential for Product Managers to adopt several critical insights that can significantly impact the journey from ideation to a successful market offering.

• **Elevate Product Discovery**: Prioritize the product discovery phase, dedicating plenty of resources to deeply understand customer needs and market dynamics. This alignment is foundational, ensuring your product vision and solutions are continuously refined to meet real user demands. Treat product discovery as an ongoing dialogue with your market, fostering a product that is both responsive and relevant.

• **Solve the Core Problem**: The essence of product management lies in solving problems. Focus your efforts on identifying and addressing the most significant user challenges. This targeted approach ensures your solutions are not only valued but deemed indispensable by your users.

• **Advocate for Product-Market Fit**: Guard against the allure of personal bias towards your ideas. The essence of product success is a robust alignment with market needs. A product that resonates with market demand is a product poised for triumph.

• **Implement Discovery Frameworks**: Utilize structured product discovery models to streamline the ideation and development process. These frameworks offer a methodical way to brainstorm, define, refine, and deliver solutions that genuinely address user needs and challenges.

• **Prioritize UX Design**: The impact of UX design on your product's success is paramount. Strive for a product that excels not only in aesthetic appeal but in usability, functionality, and user satisfaction. Incorporating principles of UX design across conceptual design, information architecture, and interaction design can significantly elevate the user experience.

• **Leveraging User Feedback**: Engage in continuous feedback loops with your users throughout the discovery and development process. Employ user research, usability testing, and prototyping as tools to unearth insights into user behaviors, needs, and preferences, refining your product based on these learnings.

As we progress, the forthcoming chapter will delve into the nuts and bolts of product development. We'll explore strategies for crafting a compelling product roadmap, the details of building a Minimum Viable Product (MVP), and the application of agile methodologies. This next chapter aims to arm you with actionable strategies and insights to turn your product concepts into reality, navigating the path from visionary ideas to market successes efficiently.

Stay tuned as we continue our journey, shedding light on transforming groundbreaking ideas into products that captivate and succeed in the competitive landscape.

CHAPTER 3
BUILD YOUR PRODUCT

Now we are moving our journey from the drawing board to the real world. After diving deep into research and wrapping our heads around what our customers truly need, we've arrived at a pivotal stage: turning all those insights and strategies into a tangible product that delivers real value to your audience.

Building a product is much more than just a list of features mended together. It involves detailed planning, skillful execution, and constant fine-tuning of our creation. Our first milestone on this journey is the product roadmap. Think of it as your treasure map, charting the path from concept to launch, making sure that every step we take is aligned with our grand vision and strategy.

One of the critical landmarks ahead is crafting a Minimum Viable Product (MVP). This stripped-down version of your product, equipped only with its core features, serves as our reality check to confirm we're on the right track, offering us a chance to get real-world feedback and validate our hypotheses early. This lean approach to building—test, learn, refine—ensures that we're ready for the full-scale product, we're going exactly where our users need us to be.

But let's not forget, creating a product is a team effort. It demands syncing up with our team and making sure we're all steering in the same direction, aligned with what our stakeholders expect. This is where Agile development methodologies excel. Agile is all about embracing change, working together efficiently, and making steady progress. It's perfectly suited for the ever-changing world of product development, allowing us to deliver value in bite-sized pieces and stay open to feedback, ensuring we're always moving closer to our users' hearts.

In this chapter, we're diving into the process of making your product a reality. We'll navigate through using product roadmaps effectively, unveil the strategic power of MVPs, and learn how to integrate Agile principles into your development process. By the end of this journey, you'll be equipped to turn your vision into a product that not only exists in the market but succeeds, adapting gracefully to every new discovery along the way.

The Product Roadmap

Jeff Bezos once advised to 'be stubborn on vision but flexible on details,' a philosophy that perfectly captures the essence of a product roadmap. Serving as much more than a plan, the product roadmap acts as your strategic compass, aligning your ambitious vision with the concrete steps required to bring it to life. It charts the path of your product's development, highlighting the key goals and milestones along the way, yet remains agile, ready to shift with new discoveries, market changes, and the unavoidable surprises that come with innovation.

Many Product Managers feel overwhelmed by creating a roadmap. Balancing the expectations of various stakeholders and squeezing a lot of ideas into limited timelines can feel like trying to solve a puzzle where the pieces keep changing. If you've ever found yourself struggling with a roadmap that seems more like a wish list than a workable plan, it's a sign to pause and recalibrate. Remember, a roadmap is your guide, not your constraint. It's meant to trigger dialogue, drive teamwork, and invite ongoing refinement.

Marty Cagan, in his book "Inspired," highlights two hard truths of product development that are especially relevant when thinking about product roadmap. First, you'll likely find that at least half of the ideas you plan won't deliver the expected value. And second, for those ideas with promise, reaching their full potential often requires multiple iterations. This reality can be distressing especially for small and medium-sized businesses where every resource counts, and the pressure isn't just about 'time to market' but more about reaching profitability—'time to money'—as swiftly as possible.

This section is all about clarifying the process of building a product roadmap. We'll tackle how to weave your big-picture goals with the nitty-gritty of day-to-day development, ensuring your roadmap is a living document that guides your journey without constraining your ability to adapt and evolve. Let's dive into creating a roadmap that's ambitious yet anchored in reality, a roadmap that empowers your vision while staying agile in the aspect of product development's constant change.

Crafting Your Strategic Product Roadmap

As a Product Manager, one of your key tasks is to forge a roadmap that is both achievable and robust, a document that aligns your team and stakeholders around the product's vision, goals, and execution path. This roadmap should not only prioritize the most impactful features based on well-defined objectives and user needs but also maintain the flexibility to pivot as new information comes to light. Here are essential steps to guide you in creating a roadmap that leads to success:

Start with Your Vision and Goals: Tie up your roadmap with the product vision and objectives outlined initially. Every feature and milestone plotted should trace directly back to solving the core problem your product addresses and delivering value to your users.

Prioritize Customer Needs: Ground your roadmap in the deep understanding of customer pain points and needs, derived from exhaustive research and discovery efforts. Evaluate the relevance and potential impact of each feature in solving these problems, assessing it against the feasibility and resources required.

Embrace Team Collaboration: The roadmap should be a collective effort, incorporating perspectives from engineering, customer service, sales, and leadership through brainstorming and regular feedback. This inclusive approach ensures a diversified viewpoint and fosters comprehensive planning.

Organize with Themes and Initiatives: Structure your roadmap around broad themes or objectives, breaking them down into specific initiatives or projects like 'User Onboarding Improvement' or 'Performance Enhancement.' This categorization clarifies the strategic direction and rationale behind prioritizing certain features or improvements.

Define the Timeline: Outline a realistic timeline, usually spanning from six months to a year, taking into account market trends, competitive landscape, and your capacity. Break this timeline into shorter intervals, like quarters or release cycles, to manage development phases and facilitate ongoing assessment.

Choose the Right Visualization: Select a roadmap format that resonates with your team and stakeholders. Whether it's a Gantt chart, a Kanban board, or simple timelines, the key is to present the roadmap in an easily digestible and visually appealing manner that highlights priorities and stages of development.

Communicate and Adapt: View your roadmap as a living document. Keep stakeholders in the loop with regular updates and be open to reshaping the roadmap based on fresh market insights, technological shifts, or internal feedback. Clear, ongoing communication is vital for ensuring everyone is aligned and ready to adapt.

By following these steps, your roadmap will not just serve as a directive for developing your product but will also reflect a keen focus on satisfying customer needs, smart feature prioritization, and cohesive team effort towards realizing your strategic vision. Next, we'll delve into how digital tools can streamline and enrich the roadmapping process, making it an even more effective guide for your product development journey.

Choosing the Product Roadmapping Tools

As we dive into the practical aspects of bringing our product roadmap to life, it's essential to leverage digital tools that streamline the process, boost communication, and enhance transparency across all teams and stakeholders. These tools benefit in crafting visually prominent roadmaps and making strategic decisions based on collective insights. Here's a look at some standout tools that are reshaping how Product Managers approach roadmapping.

Productboard: A standout choice for those keen on aligning their product closely with user needs. Product board excels in gathering user feedback, identifying trends, and making evidence-based prioritization decisions. Its strength lies in its ability to create dynamic, interactive roadmaps that clearly communicate the strategic plan to different audiences, ensuring everyone is on the same page.

Aha!: This tool is a powerhouse for visualizing and sharing your product's journey. Aha! brings to the table robust functionalities like idea management, strategic planning, and detailed roadmap visualization. It's designed to cater to various roadmap styles, offering customization that ensures your roadmap not only guides your team but also engages stakeholders by clearly showcasing the product's future path.

Airtable: For those who appreciate the simplicity of spreadsheets but need more power, Airtable is a perfect match. It blends the straightforwardness of spreadsheet applications with the depth of a full-fledged database, allowing for a highly customizable roadmap creation experience. Its visual and organizational capabilities make it an adaptable choice for managing features, tracking progress, and scheduling releases.

Air focus: Tailored specifically for Product Managers, Airfocus shines with its prioritization and roadmapping capabilities. It guides you in concentrating your efforts on what truly matters through an intuitive scoring system, helping to distill high-impact tasks and features. Whether you prefer Kanban boards, Gantt charts, or simple timelines, Air focus offers the flexibility to visualize your roadmap in a way that best suits your project's needs.

These tools are invaluable helpers in the Product Manager's search to articulate a clear product vision, synchronize team efforts, and prioritize effectively. As we advance in building your product, remember that you are primarily delivering value to your customers. It's not always about the size or scope of your initial offering that matters, but about hitting the market with a solution that resonates. This brings us to the concept of the Minimum Viable Product (MVP), a strategy to test, learn, and refine your product with minimal upfront investment. Next, we'll delve into the MVP, exploring its significance in validating your ideas, reducing risks, and accelerating the delivery of value to your users. Let's explore the MVP journey together, learning how to make your product idea a reality with efficiency and impact.

The Minimal Viable Product (MVP) Strategy

In the landscape of product development, one of the most significant challenges is ensuring that a new product or feature is not just well-conceived but also well-received by users. It's an unfortunate reality that many products fail after development due to poor user adoption. You might argue, "I've done the homework, identified key pain points, and their solutions. Why didn't it catch on?" The misstep usually lies in overcommitting to a product based on initial research and discovery, only to find user adoption lagging. This gap between expectation and reality is where the concept of the Minimal Viable Product (MVP) becomes crucial.

Consider the case of Google Glass. This innovative wearable technology was anticipated to revolutionize user interaction with digital information. Despite the initial excitement, it failed to gain traction due to privacy issues and limited practical use-cases, leading to its discontinuation. Google Glass is a classic example of a product that, while technologically advanced, didn't align with the actual needs and concerns of its potential market.

The essence of an MVP is to test the waters before diving in. It's a streamlined version of your product, designed with just enough features to attract early adopters and validate the overall product concept. Deploying an MVP allows you to gather critical feedback from this initial user base, refine your product, and make informed, data-driven enhancements.

Amazon's journey is a testament to the effective use of the MVP approach. Starting as an online bookstore, Jeff Bezos's strategy was to keep overheads low. Instead of storing books, Amazon operated on a demand-response basis, sourcing books as orders were placed. This lean approach enabled Amazon to validate the online book-selling market with minimal investment. As demand increased, Amazon gradually expanded its offerings and infrastructure. This careful, feedback-driven expansion from books to an array of products and services exemplifies how starting small—with a clear focus on learning from user interactions—can underpin monumental success.

In the following sections, we'll dive into the nuances of MVPs, exploring how they can serve as a launchpad for your product, allowing you to test, learn, and adapt efficiently. Leveraging MVPs effectively can transform your product from an idea to a market-loved solution, ensuring you build not just for the sake of creating but for meaningful user engagement and success. Let's unpack the MVP concept further, understanding its pivotal role in turning great ideas into successful products.

MVP Strategies for Validating New Ideas

MVPs stand as a critical tool for initiating new products, offering a practical approach to validating innovation. Take IBM's venture into voice-command technology as a prime example. Eager to explore computer operation via voice commands, IBM conducted a clever experiment where participants interacted with what they believed was a voice-responsive computer. In reality, their commands were manually executed by someone using traditional input methods out of sight. This experiment revealed a crucial insight: despite the appeal of advanced speech-to-text capabilities, users found voice commands less efficient and more awkward than standard inputs. This exposure emphasized that for technology to be embraced, it must not only innovate but also align with user preferences for efficiency and ease of use.

Selecting the optimal MVP type is pivotal in the journey of product development, necessitating a careful balance of your available resources, time constraints, and the unique attributes of your product and target market. Each MVP model presents its own set of benefits, tailored to different scenarios and stages of the idea validation process. Let's explore different types of MVP.

Types of MVP

When it comes to selecting the right Minimum Viable Product (MVP) for your project, the decision depends on the unique needs and goals of your product. Various MVP types offer different insights and benefits. Here's a closer look at some common MVP models, each paired with real-world examples to illuminate their practical applications:

Single-Feature MVP: This MVP focuses on a singular, core feature pivotal for solving a key user problem. It's a focused approach to measure interest and functionality before broadening the product scope. Consider Slack's origins; it started as a chatbot named "Tiny Speck," to streamline team communication and collaboration, which, through feedback and iteration, grown into the multifaceted collaboration platform we utilize today.

Concierge MVP: Here, the service or solution your product aims to deliver is manually executed. It's a hands-on way to confirm market demand and gather user insights without the initial complexity of full-scale development. Zappos exemplifies this approach. Initially, the founder confirmed the viability of selling shoes online by manually fulfilling orders from local stores, a step that validated the online demand for shoes before the establishment of their extensive e-commerce system.

Fake Door MVP: This MVP simulates your product's functionality, giving users the impression of a fully automated service. It allows you to test user interactions and collect feedback without building out the backend. Groupon, for instance, started as a simple WordPress site where daily deals were posted. When a customer bought a deal, the team manually emailed them a PDF coupon, enabling Groupon to validate their business idea before investing in a custom-built platform.

Landing Page MVP: A straightforward landing page that outlines your product's benefits and captures user interest through sign-ups or pre-orders. This method was essential for Buffer, a social media tool, which validated its market demand through a simple webpage and sign-up form, gathering a foundational user base even before product completion.

Explainer Video MVP: This is a short video that explains your product's value proposition. It can be used to measure interest and collect sign-ups before building the actual product. Dropbox successfully used this type of

MVP by creating a 3-minute video demonstrating how their product would work. The video led to a significant increase in sign-ups on their beta waiting list, validating the demand for the product.

Mockup MVP: Detailed, interactive mockups of your product presented to users or investors for feedback. Tools like Balsamiq, Figma, and InVision are popular tools for creating such prototypes. InVision itself began with a mockup MVP, using an interactive prototype to secure feedback and initial orders ahead of development.

Each of these MVP models serves as a strategic step, allowing you to validate concepts, engage early users, and refine your product with minimal initial investment. Understanding and choosing the right MVP type can significantly influence your product's path to market success, providing clarity and direction in the often-uncertain early stages of development. For example, while a Landing Page MVP might be the perfect tool for evaluating initial interest in a novel concept, a Single-Feature MVP could be more effective for studying a particular element of an already existing product. The mastery lies in choosing an MVP approach that not only aligns with your strategic goals but also yields the most meaningful and actionable feedback.

Through strategic MVP selection, you're equipped to navigate the complexities of introducing innovative solutions, ensuring that every new venture is not just a leap of faith but a measured step towards fulfilling genuine user needs and preferences.

Building Your MVP: A Step-by-Step Guide

As you begin on this journey, the primary question to consider is: What is the fundamental objective of your MVP? Is it to explore the viability of cutting-edge technology, assess the potential of a new feature, or measure market interest? Pinning down this goal is your crucial starting point.

An MVP isn't about delivering a flawless, fully featured product right out of the gate. Instead, it's about encapsulating just enough functionality to attract early adopters, prove your concept's worth, and lay the groundwork for future enhancements. Your MVP should represent your product's fundamental value proposition, emphasizing practicality over perfection. This approach ensures your MVP acts as a dependable guide for your product's continued development.

Here's a step-by-step guide tailored for digital products on building your MVP. If you're working on a physical product, you'll need to adapt these steps to fit the specific challenges of tangible goods:

Identifying Key MVP Features: Begin by pinpointing the essential features that will test your product's viability in the market. Focus on functionalities that are central to your product's value. Engage your team in brainstorming to explore various feature ideas that support your product's benefits. Aim to generate a broad list of potential features without yet assessing their feasibility or impact.

Feature Evaluation and Prioritization: With your feature list in hand, categorize these features based on the benefits they deliver. Within each category, highlight the three to five features that most closely align with your key benefits. This initial prioritization is subject to change, depending on the feedback you receive down the line.

Mapping the User Journey: Gain a deep understanding of the user journey, detailing every interaction and step a user takes with your product. This process should center around the user's goals, the challenges they encounter, and their aspirations. Ensure your MVP's essential features address these user needs effectively.

Sketching the Interface: Move on to sketching basic wireframes or interfaces for your product, focusing on simplicity and usability. These initial sketches should capture your MVP's core features and how users will interact with them. Utilize either traditional sketching tools like pen and paper or digital platforms to bring your concepts to life.

Creating Interactive Mockups: Progress from basic sketches to interactive mockups that offer a more realistic user experience. Utilize digital design tools to create clickable prototypes. This step is crucial for gathering accurate feedback and fine-tuning your MVP's design.

Prioritizing Functionality Over Design: In this MVP phase, the spotlight should be on functionality and user experience, rather than complex design details. While aesthetics plays a role, the foremost objective is to verify if the MVP addresses the problem it's designed to solve. Adopt a minimalist design philosophy, steering clear of investing heavily in detailed visuals at this stage.

Spotify's MVP Journey: Tuning into User Needs

The story of Spotify's initial steps towards creating their MVP sheds light on a strategic approach that perfectly blends vision with user-centric functionality. Spotify set forward with a straightforward mission: "To unlock a world of music, offer personalized tunes, and ensure frictionless listening joy." Central to this mission was pinpointing exactly what users of a music streaming service might need, focusing sharply on three essential needs: an exhaustive music collection, customized music suggestions, and a seamless user interface.

Feature Identification and Categorization: Spotify's team embarked on a creative brainstorming venture, eventually sorting potential features into groups that mirrored their core value proposition:

Benefit Category 1: Access to a vast library of music:

Feature 1: Search and play any song or artist on demand.

Feature 2: Curated playlists sorted by genres, moods, and activities.

Feature 3: Offline listening for premium subscribers.

Benefit Category 2: Personalized recommendations:

Feature 1: Recommendations powered by algorithms that consider listening history.

Feature 2: A weekly playlist called "Discover Weekly," featuring personalized song suggestions.

Feature 3: "Daily Mixes" that blend favorite genres and artists.

Benefit Category 3: Seamless listening experience:

Feature 1: Cross-device synchronization for uninterrupted playback.

Feature 2: A user-friendly interface with intuitive navigation and controls.

Feature 3: High-quality audio streaming options.

Prioritizing MVP Features: In the next step, Spotify carefully reviewed and prioritized these features, balancing their potential impact against development feasibility. They identified critical features for their MVP that were fundamental to their value proposition and crucial for engaging early users. These included the ability to search and play any song, sophisticated algorithm-powered recommendations, and cross-device synchronization, which were not just central to their core offering but also crucial in attracting early adopters and collecting initial feedback.

As Spotify continued its journey, gathering user feedback and adjusting to market dynamics became an ongoing process. They gradually expanded their feature set, responding to users' evolving needs and preferences. This adaptive strategy enabled Spotify to transform from a basic MVP into the comprehensive and beloved music streaming platform it is today.

Strategic MVP Integration in Product Evolution

An MVP is not only helpful for launching new products or exploring new concepts; it's equally vital for mature products that have been in the market for a while. This strategy becomes particularly significant when you're planning to add new features to your already established product.

It's critical to remember that just because you have the resources to develop and roll out a new feature, it doesn't guarantee it will be embraced by your users. Even with a solid user base, investing in a feature that doesn't resonate can lead to wasted resources and misdirected product development.

To harness MVPs effectively throughout your product's life, especially post-launch, it's crucial to integrate them into your ongoing development process. After wrapping up the discovery phase and pinpointing a prospective new feature or improvement, the MVP serves as your proof of concept.

Incorporating MVPs into your regular product development rhythm ensures that every new feature is not just born out of internal brainstorming but is rigorously tested against real user feedback and insights. This method fosters a product evolution that's deeply rooted in user-centric principles, ensuring new additions are in lockstep with your audience's current needs and desires.

Mastering Interview skills for MVP Testing

Diving into MVP feedback is a critical part of its journey, and conducting insightful customer interviews stands as a cornerstone of this process. For you, the Product Manager, improving your interview skills is not merely about enhancing MVP testing—it's about enriching your toolkit for continuous product evolution and user engagement. Reflect on the "Mom Test" principles we discussed earlier, and consider these guidelines to elevate your interview techniques:

Encourage Open Dialogue: Craft your questions to encourage detailed responses about the users' experiences and feelings. Avoid the yes-or-no traps that narrow down insights, limiting your understanding of user experiences and needs.

Past Behavior as a Predictor: Focus on users' actual past behaviors instead of hypothetical future possibilities. Remember, the way people have acted historically is often a more accurate forecast of what they'll do next, not the hypotheticals they imagine.

Chase Concrete Stories: Your aim should be to uncover specific instances and narratives. These stories shed light on the real-life scenarios where your product fits, moving away from opinions that might not hold up in practice.

Beware of Bias: Craft your questions to avoid leading the user towards a 'desired' answer or unintentionally seeking confirmation for your product idea. The real treasure lies in uncovering the user's true needs and challenges that your MVP seeks to solve.

Learn with Every Conversation: Approach each interview as a step to deeper understanding. Collect insights to refine both your product direction and your interview approach, iterating towards more meaningful engagements.

Post-interview, take time to refine the feedback, looking for trends and actionable insights. This insightful process will spotlight critical user needs and the elements of your MVP that resonate with your audience. Leverage these insights for iterative MVP refinement, ensuring your product continuously aligns with genuine user demands and expectations.

A Case Study on Fitness Apps

Picture this: you're building a fitness app tailored for the busy life of professionals. Instead of asking leading questions like, "Would you use a fitness app made just for busy folks?" – which might prompt superficially positive but ultimately unhelpful feedback – aim for real, tangible insights into their daily struggles and routines. Here's how you can dig deeper:

Dive Into Their Current Routine: "Walk me through how you managed your fitness routine last week." This question isn't about hypothetical scenarios; it's rooted in the real world, encouraging users to share their actual experiences, habits, and where they might be hitting roadblocks.

Reflect on Previous App Experiences: "Share your experience with the last fitness app you tried." This inquiry opens the door to valuable lessons from past attempts, offering valuable data on what features they might have found useful or what aspects may have led them to stop using the app.

Pinpoint the Challenges: "What's been the biggest difficulty in keeping up with your fitness within a packed schedule?" Here, you're focusing on the exact pain points your app aims to improve. Direct insights into their challenges empower you to tailor your solution precisely to their needs.

These kinds of questions are strategic in that they uncover real-life, actionable information. The responses provide a window into the users' daily lives, revealing their actual behaviors, needs, and the challenges they face in maintaining a fitness routine within a busy professional life. This information is invaluable for building a fitness app that not only aligns with the users' lifestyle but also effectively addresses their specific fitness challenges.

Rethinking the MVP: A Reality Check

As you navigate the MVP development journey, take a moment to pause and reflect. Ask yourself: Does your MVP truly adhere to the Minimum Viable Product character? It's a common issue for MVPs to expand into nearly finished products. These products are loaded with features and complex processes but are still tagged as MVPs. This often happens when revenue or sales become the main success indicators for the MVP. Beware, as this focus might blur the true purpose of an MVP and lead to complexities later on.

Launching a nearly complete product as an MVP deviate from the heart of lean startup methods and agile values. The real beauty of an MVP lies in its power to test assumptions, gather user insights, and guide future enhancements with solid, data-backed decisions. It champions a cycle of ongoing refinement and adaptation based on what users really think and need, significantly boosting your product's chances of truly resonating with your audience. Rushing out a nearly done product risks skipping over these essential feedback loops, potentially leading to wasted resources and missed opportunities for crucial insights.

Getting your MVP off the ground is an important milestone, but remember, it's only the beginning. Once your MVP proves its worth, it's time to broaden and fine-tune your product, in sync with your dev team's efforts.

Next up, we're diving into Agile development. Agile is more than just a buzz in the tech world; it's a crucial mindset for any Product Manager aiming to deliver products that genuinely meet, and exceed, user expectations. In our upcoming section, we'll break down why Agile is such a key player in product development and how its principles can help lift your product development process from good to exceptional. Get ready to see how Agile can become a cornerstone in realizing dynamic, user-focused development success.

Agile Development: A Revolution in Building Products

Jeff Sutherland, one of the minds behind Scrum, once shared, "Agile development isn't just a process; it's a whole new way to think about creating products." Agile is all about embracing change and keeping a laser focus on delivering real value to customers. It's become a cornerstone in software development and beyond, empowering teams to adapt swiftly to changes in market demands and user expectations.

At its heart, Agile is about being ready to pivot, to experiment, and to learn continuously. It's built on principles that value teamwork, iterative development, and ongoing feedback. This approach breaks away from the old-school, straight-line way of building products. Instead, Agile advocates a cycle of planning, doing, checking, and acting, which keeps your work aligned with real-world needs and ready to adjust at a moment's notice.

The Agile movement has generated various methodologies like Scrum, Kanban, and Lean Development. Each not only brings its flavor to the Agile philosophy but also shares the core idea: to deliver work in small, manageable increments and be ready to shift gears based on feedback and changes.

For you, the Product Manager, diving deep into Agile is non-negotiable. It arms you with strategies to steer your team towards focusing on what customers truly value, working collaboratively, and staying nimble in the face of change.

As we move forward, we'll covering the layers of Agile development. We'll explore different Agile frameworks and show how you can integrate Agile principles into your product management approach. The goal? To build products that don't just meet expectations but exceed them, standing out in a fast-paced market.

The Evolution of Agile Development

Agile development reshaped the landscape of software engineering, originating from the challenges faced by developers in the late 20th and early 21st centuries. Back then, the Waterfall model was the dominant paradigm in software development —a linear, step-by-step approach that, while organized, often fell weak when it came to flexibility and responding to change. Its rigid structure made accommodating changes during the development process both expensive and difficult. Its biggest pitfall was the assumption that every requirement of a project could be known from the start, leading to projects that were slow, over budget, and not always what the user needed by the time they were launched.

In response to these dilemmas, February 2001 saw a pivotal moment in software development history. Seventeen forward-thinking software developers and project leaders met in Snowbird, Utah, united by a common mission: to craft a development methodology that was as dynamic and adaptable as the digital worlds' demands. This meeting concluded in the creation of the Agile Manifesto, setting out values and principles that emphasized adaptability, team collaboration, and keeping the customer at the heart of the development process.

From this groundbreaking summit, Agile evolved into various methodologies, each with its own flavor but all rooted in the manifesto's philosophy. Scrum, with its sprints and specific roles; Kanban, focusing on continuous delivery and efficiency; and Lean development, aiming to deliver maximum value while minimizing waste, are just a few examples.

Agile's impact didn't stay limited to software development. Its principles of flexibility, customer focus, and efficiency have spread across industries, transforming project management and organizational practices worldwide. Agile's growth from a software development fix to a global project management revolution highlights its versatility and effectiveness in promoting projects that truly meet user needs and keep pace with market changes.

Core Values and Principles of Agile Methodology

Agile is more than just a methodology—it's a mindset that emphasizes adaptability, collaboration, and customer focus in product development. Understanding the core values and principles of Agile is crucial for any Product Manager aiming to harness its full potential. Let's dive into the foundational values that shape Agile:

Prioritize People Over Processes: Agile reminds us that the heart of any project is its people. It values the team's interactions and collaboration more than rigid processes. For you, as a Product Manager, this means creating an environment where open communication and teamwork are vital. This approach not only fosters innovation but also keeps your team motivated and focused on common goals.

Focus on Functional Software Over Extensive Documentation: In the fast-moving tech world, getting a working product into users' hands is often more valuable than having detailed documentation. This principle guides you to focus on delivering products that solve user problems effectively, with documentation serving to support rather than block the development process. It's your job to ensure that your team strikes the right balance, focusing on building solutions that truly address user needs.

Engage Customers Over Enforcing Contracts: Agile stresses the importance of continuously engaging with customers rather than adhering rigidly to contracts. This ongoing dialogue with your customers allows you to evolve the product based on real feedback and changing needs, ensuring that what you build remains relevant and highly valued. It's about building partnerships rather than just fulfilling contract terms.

Adapt Change Over Strict Plan Adherence: The tech landscape changes rapidly, and Agile prepares you to navigate and respond to these shifts with agility. This value is about being ready to pivot when necessary, making sure your product stays aligned with market demands and user expectations. It's your role to lead your team through changes, making informed adjustments to your plans and strategies to keep your product competitive and relevant.

By embedding these values into your daily practices, you prepare your team and product for success in a dynamic world. Agile isn't just about managing projects—it's about fostering a culture that values innovation, collaboration, and responsiveness to change.

The Twelve Guiding Principles

These core values lead us to Agile's twelve guiding principles, essential for any Product Manager to fully integrate Agile in the team's practice. Let's dive deep into each principle and how it can shape your approach to product development.

Prioritizing Customer Satisfaction: Agile puts the spotlight on delivering value to customers through frequent releases of functional software, building trust and a strong value proposition with each update.

Welcoming Change: Agile teams succeed on flexibility, readily adapting to changes even late in the development cycle to ensure the product stays relevant and competitive.

Regular Delivery: Agile urges the consistent release of product iterations, enabling rapid feedback and the ability to pivot as needed, ensuring a tight feedback loop with your users.

Stakeholders Collaboration: Keeping a close and continuous collaboration between developers and stakeholders aligns product development with business goals, ensuring everyone is moving in the same direction.

Empowering Teams: An environment that trusts and supports teams to manage their workload leads to more efficient and motivated team members, driving the project forward with a sense of ownership and commitment.

Direct Communication: Favoring face-to-face interactions ensures misunderstandings are minimized, and clarity around project goals and tasks is maintained, nurturing a unified team environment.

Measuring Progress with Working Software: In Agile, tangible, working software is the true measure of progress, focusing on delivering functional features over completing tasks that don't lead to immediate user value.

Sustainable Development: Encouraging a balanced workload ensures teams can maintain their pace and productivity consistently, avoiding burnout and fostering a healthy work environment.

Technical Excellence and Good Design: Agile stresses the importance of quality and design not just for the product's current success but for its future adaptability and growth.

Simplicity: Efficiency is key in Agile, focusing on what's essential and avoiding unnecessary work that doesn't contribute to customer value.

Self-Organizing Teams: Giving teams the self-governance to organize their work encourages innovation, increases accountability, and leads to more effective problem-solving and product development strategies.

Reflect and Adjust: Regular retrospectives allow teams to reflect on their processes and make adjustments, fostering a culture of continuous improvement and learning.

In essence, Agile is not merely about managing change but embracing and leveraging it for better outcomes. Reid Hoffman, the co-founder of LinkedIn, encapsulated this sentiment well: "If you are not embarrassed by the first version of your product, you've launched too late." Implementing Agile is about prioritizing speed and adaptability over perfection. Agile also underscores the importance of teamwork, resonating with Steve Jobs' belief, "Great things in business are never done by one person. They're done by a team of people." As a Product Manager, your role is pivotal in fostering an environment where such collaboration and continuous improvement can thrive, ultimately leading to the creation of superior and relevant products.

Agile is all about leveraging change for better outcomes. It emphasizes that releasing a product that may not be perfect but is out in the market gathering real user feedback is more valuable than waiting for perfection. Reid

Hoffman, the co-founder of LinkedIn, summarized this sentiment well: "If you are not embarrassed by the first version of your product, you've launched too late."

It is a testament to the power of teamwork, echoing Steve Jobs' belief that "Great things in business are never done by one person. They're done by a team of people." You're at the helm of nurturing this collaborative and iterative environment, guiding your team to create products that not only meet but exceed user expectations.

Implementing Agile: Steering the Transition

Transitioning to Agile methodologies marks a pivotal shift in your approach to product development. It's a journey filled with potential, aimed at enhancing adaptability, focusing on the customer, and embracing iterative improvement. Yet, embarking on this transition, especially within different organizational landscapes, presents unique challenges.

For startups and smaller teams, Agile often interconnects well with their inherent flexibility and streamlined operations. These settings are naturally more receptive to change, making the adoption of Agile a catalyst for increased efficiency and a faster market response.

In contrast, larger corporations face more significant obstacles due to their scale, established hierarchies, and established practices. Here, Agile's principles of flexibility and team self-governance can sometimes clash with the status quo, posing challenges that demand strategic navigation. Here's how to tackle some of the most common challenges:

Cultural Resistance

Challenge: Established norms and a top-down management approach may resist the shift towards Agile's team empowerment and collaborative attitude.

Strategy: Craft a change management strategy centered on open dialogue and education. Engage with leadership at all levels to support Agile, addressing concerns and highlighting the benefits for both teams and the organization.

Organizational Structure

Challenge: Rigid hierarchical setups can slow swift decision-making that Agile thrives on.

Strategy: Introduce cross-functional teams to break down silos. Promote a culture of open communication and shared decision-making, underscoring the value of a more dynamic structure to leadership.

Stability and Flexibility

Challenge: The balancing act between maintaining stability and incorporating Agile's flexibility can be tricky.

Strategy: Identify processes that can adapt to Agile without losing essential stability. Champion a culture that allows for controlled experimentation within organizational limits.

Financial Planning

Challenge: Agile's variable scope can clash with traditional financial models built on precise forecasts and budgets.

Strategy: Keep finance teams in the loop, explaining Agile's iterative nature and its implications for budgeting. Collaborate on adaptable financial strategies that accommodate Agile projects.

HR Alignment

Challenge: Conventional HR practices may not fully support the Agile way of working.

Strategy: Work with HR to realign hiring, evaluation, and incentive systems with Agile values. Focus on qualities like adaptability and collaborative skills in recruitment, and tailor performance reviews to reflect Agile's team-centric and iterative approach.

In summary, while the journey to Agile can be complex, particularly in larger organizations, the benefits of increased flexibility, improved collaboration, and customer alignment make this a worthwhile endeavor. By recognizing and addressing the challenges head-on, organizations can successfully navigate this transition and harness the full potential of Agile methodologies.

Exploring Agile Methodologies

Agile development is versatile, offering various methodologies tailored to different team needs, project scopes, and organizational cultures. Let's dive into some of the most prominent Agile methodologies and their unique attributes:

Scrum: Highly popular, Scrum structures development in short, time-boxed periods called sprints, typically lasting two to four weeks. It features roles such as the Scrum Master and Product Owner and includes practices like Daily Stand-ups and Sprint Reviews to ensure progress and adaptability.

Kanban: Originating from Toyota's production system, Kanban emphasizes visualizing workflow and limiting work-in-progress. This approach is highly flexible and allows for continuous delivery without overloading team members.

Lean Software Development: Inspired by Lean manufacturing principles, this approach aims to boost efficiency by cutting waste and maximizing value for the customer. It encourages team empowerment, making decisions at the last responsible moment, and aims for speedy delivery.

Extreme Programming (XP): XP prioritizes technical excellence and customer satisfaction. It advocates for frequent releases in short development cycles, aiming to improve productivity and introduce checkpoints for adopting new customer requirements.

Feature-Driven Development (FDD): FDD combines Agile with more traditional aspects of software development. It breaks projects into discrete features that can be developed in parallel, simplifying progress tracking and complex project management.

Dynamic Systems Development Method (DSDM): One of the earliest Agile methodologies, DSDM is part of the Agile Alliance. It emphasizes the full project lifecycle and encourages active user involvement in a cooperative and collaborative manner.

The choice of an Agile methodology depends on several factors, including the specific dynamics of your team, the nature of the project, and the overall environment of your organization. While each methodology brings its strengths to the table, they all meet on a singular objective: streamlining the development process to be more agile, efficient, and in tune with customer requirements.

In our journey, we'll focus on Scrum and Kanban, two methodologies that have seen broad implementation across the tech industry. We'll dive into how these frameworks can be practically applied to enhance your software development efforts, ensuring that your projects are both dynamic and customer-focused. Let's unpack these methodologies further to see how they can be best utilized in your development journey.

Understanding Scrum

Scrum stands as a cornerstone in the Agile methodology landscape, well-known for its straightforward yet powerful approach to project management. It's designed to foster a culture of continuous improvement, experimentation, and tight feedback loops, making it a valuable asset for teams aiming to evolve and refine their projects dynamically.

At its core, Scrum is structured around a Scrum Team, which includes the Product Owner, the Scrum Master, and the Development Team. These roles form the backbone of any Scrum project, each contributing to the project's success in unique ways. Scrum operates on the principles of transparency, inspection, and adaptation, promoting an environment where teamwork, learning, and iterative progress are paramount.

The Evolution of Scrum

Scrum's roots go back to the mid-1980s when it first appeared as a software development approach. The concept gained traction from a ground-breaking article, "The New New Product Development Game," published in the Harvard Business Review in 1986. Authors Hirotaka Takeuchi and Ikujiro Nonaka likened this new approach to a rugby game, where a self-organizing team collaborates toward a common goal. This was a shift from the sequential, siloed approaches traditionally used in project management.

The article highlighted companies like Honda, Canon, and Fuji-Xerox, which had achieved success by adopting this team-based approach. It emphasized the importance of cross-functional, self-organized teams working in short, iterative cycles to increase flexibility, adaptability, and creativity.

The term "Scrum" comes from rugby and refers to a formation where players group together to gain possession of the ball. Takeuchi and Nonaka used this analogy to underscore the collaborative and adaptive nature of their proposed product development approach.

In the early 1990s, Jeff Sutherland, along with John Scumniotales and Jeff McKenna, fine-tuned the Scrum framework at Easel Corporation. They integrated Scrum principles into their software development practices, evolving the framework through hands-on implementation and experimentation.

As Scrum gained traction, Jeff Sutherland and Ken Schwaber collaborated to formalize the framework and document its principles and practices. They co-authored the influential book "Agile Software Development with Scrum" in 2001, offering a comprehensive guide for implementing Scrum in software development projects.

Today, Scrum serves as a recognized framework for managing complex projects. It helps organizations embrace change, foster transparency, and continually improve both products and processes. Its rich history and proven effectiveness make Scrum a cornerstone of Agile project management.

Scrum Roles Simplified

In Scrum, the team is solid and self-organizing, featuring three pivotal roles: the Product Owner, the Scrum Master, and the Development Team. Each role is distinct in its responsibilities and vital to the team's collective success.

Product Owner: This role acts as the liaison between the team and the product's stakeholders, including customers and users. Tasked with a deep understanding of the product vision, the Product Owner works closely with stakeholders to identify and articulate the product's requirements and its roadmap. They're responsible for maintaining and prioritizing the product backlog, ensuring it's clear, visible, and aligned with stakeholder expectations. The Product Owner plays a key role in providing clarity to the Development Team on requirements, addressing their questions, and giving feedback on their work. Their primary focus is on prioritizing the backlog to maximize value, taking into account various factors such as risk, dependencies, and stakeholder input.

Scrum Master: Serving as both a servant-leader and a facilitator, the Scrum Master guides the team through the Scrum process. This involves leading the team through key Scrum events—Sprint Planning, Daily Scrums, Sprint Reviews, and Sprint Retrospectives—while ensuring adherence to Scrum principles. The Scrum Master is dedicated to creating an environment where the team can self-organize and work efficiently, tackling any obstacles that might slow them down. Their goal is to ensure the team can deliver value effectively and efficiently.

Development Team: They possess all the necessary skills—designing, developing, testing, and releasing—to create and deliver increments of the product that are ready to ship. Working closely with the Product Owner, they select items from the product backlog during Sprint Planning and break these down into actionable tasks. The team meets daily in Scrum meetings to coordinate efforts, address any challenges, and adapt their plans as needed. Through collaboration and shared responsibility, they maintain high standards of quality and completeness in their work.

Each of these roles is vital to the Scrum team's overall success, ensuring that the project moves forward smoothly, obstacles are addressed promptly, and the final product aligns with the user's needs and expectations.

How Does Scrum Work?

Scrum enhances teamwork with a structured yet flexible framework, kicked off with what we call a Sprint. Sprints are intensive work periods, typically lasting 2-4 weeks, where the team focuses on a carefully selected set of tasks aimed at achieving a specific goal.

Sprint Planning: This is where it all starts. The team, together, picks tasks from the product backlog that they commit to completing in the Sprint, guided by a shared Sprint Goal.

Daily Stand-up (Daily Scrum): This quick, daily meeting keeps everyone on the same page. It's a chance for the team to sync up, tackle obstacles, and make sure they're on track to hit their Sprint goals.

Sprint Review: At the Sprint's end, it's show-and-tell time. The team showcases what they've accomplished, inviting feedback from stakeholders to ensure the work aligns with user needs and expectations.

Sprint Retrospective: This is a moment for reflection. The team gathers to look back on the Sprint, discussing what went well and what could be better. It's all about continuous improvement, adjusting strategies and methods to make the next Sprint even more effective.

Through these events, Scrum creates a steady beat of productivity and progress, ensuring everyone moves together towards common goals. It's a cycle of planning, doing, checking, and adjusting, helping the team refine their work and processes bit by bit.

We will go into Scrum ceremonies in detail in next chapter. Now, we'll take a closer look at Kanban, another Agile favorite. Known for its visual workflow management, Kanban is all about keeping work flowing smoothly and efficiently.

The Kanban Framework

In the Agile world, Kanban stands out by making work tasks visible, limiting the number of tasks team can handle at once, and improving task flow. Originally developed for manufacturing, Kanban has grown to be utilized in software development, project management, and many other areas, showcasing its flexibility and effectiveness across different fields.

At the core of Kanban is the practice of visually managing work. This method uses boards and cards to display tasks, their progress, and their current status clearly. The name 'Kanban,' meaning 'visual card' or 'signboard' in Japanese, emphasizes the importance of transparently viewing work tasks, their conditions, and the team's capacity to manage them.

The History of Kanban

Kanban's origins trace back to the 1940s with Taiichi Ohno at Toyota. Facing challenges like overproduction, excessive inventory, and inconsistent workloads, Ohno found inspiration in the way supermarkets restock items based on customer purchases. He applied a similar principle to Toyota's manufacturing processes, introducing a system where visual signals, or Kanban, indicated the need for more materials, thereby streamlining production and minimizing waste.

For many years, Kanban was primarily associated with manufacturing. However, in 2004, David J. Anderson adapted Kanban for the IT industry. Today, Kanban is recognized globally as a straightforward yet powerful approach for visualizing work, managing workflow, and encouraging continuous improvement in various sectors. Its simplicity, adaptability, and focus on transparency have made it a key strategy for teams and organizations aiming to improve productivity, efficiency, and performance.

Key Principles of Kanban:

• **Visualize Workflow:** At the heart of Kanban is the Kanban board, a tool for visually mapping out the workflow. This board, whether physical or digital, displays tasks as cards moving through different stages such as

"Backlog," "To Do," "In Progress," "QA in Progress," and "Done." This visual layout offers a quick, clear view of each task's progress and current status.

• **Limit Work in Progress (WIP):** A critical element of Kanban is limiting the number of tasks being worked on simultaneously. By setting WIP limits for each stage of the workflow, teams can avoid bottlenecks, reduce multitasking, and focus more effectively on task completion. For example, a WIP limit of three in the "In Progress" column means only three tasks can be tackled at once. Setting these limits may require some practice but proves beneficial in streamlining work.

• **Manage Flow:** Managing the movement of tasks through the workflow is vital in Kanban. The aim is to establish a steady, uninterrupted flow, reducing delays and shortening cycle times. Teams use Kanban to analyze and adjust their workflow, reallocating resources as needed for efficient and consistent delivery.

• **Make Policies Explicit**: Kanban advocates for clearly defined policies for each stage of the workflow. These policies might include criteria for task completion or guidelines for task assignments. For example, a policy could state that a task must pass a code review and meet specific quality benchmarks before moving from "In Progress" to "Ready for QA." Such transparency minimizes confusion, fosters accountability, and maintains work quality.

• **Continuous Improvement:** Kanban encourages a mindset of continuous enhancement. Teams regularly evaluate their processes, identify improvement opportunities, and implement changes. By analyzing the Kanban board, generating metrics, and utilizing visual indicators, teams continuously refine their workflow, adjust to changing needs, and boost overall efficiency.

Why Kanban for a Product Manager?

Kanban, with its focus on visual workflows and limits on work-in-progress, brings several advantages to the role of a Product Manager. Key benefits include:

Real-Time Adaptability: Unlike Scrum's fixed sprints, Kanban permits adjustments in real-time, allowing you to shift priorities in response to customer feedback or market changes without major disruptions.

Enhanced Efficiency: The clarity provided by Kanban boards aids in monitoring progress, spotting bottlenecks, and optimally allocating resources. It facilitates quick identification of underperformance or inefficiencies for timely improvement.

Continuous Delivery Focus: Kanban's emphasis on steady flow and ongoing improvement supports frequent updates, feature rollouts, and bug fixes, aligning with the Product Manager's objective of rapid market delivery and consistent customer value.

Improved Team Collaboration: The centralized Kanban board encourages transparent communication, which is especially beneficial for the cross-functional teams which are common in digital product development.

Flexibility: Kanban's adaptability to various organizational structures and absence of rigid roles or rituals makes it an excellent fit for collaboration across different departments, such as marketing, sales, and customer service.

Transparency: The visual nature of Kanban enhances organizational transparency. It allows stakeholders to easily understand ongoing tasks, upcoming projects, and completed work, which is crucial for effective digital product management.

Better Forecasting: By tracking cycle times, or the time taken to complete tasks, Kanban provides valuable data for predicting future performance and making more accurate delivery forecasts.

Scrum or Kanban: Which One's Best for You?

Choosing between Scrum and Kanban involves evaluating your project's specific needs, your team's workflow, and your organizational culture. Both methodologies fall under the Agile umbrella but offer distinct approaches suited to different project environments. Let's break down when you might lean towards Scrum or Kanban.

Choose Scrum When:

Your project is complex and has everchanging requirements. Scrum's structure excels in environments where priorities can change quickly, offering a framework that can pivot as needed.

You're working with fixed deadlines or release cycles. Scrum's sprint cycles create a rhythm of delivery and review, providing predictability in scheduling and output.

Your team is cross-functional and covers all stages of product development, from conception to launch. Scrum encourages comprehensive collaboration and shared responsibility.

Regular stakeholder feedback is crucial for your project's success. Scrum facilitates feedback loops at the end of each sprint, allowing for iterative improvements based on direct input.

Your project benefits from high levels of team interaction and coordination. Scrum's daily stand-ups and sprint retrospectives foster communication and continuous refinement.

Select Kanban When:

Flexibility and responsiveness are your top priorities. Kanban's continuous flow model lets you adjust priorities on the fly, making it easier to handle urgent tasks or changes without disrupting your entire workflow.

You're managing ongoing tasks like support or maintenance, where work comes in a steady, unpredictable stream. Kanban allows you to prioritize and tackle these as they arise.

Your project or team doesn't fit neatly into the sprint-based structure of Scrum. Kanban's flexibility and lack of rigid time frames can accommodate a wide range of working styles and project paces.

You're looking to identify and reduce bottlenecks in your process. The visual nature of Kanban boards highlights where tasks slow down or pile up, helping you streamline your workflow.

Your team is smaller, or your roles are more fluid. Kanban's simplicity and adaptability can be easier to integrate into teams where members wear multiple hats or where project scopes are more open-ended.

In essence, the decision between Scrum and Kanban depends on your project's specific demands and your team's working style. Scrum provides a structured framework ideal for projects with clear iterations and a need for regular stakeholder feedback. In contrast, Kanban offers flexibility and continuous delivery, perfect for ongoing tasks and projects requiring high adaptability.

Hybrid Approaches:

It's important to recognize that different teams within the same organization might benefit from different Agile methodologies, depending on their specific requirements. For instance, a team building new features and diving deep into testing may find their solution in Scrum, due to its structure and focus on iterative development. Meanwhile, a support team, constantly managing incoming requests, may find Kanban to be their secret to staying agile and responsive.

Allowing teams to choose the Agile methodology that best fits their context empowers them to optimize productivity and adapt to specific challenges, contributing to the organization's overall success. Regardless of the chosen methodology, maintaining robust communication and collaboration among teams employing different approaches is key to ensuring organizational cohesion and alignment.

Chapter Conclusion and Reflection

As we close this chapter, let's take a moment to reflect on the significant progresses you've made on the path to building a standout product. This journey has taken us through the foundational pillars of product development: the creation of a Minimum Viable Product (MVP) and the design of a strategic product roadmap.

We've explored the concept MVP, understanding it as more than just a product version—it's your first real conversation with your market, offering just enough value to check interest and gather crucial feedback. Then, we navigated into the critical components of the product roadmap, a crucial document that captures your vision and plots a course for turning that vision into reality.

Our journey didn't stop there. We ventured into the world of Agile development, tracing its origins, and uncovering its pivotal role in modern product development. The Agile Manifesto was not just a document; it was a declaration of a more dynamic, responsive approach to creating products. Embracing Agile means more than changing how we work; it's about changing how we think about work, prioritizing collaboration, flexibility, and the relentless pursuit of customer value.

Reflection for Product Managers

Now is the perfect moment to pause and consider the journey ahead. You're not just building a product; you're leading the charge towards something new and potentially game-changing. Your role as a Product Manager is critical.

Champion the MVP Philosophy: Embrace the MVP not just as a phase in product development but as a mindset of continuous learning and adaptation. Let it remind you that understanding your customer's core needs covers the way for meaningful innovation.

Master the Art of Roadmapping: Your product roadmap is your storybook, illustrating where you want to go and how you plan to get there. Infuse it with clarity, flexibility, and a deep connection to your product's vision. It's your narrative that rallies your team and stakeholders around a shared journey.

Cultivate an Agile Mindset: Agile is more than methodology—it's your strategic advantage in a competitive landscape. It empowers you to navigate change with style, prioritize value delivery, and foster a culture of transparency and collaboration. Agile is your toolset for building not just a product, but a legacy of innovation and customer-centricity.

Embrace Change as a Constant: In the realm of product development, change is the only constant. View every pivot, every new customer insight, and every technological advance as an opportunity to refine and enhance your product.

Foster Team Collaboration: Remember, great products are rarely the result of independent genius. They are born from the collective effort, diverse perspectives, and unwavering commitment of your entire team. Cultivate an environment where every team member feels valued, heard, and empowered to contribute their best.

As we turn the page to "The Art of Agile Management," prepare to dive deeper into the Agile world. We'll explore Scrum artifacts, backlog management, and prioritization techniques, equipping you with the knowledge and tools to navigate the Agile landscape with confidence. Your journey as a Product Manager is a testament to the power of vision, adaptability, and relentless pursuit of excellence. Let's continue to build products that matter, products that resonate, and products that endure.

CHAPTER 4
AGILE MANAGEMENT &
PRIORITIZATION

Agile management is more than following rules. It involves adopting a mindset that values adaptability, teamwork, and a deep commitment to satisfying customers. So, what does it take to manage an Agile process effectively? How can you ensure your team not only embraces this methodology but also excels in it? Moreover, what role do you play in guiding this process towards success?

In this chapter, we dive into the attractive world of Agile management, with a special focus on Scrum, a methodology renowned for its effectiveness in enhancing operations and driving product evolution. Understanding and applying Scrum principles can transform your product development process. This transformation enables a more effective and dynamic approach to meeting customer needs. We'll cover how to excel in using Scrum, focusing on creating and managing a product backlog, writing compelling user stories, leading impactful Scrum ceremonies, and most importantly, mastering the skill of feature prioritization.

We dedicate a section of this chapter to advanced strategies for feature prioritization and stakeholder management—key aspects of your role as a Product Manager. These insights will arm you with the tools to make well-informed decisions, align team efforts with business objectives, and manage stakeholder expectations effectively.

Let's start on this journey together to uncover the secrets of successful Agile management and prioritization.

Product Backlog Management

In Agile product development, everything begins with the backlog. Think of the Product Backlog as your dynamic, prioritized list of everything the product might need—features, enhancements, bug fixes, and technical tasks. It stands as your single source of truth, constantly evolving with user feedback, market trends, and shifts in business strategy. It's not just a to-do list; it serves as the foundation of the Agile methodology, which requires regular refinement and re-prioritization.

For Agile teams, you should maintain the Product Backlog as a crucial guide for both the immediate next steps in development and as a strategic tool for comprehensive planning and smart release management. More importantly, it acts as a collaboration hub, aligning the product team and stakeholders around shared goals and a clear vision.

Effectively managing the Product Backlog requires you to organize and break down the work into manageable tasks. Let's explore some best practices:

Start with Themes: Themes are broad categories that capture the essence of a feature or requirement, providing clarity and a unified direction, especially in complex projects. For instance, "Launch new loyalty program" or "Improve order management experience."

Define Epics: Epics are large work blocks that break down into smaller, manageable tasks called user stories. An Epic focuses on a single feature or a significant update, covering all related tasks. For instance, under the "Improve order management experience" theme, you can add "Integrate live tracking" or "Revamp order detail page."

Craft User Stories: These are detailed tasks derived from Epics, written from the user's perspective. They outline a specific functionality or feature, answering 'who,' 'what,' and 'why.' For example, under the Epic "Integrate live tracking," you might find "Integrate Google Maps" or "Add live tracking widget on home page."

Continual Refinement and Grooming: This ongoing process keeps the backlog relevant and aligned with project goals. It involves adding new tasks, removing outdated ones, re-prioritizing based on current needs, and breaking down large items into actionable steps.

Strategic Prioritization: This vital step is prioritizing Epics and User Stories by considering factors like customer impact, effort required, and alignment with overall business objectives.

In Agile development, the Product Backlog is structured hierarchically with Themes at the top, then Epics, and finally User Stories. This hierarchy provides a clear, organized view of the project's workload, streamlining the prioritization process and making it easier to manage the development lifecycle.

Product Backlog vs. Sprint Backlog

In Agile product development, two essential backlogs form the cornerstone of effective product management: the Product Backlog and the Sprint Backlog. Each plays a critical and unique role in guiding Agile teams from broad planning to detailed execution.

The Product Backlog: Think of the Product Backlog as a comprehensive repository for all possible tasks that could enhance the product over its lifecycle. It's a vast collection of potential features, improvements, and bug fixes, each ranked by its value and potential impact. The Product Manager uses this backlog for long-term strategic planning, ensuring every team effort is in sync with the product's overarching vision and objectives.

The Sprint Backlog: The Sprint Backlog, in contrast, is a tactical tool designed for the upcoming sprint. It originates from the larger Product Backlog and consists of a select group of tasks the development team is committed to addressing in the next sprint cycle. This backlog is time-specific, aligning with the sprint's timeframe, and includes definite user stories and tasks that the team has agreed to tackle, explore, and implement.

While the Product Backlog offers a broad, long-term view of potential future enhancements for the product, the Sprint Backlog narrows the focus to the immediate, actionable tasks. The first is about strategic, focusing on the big-picture, while the latter concentrates on tactical, short-term execution. Together, they ensure a well-rounded approach to Agile product development, marrying visionary thinking with practical, immediate action.

The Art of Writing User Stories

In Agile and Scrum, user stories are essential tools for Product Managers. They capture user needs, steer development teams, and ensure the delivery of real value. User stories shift focus from technical specifications to a user-centered dialogue, fostering a deeper, more empathetic understanding of the end-users' true needs.

Defining a User Story

A user story is a concise, clear feature or requirement description from the user's viewpoint. It's expressed in natural language, making it clear to technical and non-technical stakeholders alike. This clarity keeps everyone on the same page, concentrating on delivering value to the user.

User stories clarify the needs, goals, interactions, and expected benefits of the customers. This user-centric approach deepens the team's understanding of user behavior, inspiring the creation of features that are both valuable and meaningful.

The Structure of a User Story

A common format for starting user stories is: "As a [type of user], I want [goal], so that [benefit]." This structure is purposely designed to pinpoint who the user is, what they want to achieve, and why it's important.

Type of User: Specify the user or persona benefiting from the feature, whether an external customer or an internal role, like a marketing or administration member. Detailing this helps the development team understand their audience.

Goal: Detail the user's specific aim. This should be concise and measurable, offering the development team a clear target.

Benefit: Describe the advantage or value the user gains from this feature. Knowing this motivates the development team, informing their work and choices.

When these elements are combined, user stories exceed simple requirements; they become stories that add empathy and strategic focus into the development process. They align teams with user needs, ensuring the final product truly serves its intended users.

Optimizing User Stories

With the user-centered opening of a user story, it's crucial to delve into the specifics of the feature. This involves detailing the business requirements, expected user interactions, and how to navigate various scenarios. Clarifying the user journey at each step and outlining error handling is essential. A user story should be a comprehensive document that covers every facet of the feature, including design, calculations, logic, and all user communications.

User stories are fundamental in Agile development, demanding full detailing of features and focused consideration of key elements before transitioning to the development team. These stories are influential in aligning development activities with user needs and business objectives. Here are vital factors to consider when crafting user stories:

User-Centric Approach: At the core of a user story is its emphasis on the end-user. It's vital to specify whom the story is for, and the particular user needs it addresses. This approach fosters empathy in development and ensures the product's value and relevance to the user.

Complete Reference: A user story should act as a comprehensive reference, covering all necessary resources such as designs, texts for various scenarios like error messages, business logic, calculations, and links to useful documentation, like third-party integration guides.

Testability: A well-crafted user story is testable, with clear criteria to indicate successful implementation and functionality achievement. Testability is key for confirming that the feature meets its intended purpose and quality standards.

User Acceptance Criteria (UAC): UAC is a cornerstone of Agile development, defining what 'Done' looks like for a story or feature. It sets the conditions that the software must meet for user or stakeholder approval, covering functionality, performance, usability, reliability, and compliance. UAC also lays the groundwork for test cases that validate the feature's alignment with its intended goals.

Independence of Stories: Ideally, user stories should be independent, allowing for development and testing without reliance on others. This independence enhances prioritization flexibility, eases estimation, and minimizes development delays due to dependencies.

In essence, user stories translate user needs into clear, concise, and actionable terms. Moreover, user stories evolve through the development process as feedback is gathered from users and stakeholders. They are vital for effective product development, offering a straightforward understanding of objectives and ensuring the development team's alignment with project goals. Let's review an example.

User Story Title: Quick Reorder Feature

As a returning customer, **I want** to be able to quickly reorder products from my previous purchases **so that** I can save time and effort when shopping for the same items again.

- **Business Requirements**:
    - The "Reorder" feature should be accessible from both the user's order history and a dedicated section in the user profile.
    - Users should be able to select which items from a past order they wish to reorder.
    - The system should automatically add selected items to the

user's cart and take them directly to the checkout page.

- **Technical Requirements**:
  - Update the database schema to support tracking individual order histories.
  - Implement backend logic for fetching previous orders and processing reorders.
  - Ensure that the feature is integrated with the current payment systems and promotional discounts are applied if applicable.
- **Design**:
  - Link to Mockup for Reorder Feature (This would be a link to an external design tool like Figma or Sketch, showing wireframes or UI mockups of the feature.)

User Acceptance Criteria (UAC)

1. **View Past Orders**:
   - Given I am logged in, when I visit my profile, then I should see an option to view my past orders.
2. **Select Items to Reorder**:
   - Given I have selected a past order, when I click on 'Reorder', then I should be able to select items I wish to purchase again.
3. **Add to Cart**:
   - Given I have selected items for reorder, when I confirm my selection, then the items should automatically be added to my shopping cart.
4. **Checkout Process**:
   - Given items are added to the cart via the reorder feature, when I proceed to checkout, then the checkout page should reflect the current items with correct prices and applicable discounts.
5. **Order Completion**:
   - Given I am on the checkout page, when I complete the payment process, then I should receive confirmation of my

reorder.

Error Handling

- If no items are available for reorder (out of stock), display a message: "Some items in your order are currently out of stock. Please remove these items to proceed."
- Handle errors during checkout, such as payment failures or network issues, with appropriate error messages and recovery options.

Dependencies

- Coordination with the backend team to update APIs for handling order data.
- Database updates to store and retrieve order history efficiently.
- Design team inputs for creating UI/UX compliant with brand standards.

Metrics to Track

- Number of reorders made using the feature.
- User feedback on the reorder functionality.
- Conversion rate changes due to the feature implementation.

A crucial aspect of managing user stories in a Scrum team is estimating each story's development effort. While challenging, mastering effective estimation techniques is essential for fostering team collaboration and optimizing project planning.

User Story Estimation

Estimating the complexity of user stories is a crucial part of Agile product management, helping to measure the necessary effort and resources for story completion. This estimation usually occurs during backlog grooming sessions, where team members collaboratively assess each story.

The goal of user story estimation is to understand the relative effort involved, not to calculate the exact time for completion. 'Story points estimation' is a common method, assigning points to stories based on their complexity, effort, and associated risks. A story with more points suggests higher complexity compared to one with fewer points.

Agile teams often use the Fibonacci sequence (1, 2, 3, 5, 8, 13) to assign story points, reflecting the growing uncertainty and complexity in larger stories. Estimation is a collective activity, where each team member, after carefully understanding the story, presents their estimation. Variations in these estimates spark discussions, leading to a deeper exploration of the story's complexities. The aim is to reach a harmony that reflects a well-rounded view of the story's complexity.

Estimations are flexible and should be revisited as new details emerge or when requirements evolve. This adaptability ensures that the backlog remains relevant, and that sprint planning is both realistic and feasible.

'Planning Poker' is a popular technique for estimating story points in Agile. After discussing a user story, team members independently assign points based on their perception of the total effort required. These points typically following the Fibonacci sequence. Revealing these estimates simultaneously, any significant discrepancies trigger further discussion, enhancing the teams understanding of varying perspectives ultimately leading to an agreement.

In summary, user story estimation is a dynamic, collaborative process in Agile management, emphasizing relative effort rather than exact durations. It encourages team engagement, nurtures shared understanding, and remains adaptable to changes, all crucial for effective sprint planning and product management.

The next section will explore Scrum Ceremonies, exploring their roles in maintaining team alignment, guiding workflows, and adapting the product to align with user needs and market changes. Understanding these ceremonies is key to understanding the essence of Agile management and ensuring a successful Agile process.

Scrum Ceremonies: Optimizing Team Collaboration

Scrum ceremonies are essential in structuring team efforts and enhancing collaboration within the Scrum framework. Each ceremony has a specific role, contributing significantly to the success of product development. By following a fixed schedule and fulfilling specific functions, these ceremonies enhance transparency, encourage regular review, and facilitate adjustments throughout the development process.

Sprint Grooming

Sprint Grooming, or backlog refinement, is vital in Scrum, involving the Product Owner, Scrum Master, and Development Team. The goal is to maintain a well-organized, prioritized Product Backlog that's prepared for upcoming sprints.

In these sessions, the team examines high-priority items in the Product Backlog. The Product Owner details each user story, explaining the problem, purpose, user interactions, and anticipated outcomes. The team discusses to resolve ambiguities and delve into the technical details of the story, including various scenarios and edge cases. Part of this process involves estimating the story's complexity with story points, offering insight into the expected workload for the next sprint and aiding in its planning.

Additionally, the team refines user stories, breaking larger tasks into smaller, manageable pieces. This clarification aids in planning and provides a clearer workload perspective. Note that Sprint Grooming is an ongoing activity, crucial for keeping the backlog clear and manageable, thus ensuring smooth sprint planning.

While the Scrum Guide doesn't prescribe a specific duration for grooming, the general recommendation is to spend about 5-10% of the total sprint time on this task. For example, in a standard two-week sprint, this would mean dedicating 4-8 hours to grooming. The goal is to enter the Sprint Planning meeting with a "ready" backlog, marked by well-defined, prioritized, and estimated user stories, facilitating an efficient sprint planning process.

Sprint Planning

Sprint Planning sits at the heart of the Scrum process, marking the beginning of each sprint. It's a collaborative session where the team decides on the work scope for the upcoming sprint and formulates an initial execution plan.

Involving the Product Owner, the Scrum Master, and the Development Team, the planning begins with the Product Owner presenting the sprint goal and introducing top-priority, groomed, 'ready' user stories from the Product Backlog. The Product Owner details these stories and their acceptance criteria, outlining the team's upcoming tasks.

The Scrum Master facilitates the session, ensuring the team understands the sprint goals and expectations. The Development Team evaluates the work, considering their previous sprint velocities to measure the feasible workload for the new sprint.

A pivotal aspect of Sprint Planning is creating a high-level plan for the sprint's work, discussing technical strategies, identifying dependencies, and noting potential risks. Aligning team roles is crucial, such as synchronizing Front-End and Back-End developers and setting clear timelines for QA.

The session concludes in the Sprint Backlog, a comprehensive list of items the team commits to, anchored by a defined sprint goal. It's essential that all team members leave the planning meeting with a unified understanding of the sprint's objectives and a clear direction for the tasks ahead, establishing a solid foundation for a productive sprint.

Daily Scrum

The Daily Scrum, or daily stand-up, is a key daily meeting in Scrum, designed to be brief yet effective, keeping the team aligned and focused. This 15-minute check-in helps maintain sprint momentum, with a consistent routine in time and location.

The Product Owner, Scrum Master, and the Development Team are the primary participants. The meeting centers on the Development Team, where each member shares updates on three essential questions:

What did I accomplish since the last meeting?

What will I work on today?

What obstacles are blocking my progress?

These questions guide the meeting, promoting transparency and synchronization in the team's sprint progress. The Scrum Master ensures the discussion is concise and helps address any emerging impediments. While the Product Owner may not engage directly, their presence is crucial for staying informed and making timely decisions affecting the team's work.

The Daily Scrum isn't for detailed problem-solving or extended discussions; complex issues are handled in separate sessions. Its value lies in strengthening team collaboration and self-management, ensuring daily contributions align with the sprint goal. Active participation from all team members is vital for the Daily Scrum's success in streamlining sprint coordination.

Sprint Review

The Sprint Review, or Sprint Demo, is a crucial Scrum ceremony that concludes each sprint. It's a collaborative session aimed at reviewing the completed work and collecting feedback to steer future development efforts.

For a typical two-week sprint, the Sprint Review might last around an hour, with the Scrum Master facilitating the session. Participants include the Product Owner, the Development Team, and key stakeholders. The Product Owner reviews completed and pending backlog items, setting the stage for the Development Team to showcase their achievements, ready to discuss and clarify the delivered features or changes.

This ceremony is centered on evaluating the sprint's product progress, allowing the team to present new features and updates, and gathering stakeholder feedback to ensure the product meets user and market needs. This feedback is crucial, guiding the team's future direction and ensuring continuous alignment with expectations and objectives.

The Sprint Review promotes a feedback loop, encouraging open dialogue and mutual understanding, essential for aligning the product's development with stakeholder expectations and market dynamics. It's a forum where the collective assessment of progress, addressing of gaps, and strategic planning for the next sprint occurs, essential for crafting a product that not only meets but exceeds expectations.

Sprint Retrospective

The Sprint Retrospective concludes the cycle of Scrum ceremonies, offering a reflective space for the Product Owner, Scrum Master, and Development Team to assess the sprint's outcomes. This session is dedicated to discussing successes, challenges, and identifying improvement opportunities.

It's a forum for open, honest dialogue, aimed at constructive reflection rather than pointing fingers or assigning blame. The team reviews the sprint to extract learnings and strategies for improvement, fostering a culture of continuous improvement. Celebrating successes, examining obstacles, and strategizing on overcoming them are key discussion points, often leading to considerations for process or workflow enhancements to optimize future sprints.

This retrospective is crucial for the Scrum process's health and effectiveness, providing a platform for the team to express concerns, acknowledge achievements, and propose enhancements. Ensuring these discussions translate into actionable plans is vital, enabling the team to refine their practices and enhance their performance in upcoming sprints.

By emphasizing continuous reflection and adaptation, the Sprint Retrospective is helpful in the Agile journey, empowering teams to evolve their practices, thereby consistently improving their work quality and delivering greater value to customers.

Enhancing Scrum Team Performance

In Scrum, a subset of the Agile framework, continuous evaluation and enhancement of team performance are vital. It's not merely about task completion; it's about refining processes and boosting productivity. By tracking performance metrics in each sprint, Scrum teams can make data-driven decisions to foster progress and improvement. Key metrics include:

Velocity: This metric measures the amount of work a team can accomplish in a sprint, quantified by the story points of all completed tasks. Velocity is pivotal for planning and forecasting future workloads. By analyzing velocity over multiple sprints, teams can understand their productivity patterns and implement strategies to enhance their output, such as refining estimation processes or breaking down tasks.

Burndown Chart: The Sprint Burndown Chart is a visual tool representing the amount of work remaining in a sprint over time. It's an excellent indicator of whether the team is on track to complete their tasks. Variances in the chart's slope can signal progress or highlight areas needing attention. Regular review of the Burndown Chart enables teams to adjust their efforts dynamically to meet sprint objectives.

Cycle Time: This metric measures the time taken from the start to the completion of a task. It encompasses all stages of a sprint, including development, testing, and review. Monitoring cycle time helps identify workflow efficiencies and inefficiencies, offering insights for process optimization.

Sprint Goal Success: This metric assesses the team's success in achieving the sprint's objectives. It underscores the importance of aligning with the sprint goal, promoting a shared sense of purpose and commitment among team members.

Quality Metrics: These include indicators like defect density, test coverage, and customer-reported issues, allowing teams to measure the quality of their output. Focusing on these metrics can lead to improvements in testing, code reviews, and overall product quality.

Balancing these quantitative metrics with qualitative reviews and team reflections ensures a comprehensive performance assessment, enabling

Scrum teams to refine their cooperation, streamline workflows, and deliver superior results. Utilizing these metrics effectively allows teams to surpass sprint goals and continuously improve their Agile practices.

Streamlining Tasks with Digital Tools

In the dynamic world of product management, staying organized and keeping track of countless tasks is a challenge. This is where digital task management tools come into play! Digital tools are crucial for organization and task tracking. These tools are key for efficient coordination and progress monitoring.

JIRA by Atlassian: A staple in many software development teams, JIRA excels in creating and tracking user stories, defining tasks, and monitoring progress through adaptable boards. It's tailored for Agile methodologies like Scrum and Kanban and offers comprehensive analytics to track team performance, including burndown charts. JIRA's integration with other Atlassian products further enhances its utility.

Click Up: Gaining popularity for its unified workspace, ClickUp allows for comprehensive task planning, organization, and collaboration. It accommodates different work styles with multiple views like lists, boards, and Gantt charts. Features such as task prioritization, time tracking, and workflow automation make it a compelling choice for managing diverse product development activities.

Notion: Known for its versatility, Notion is a multifaceted tool for note-taking, data management, and project planning. Its customization capabilities allow Product Managers to create tailored roadmaps, manage backlogs, and collaborate efficiently. With a variety of templates and an intuitive interface, Notion simplifies project and task management.

Asana: Focused on helping teams organize and manage their work, Asana's user-friendly platform is ideal for creating tasks, assigning roles, and setting deadlines. Its timeline feature visualizes project schedules, while its robust reporting tools help in monitoring productivity and identifying bottlenecks.

Choosing the right tool depends on the team's specific requirements, project complexity, and management preferences. Align with your team members, and other teams and find out the best tool can fit your company and ensure the smooth implementation across all teams.

Scrum and all the ceremonies we've discussed are foundational to effectively managing your product. As we transition back to the subject of backlog management, remember that maintaining a dynamic and current backlog is central to your journey in product management. A well-prioritized backlog ensures that every user story is aligned correctly according to its importance and urgency. Coming up next, we will explore backlog prioritization within Agile management. This is a critical skill that helps you navigate the complexities of product development, ensuring that your team is always working on the most impactful tasks first.

Prioritization in Agile Product Management

In Agile product management, aligning development efforts with customer needs, business goals, and resource availability is an ongoing challenge. At the heart of this challenge is backlog prioritization, a critical and strategic process where product backlog items are ranked based on factors like business value, user requirements, and market trends. This process is essential in steering the product development journey effectively.

Prioritization comes with its set of challenges, particularly balancing the diverse priorities and expectations of stakeholders—customers, executives, developers, and marketers. Each group has its unique perspective and demands, making it crucial to find a balance that aligns with overarching organizational objectives.

Another significant challenge is identifying the features that will deliver maximum value to users and the business. Given the constraints of time and resources, focusing on high-impact initiatives is crucial. Strategic prioritization ensures that resources are used wisely, aligning efforts with key business objectives, and preventing the dilution of efforts, which is essential for delivering a solid product experience.

Without careful prioritization, there's a real risk of compromise to the pressure of conflicting requirements, which can lead to investing in low-impact features or constant priority shifts, resulting in resource wastage. Adopting a solid prioritization technique is fundamental, enabling data-driven decisions that align feature development with product strategy, company goals, and customer expectations.

Let's dive into various models and strategies for effective backlog prioritization, such as the MoSCoW model, Value versus Effort analysis, the KANO model, and the RICE framework. Each approach offers a unique lens for assessing and ordering backlog items, providing you with the strategy to make choices/decisions that drive your product toward success in the market.

The MoSCoW Model

The MoSCoW model is a prioritization technique extensively utilized in product management, business analysis, and software development. It categorizes features or tasks into four distinct groups, represented by the acronym MoSCoW, to emphasize the most critical features:

Must-Have: These are non-negotiable features that form the product's foundation. The absence of these features means the product fails to fulfill its fundamental purpose.

Should-Have: While important, these features are not critical. They enhance the user experience and add value to the product. Their absence is noticeable but does not prevent the product launch.

Could-Have: These features are nice to have but not essential. They improve the product but are not crucial to its core functionality or user experience.

Won't-Have (at this time): Features considered non-essential for the current development cycle. They may become relevant later but are not planned for the upcoming release.

To illustrate the MoSCoW model in action, consider developing a new mobile banking app:

Must-Have Features: Core functionalities like secure login, account balance viewing, fund transfers, and bill payments are essential for the app to serve its banking purpose.

Should-Have Features: Adding features like recurring payment setup, transaction history, and balance alerts enhances the user experience and provides significant value.

Could-Have Features: Extras like customizable themes, personal finance tools, or integration with third-party apps are beneficial but not essential for the app's basic banking functions.

Won't-Have Features: While useful, features like photo check deposits are not critical for the initial release and can be considered for future updates.

MoSCoW Model: Step-by-Step Guide

Feature Listing: Start by documenting all potential features, run user research, collaborating with stakeholders, analyzing customer feedback, and interpreting relevant data.

Categorization: Work closely with your team to allocate each feature to one of the MoSCoW categories, guided by your product strategy and objectives. For example, features that add direct value to top product objectives, should be in 'Must Have' category.

Consultation and Validation: Engage with stakeholders, including marketing team, sales, executives, and customers, to validate your categorization. Their insights can provide valuable perspectives.

Finalization: Ensure that all stakeholders understand and agree with the categorization rationale.

Applying the MoSCoW model effectively streamlines your development efforts, ensuring alignment with delivering maximum customer value. This approach keeps the focus sharp on essential product features while strategically deferring or reevaluating others for future consideration.

The Value vs. Effort Model

In backlog prioritization, evaluating the potential value of a feature against the required effort is fundamental. The Value vs. Effort model is a strategic approach to prioritization in product management, focusing on the balance between the value a feature provides and the effort required to implement it. This model advocates for prioritizing features that offer high value with relatively low effort, thus optimizing resource utilization and maximizing product impact.

To employ this model, assign each feature two distinct scores: one for value and another for effort.

The Value Score

The value score reflects the anticipated benefits a feature will bring to users and the business, calculated by averaging three components:

$$Value\ Score = (Impact + Confidence + Ease) / 3$$

Impact: Assesses the expected positive influence on users or business objectives. High-impact features that significantly enhance user experience or contribute to business goals score high here.

Confidence: Represents the level of certainty about the feature's predicted impact, based on data or insights. A higher confidence score strengthens the case for a feature's potential benefits.

Ease: Evaluates how straightforwardly a feature can be implemented, considering design, development, and deployment efforts. Features that are impactful yet easy to implement score higher, indicating they can deliver value efficiently. Ease is a part of the value score since it critically influences whether a high-impact feature can be delivered effectively.

The Effort Score

The effort score quantifies the resources and time needed for a feature's implementation:

$$Effort\ Score = (Time + Resources + Complexity) / 3$$

Time: The estimated time required to develop the feature. Longer development times increase the effort score.

Resources: The human, tools, and any other assets necessary for the feature's development. Greater resource needs result in a higher score.

Complexity: The technical challenges, dependencies, and potential obstacles in developing the feature. Higher complexity translates to a higher effort score.

Visualizing these scores on a graph, with value on the y-axis and effort on the x-axis, helps identify which features should be prioritized. Features in the top-right quadrant, indicating high value and low effort, are ideal candidates for early implementation.

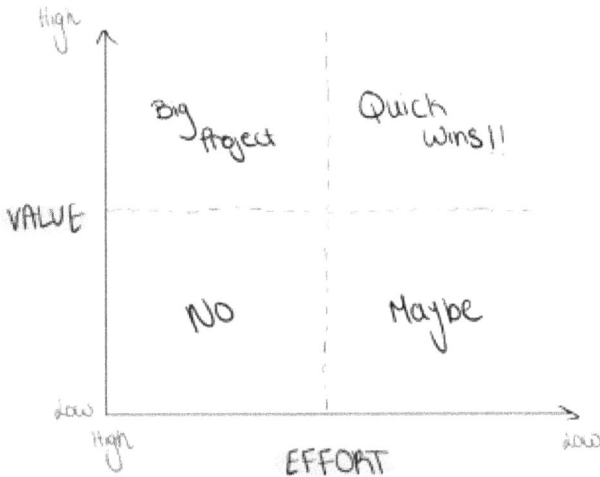

Illustrative Example: Feature Prioritization

Imagine three potential features, based on the score calculation above:

Feature A: Value Score = 8, Effort Score = 4

Feature B: Value Score = 6, Effort Score = 6

Feature C: Value Score = 9, Effort Score = 7

In this scenario, Feature A emerges as the top priority due to its high value and relatively low effort. Feature C, despite its high value, is secondary due to its higher effort requirement. Feature B, with balanced but moderate scores in both areas, ranks lowest.

In summary, The Value vs. Effort model equips Product Managers with a structured approach for effective feature prioritization. It ensures that resources are allocated judiciously, focusing on tasks that maximize impact and efficiency, thereby enabling your product to deliver optimal value to its users.

The RICE Model

The RICE model is a sophisticated framework designed by Intercom's growth squad to aid Product Managers in prioritizing features and tasks logically. RICE stands for Reach, Impact, Confidence, and Effort, each contributing a unique perspective to the evaluation process.

Reach: This measures the number of customers affected by a feature within a certain period (day, week, month). A feature with wide reach affects a large customer base, while one with low reach has a more targeted or niche impact.

Impact: This measures the potential positive effect a feature will have on important metrics like conversion rates, revenue, or user engagement. The impact is closely tied to the feature's objectives and expected outcomes.

Confidence: Reflecting the team's assurance in their reach, impact, and effort estimates, high confidence levels indicate strong trust in the accuracy of these estimates, whereas low confidence points to greater uncertainties.

Effort: This estimates the total resources needed to implement a feature, including time, labor, complexity, and other inputs. More demanding features score higher in effort.

Calculating RICE Scores

The RICE score is calculated using the formula:

RICE Score = (Reach x Impact x Confidence) / Effort

The score provides an objective measure for prioritization. For instance, a feature with a reach of 8, impact of 9, confidence of 7, and effort of 5, calculates to a RICE score of 100.8, using the formula: (8 x 9 x 7) / 5.

Teams can tailor the scoring system to their unique contexts. For example, Reach could be measured in monthly active users (MAU), while impact could utilize a scale ranging from minimal (0.25) to massive (3). Confidence could be expressed in percentages like 20%, 50%, 80%, or 100%, and effort in person-months for more precise assessments.

Adapting the RICE Model

The RICE model's strength lies in its structured yet adaptable approach. The model steers teams away from bias or assumptions and encourages data-driven decisions that serve business goals and customer needs. Consistent application of the scoring criteria and transparent processes underpin the model's success.

While RICE offers a structured prioritization approach, it's not universally applicable in its standard form. Customizing the scoring system to fit the team's specific needs and circumstances can greatly enhance its utility. The key to the RICE model's effectiveness lies in its flexibility and adaptability, allowing teams to make data-driven decisions that align with both business objectives and customer requirements.

The KANO Model

The KANO Model, developed by Dr. Noriaki Kano in the 1980s, is an insightful framework for Product Managers aiming to enhance customer satisfaction through feature prioritization. It classifies product features into three main categories, each influencing customer satisfaction in distinct ways:

Essential (Basic) Features: These are the fundamental features that customers expect by default. They may not increase satisfaction if present, but their absence leads to dissatisfaction. For example, on an e-commerce platform, basic features might include a functional search bar and secure checkout—essentials without which users would likely be frustrated.

Performance Features: These are the features that customers explicitly request and value. They have a linear relationship with satisfaction—the better these features are executed, the higher the customer satisfaction. In e-commerce example, performance features could be an advanced search engine, efficient filters, customer reviews, and fast loading times, enhancing the user experience and aiding in decision-making.

Delight Features: These features go beyond customer expectations, offering unique value that can significantly boost satisfaction. While their absence doesn't necessarily cause dissatisfaction, their presence can create memorable and engaging experiences. For an e-commerce example, delight features might include personalized shopping recommendations or innovative virtual try-on capabilities.

To apply the Kano Model, start with gathering customer input through surveys or interviews to measure their perspective on different features. Then, categorize these features into basic, performance, and delight groups. This categorization aids in directing development efforts: securing all essential features to meet basic expectations, improving performance features to elevate satisfaction, and integrating delight features to attract and fascinate customers.

It's important to note that over time, delight features might become essential as market expectations evolve. What is initially perceived as innovative can soon become a standard expectation, as seen in e-commerce market, with the transition of express delivery services from a novel offering to a standard industry practice.

The Kano Model doesn't rely on a rigid formula for feature assessment but emphasizes interpreting customer feedback to identify features that most significantly impact satisfaction. By integrating the Kano Model into product strategy, you can create a product that not only fulfills basic needs but also excels in performance and provides delightful experiences, key in a customer-focused market environment. This approach ensures a nuanced understanding of user needs, guiding the creation of a product experience that both satisfies and delights.

Reflections on Prioritization

Effective prioritization in product management exceeds just ordering features and tasks. It's about striking a sophisticated balance, aiming to deliver maximum value to customers and the business while wisely managing resources and development time. It's crucial to recognize that prioritization models are aids in decision-making, designed to enhance, not substitute, critical thinking and a profound understanding of your product and its audience.

These models are tools to support, not reduce, the insights and acumen of your team. Prioritization is an ongoing, dynamic process that must remain responsive to evolving circumstances. It's vital to integrate insights from team members and user feedback, enriching your prioritization strategy with perspectives that models alone might not fully capture.

Adopting a balanced approach to prioritization—one that leverages the structured guidance of these models while also valuing the different insights about your product and direct feedback from users—can obviously improve your decision-making. This strategy ensures your product not only meets but anticipates and surpasses user expectations, evolving in sync with their needs and contributing to your product's success.

Selecting a suitable prioritization model requires a deep dive into your company's goals, your product's strategic direction, and the resources you have. The chosen approach should align with your specific objectives, whether that's maximizing revenue with limited resources or boosting customer satisfaction across a range of features. Furthermore, the model should be tailored to your product's unique attributes, the demands of your target audience, and the specifics of your competitive environment. Effective prioritization is not one-size-fits-all; it's about finding and adapting a model that is flexible, adapted to shifts, and capable of guiding your product toward its strategic goals.

Conflict Management in Prioritization

Conflict is a natural part of the prioritization process in product management, often rising from the diverse viewpoints of stakeholders. Stakeholders come with varied perspectives, each shaped by their understanding of customer needs and anticipated business value. These differences require skillful conflict management through clear communication, collaboration, and a dedication to incorporating stakeholder feedback.

Here are some effective strategies for managing and resolving conflicts during prioritization:

1. Establish Common Goals: Start by ensuring all stakeholders align with the product's vision and objectives. This common ground can help ease conflicts that arise from differing perspectives.

2. Early Stakeholder Engagement: Engage stakeholders early in the prioritization process. Transparent communication and regular updates can foster involvement and reduce resistance.

3. Explain Your Prioritization Method: Clearly communicate the prioritization methodology to stakeholders. Understanding the reasoning behind decisions can clarify the process and minimize disagreement.

4. Use Data to Support Decisions: Focus on objective data, such as customer feedback or market analysis, to validate your prioritization choices. Data-driven decisions tend to be more justifiable and less controversial.

5. Maintain Transparency: Be clear about how decisions will affect the product roadmap, user experience, and business goals. Transparency helps prevent and resolve conflicts.

6. Foster Constructive Dialogue: Encourage stakeholders to share their views and address concerns, focusing discussions on solutions rather than assigning blame, and remain open to alternative perspectives.

7. Document and Share Decisions: After making decisions, document the outcomes and the rationale. Sharing this information provides clarity, serves as a reference, and maintains accountability.

8. Remain Flexible: Stay open to revising priorities based on new insights, market changes, or internal feedback, keeping stakeholders informed to ensure ongoing alignment.

9. Manage Expectations: Acknowledge all inputs but clarify that final decisions will prioritize the product's primary goals and user needs. Not every stakeholder will be fully satisfied, but setting clear expectations can reduce discontent.

10. Reflect and Evolve: After each development cycle, review the effectiveness of your prioritization process. Use these reflections to enhance future approaches.

Effectively navigating prioritization conflicts isn't just about agreement-building; it's about leveraging disagreements as opportunities for growth and development. While addressing conflicts, especially with senior management or team members can be overwhelming, resolving these issues constructively can propel development forward and foster a stronger, more unified team dynamic.

Handle Conflict: Step-by-Step Guide

Navigating conflicts effectively is an essential skill for Product Managers, especially within the complexities of prioritization. Here's a structured approach to managing conflicts constructively:

Maintain Calm: Stay self-controlled. A calm attitude encourages constructive dialogue and sets a positive tone for the conversation.

Active Listening: Truly listen to understand others' viewpoints before responding. Avoid planning your argument while the other party is speaking; instead, focus on understanding their perspective. This approach fosters mutual respect and aids in understanding the root of the conflict.

Present Your Viewpoint Clearly: Once you fully understanding the other party's perspective, articulate your own position concisely, starting with shared goals to build a common ground for resolution.

Emphasize Transparency: Clearly communicate the rationale behind your prioritization decisions, showing how they align with overarching company goals and contribute to the product and user benefits.

Leverage Data: Use objective data to support your arguments. Facts and statistics can serve as unbiassed elements in discussions, giving credibility and weight to your viewpoints.

Openness to Compromise: Recognize that prioritization is an evolving process. Be willing to adjust your stance if compelling reasons arise, yet clearly communicate any concerns about proposed changes.

Reflect on the Experience: After resolving the conflict, reflect on its causes and the resolution pathway. This self-analysis can yield insights for more smoothly navigating future disagreements.

Prioritization is central to effective product management, requiring a balance among user needs, business objectives, resource allocation, and market trends. While it presents challenges, it's a crucial aspect of your role, demanding a strategic approach and continuous engagement.

Acknowledge that prioritization is iterative, responding to shifts in external conditions, new insights, or market trends. This continuous cycle of evaluation and adjustment is pivotal for sustained learning and improvement, enhancing your decision-making process and contributing to the product's success.

View prioritization as an avenue to informed decision-making, aligning stakeholders around common goals, and delivering a product that not only satisfies customer needs but also drives business growth. Embrace it as a strategic opportunity to shape and steer your product's journey toward its most impactful iteration.

Chapter Conclusion and Reflection

In this chapter, we've navigated through the complicated and engaging world of Agile product management, exploring key components that underpin this dynamic methodology. Our goal has been to support you with the tools and knowledge to excel in Agile product management, from effective backlog management to adept feature prioritization.

We began with a deep dive into backlog management, highlighting its critical role in steering team efforts and defining product development. A well-maintained, dynamic backlog, consistently refined, is essential for guiding your team with precision.

The discussion then transitioned to user stories, emphasizing their importance in articulating product features from the user's viewpoint. We discovered that crafting clear, concise, and actionable user stories is fundamental for enhancing team understanding and collaboration.

Estimating user stories was our next focal point, examining techniques like story points and planning poker. The central lesson was the value of team-wide participation in estimations, fostering shared understanding and resulting in more accurate effort assessments.

We then navigated the complex landscape of feature prioritization and conflict management, addressing the challenges of aligning diverse stakeholder expectations. We offered strategies for making informed decisions, drawing on prioritization frameworks like the Value vs. Effort and RICE models to guide these choices.

As we conclude this chapter, it's clear that Agile product management is a nuanced discipline, requiring strategic insight, effective communication, and diligent process management. An interesting question arises here about the necessity of technical expertise for Product Managers, especially in their collaboration with development teams. How essential is technical knowledge for their success? This question paves the way for our next discussion, where we'll delve into the significance of technical skills within product management, further enriching our understanding of this multifaceted role.

CHAPTER 5
TECHNICAL ACUMEN FOR DIGITAL PRODUCT MANAGERS

In today's digital landscape, Product Managers often find themselves at the crossroads of technology and business, tasked with making pivotal decisions about feature development and resource allocation. This dynamic environment drives the ongoing debate: is technical knowledge essential for Product Managers?

Advocates of a technical foundation argue that it enhances collaboration with engineering teams and deepens understanding of the product's technical components. This expertise, they claim, allows Product Managers to engage more effectively with developers, fostering a seamless integration of business objectives and technical feasibility.

On the other side of the argument, some emphasize that a Product Manager's core responsibilities should focus on strategic decision-making, market analysis, and customer insights. They caution that an excessive technical focus could detract from critical business functions like understanding market dynamics, conducting competitive analysis, and designing user-centric experiences. Here, the belief is that the essential competencies of a Product Manager are rooted more in strategic insight and customer engagement than in technical prowess.

However, an agreement emerges that having fundamental technical knowledge is advantageous for Product Managers, particularly in the digital realm. Such skills can explain the technical elements of product development, enhance interactions with technical teams, and contribute to more grounded decision-making.

Despite the ongoing debate, there's a consensus that Product Managers in the digital space would benefit from acquiring essential technical skills. These skills enable effective navigation of the technical aspects of product development, foster collaboration with engineering teams, and support informed decision-making.

The level of technical expertise required can vary significantly depending on the product type. For example, managing a B2B SaaS product might demand a thorough understanding of APIs, while leading a data-driven product could require expertise in data analytics and familiarity with data-related programming languages.

This chapter dives into the essential technical skills beneficial for digital Product Managers, offering insights on how these competencies can strengthen your decision-making process, ensuring it aligns with both business strategies and user expectations.

For those managing non-technical products or who view technical skills as non-essential for their role, this chapter might be less relevant. However, it's worth noting that in the fluid realm of product management, acquiring a broad skill set can only enhance your versatility and effectiveness. Your path in learning and development is unique and ever-evolving, shaped by the specific demands of your role and the nature of the products you oversee.

Technical Competence for Product Managers

In the multifaceted role of a Product Manager, blending strategic insight with technical understanding is becoming increasingly essential. This section delves into why and how key technical skills can strengthen your effectiveness across various aspects of product management:

Enhancing Team Collaboration: Technical knowledge facilitates clearer communication with engineering teams. It enables you to share a common language and mutual understanding, leading to more effective collaboration and streamlined problem-solving processes.

Strategic Roadmap Development: Understanding the technical details of your product, from its core features to complex system integrations, is vital. This deep insight helps you accurately measure what's possible, identify potential technical obstacles, and foresee future enhancements, allowing you to construct a roadmap that is both visionary and practical.

Informed Feature Prioritization: A solid technical foundation enables you to evaluate feature decisions not just against customer desires but also technical feasibility. This balance ensures your product roadmap is a reflection of both user demand and realistic technical considerations.

Navigating Market Trends and Technological Shifts: Staying up-to-date with the latest technologies and market movements is crucial. Your technical awareness not only sparks innovation but also empowers you to evaluate the relevance and integration potential of new technologies within your product, ensuring you stay ahead in a fast-evolving landscape.

Proactive Risk Identification and Mitigation: The ability to foresee technical risks can prevent significant development setbacks. With technical insight, you can identify potential issues early on and collaborate with your engineering team to plan preventive solutions, safeguarding your project timeline and product quality.

By boosting your technical competence, you not only enhance your own role's effectiveness but also contribute to the overall success and adaptability of your product in a competitive and ever-changing digital environment.

Essential Technical Foundations for Product Managers

Acquiring a foundational understanding of technology for Product Managers doesn't require deep expertise in coding or technical details but understanding the core technical concepts to foster better collaboration and streamline the development process. Here's an overview of the critical stages in the software development workflow:

Requirements Gathering: This phase is about working in alignment with developers to define what needs to be built, focusing on the 'what' and 'why' of the product, which includes customer needs and interaction scenarios. At this stage, the emphasis is on the product's goals rather than on the technical specifics.

Designing the Architecture: After establishing requirements, the next step involves the creation of the software's architecture. This blueprint outlines the system's structure, detailing its components and how they interact. A basic understanding of this architecture is valuable for you to make well-informed decisions about the product's capabilities and limitations.

Code Writing: Developers translate the requirements and design into code during this stage. While your direct involvement in coding is minimal, being accessible to answer questions or clarify requirements is essential. Code reviews and possibly automated tests are conducted to ensure the software meets quality standards.

Testing: Following the coding phase, comprehensive testing is conducted to verify the software meets all requirements and functions as intended. This involves various types of tests, such as unit, integration, and security testing, executed by developers and QA teams. Your role is crucial in reviewing and validating the outcomes based on the user stories and User Acceptance Criteria (UAC) you've provided.

Deployment: This final phase involves releasing the product or feature to users. The coming chapter will explore deployment strategies in more detail, helping you in planning effective releases and managing user expectations.

Developers also utilize version control systems like Git or BitBucket to manage code changes and facilitate collaboration. Even a basic understanding of these tools can significantly enhance your interactions with the development team and offer insights into the development dynamics.

> By familiarizing yourself with these stages and tools, you're better equipped to navigate the technical aspects of product development, bridging the gap between business strategy and technology. This knowledge not only improves your communication with the development team but also informs your strategic decisions, contributing to a more efficient and effective product development process.

Different Roles within the Development Team

While it may be considered basic knowledge, understanding the composition and structure of the development team is fundamental for Product Managers. A clear knowledge of each team member's role can significantly enhance collaboration and streamline project management. Here's an overview of the key roles within a development team and their contributions to the product's lifecycle:

Front-End Developers: These professionals focus on the user interface and user experience aspects, creating the parts of the product that users directly interact with. Their work is crucial for ensuring the product is intuitive and user-friendly, with expertise varying from web development to mobile application interfaces.

Back-end Developers: They handle the server-side of the product, dealing with the database, server configuration, and the backend logic that powers the application. Their work is essential for the product's functionality, handling data management and backend processes that enable the front-end to operate effectively.

Full-Stack Developers: These developers have a broad skill set, capable of working on both the front-end and back-end. In smaller teams or in projects where agility is required, they are valuable, providing a comprehensive approach to development across the entire technology stack.

Quality Assurance (QA) Engineers: The guardians of product quality, QA Engineers rigorously test the product to identify any defects, performance issues, or deviations from the requirements. Their role is vital to ensure the product adheres to the highest quality standards and offers a flawless user experience.

DevOps Engineers: Specializing in optimizing and automating the development lifecycle, DevOps Engineers focus on improving the software deployment pipeline, including Continuous Integration/Continuous Deployment (CI/CD) practices. They manage the infrastructure to ensure the product's performance and reliability are top-notch.

Technical Lead: This individual guides the technical direction of the project, ensuring the technical quality and progress align with the project goals. They mentor the development team, provide technical oversight, and serve as a crucial link between the technical staff and the product management, facilitating clear communication and alignment on project objectives.

Fundamentals of System Interactions

Understanding the details of system interactions is invaluable for Product Managers, providing insight into how various components of a product interconnect to deliver functionality. This understanding enhances your decision-making capabilities. Let's review some key system interaction components:

APIs (Application Programming Interfaces): APIs facilitate communication between different software applications, enabling them to communicate without requiring a deep understanding of each system's internal mechanics. These interfaces lay down a set of rules and protocols governing how software components should interact. They enable different systems to exchange data and functionality efficiently, enhancing software interoperability and capabilities. Understanding APIs integration can empower you to leverage these connections, aligning your product more closely with user needs.

Web services: These services offer standardized methods for facilitating communication and data exchange between various software applications or systems via the Internet. Web services use a set of protocols and standards that enable applications to share data and functionalities, regardless of the programming languages or platforms they use. Here are some of the primary types of web services:

SOAP (Simple Object Access Protocol): SOAP is a robust method for sending messages over the Internet, often using XML. Though it is powerful, SOAP can be complex and resource-intensive.

REST (Representational State Transfer): REST offers a simpler, more efficient way for systems to interact. It uses standard HTTP methods, making it easier to operate.

GraphQL: This modern technology allows clients to specify the data they need, leading to more efficient data management.

gRPC: This open-source framework focuses on high-performance communication. It uses Protocol Buffers and supports a wide range of formats and programming languages.

Integration Patterns: These frameworks ensure seamless interactions between software systems, outlining data sharing, initiating communication, and error handling strategies. Understanding these patterns can guide integration with external systems or internal module interactions. Notable patterns include:

Synchronous Integration: In this setup, one system sends a request to another and waits for a response before moving on. This method is similar to a face-to-face conversation where each participant waits for the other's reply before proceeding. While synchronous integration provides immediate feedback, it may slow down system performance, as the system has to wait for each response.

Asynchronous Integration: Here, the system sends a request and continues with other tasks without waiting for a reply. It handles the response whenever it arrives, similar to how email correspondence works. This approach can improve performance because the system doesn't sit idle while waiting for responses.

Batch Processing: This pattern accumulates data over a defined period or until specific conditions are met, then processes all the data at once. Batch processing is efficient for handling large data volumes but isn't suitable for scenarios requiring real-time processing.

Real-time Processing: In contrast, real-time processing happens immediately as data arrives. This pattern is vital for situations that demand instant data processing and action.

> **Databases:** Databases play a critical role in storing and retrieving your product's data. A fundamental understanding of databases isn't about mastering complex queries but appreciating the core elements that make up a data system. These include data sources, data pipelines, and data storage solutions. A knowledge of these components will guide you in making well-informed decisions about data-centric features and help you understand how product changes could affect data handling.

Data Sources: These are the starting points where data originates. Whether it's users interacting with your product, data from third-party APIs, or other external inputs, identifying your data sources is crucial for understanding your product's data structure and its origins.

Data Pipelines: These mechanisms move and transform data from its source to its ultimate storage or display. Understanding the role of data pipelines can help you spot potential bottlenecks or challenges in your product's data flow.

Data Storage: This refers to the locations and methods used to store your data. Options include cloud storage services like Amazon S3 or Google Cloud Storage, as well as on-premises solutions. Different storage methods offer various benefits and understanding them allows you to make educated choices about how to store your product's data most effectively.

Balance Technical Knowledge with Managerial Responsibilities

While technical knowledge is undoubtedly beneficial for Product Managers, striking the right balance between this expertise and your core managerial responsibilities is key. Here's a refined approach to maintaining this balance:

Effective Communication and Decision-Making: Utilize your technical insights to engage in meaningful dialogues with developers, asking relevant questions and making decisions that are informed by a deep understanding of the product's technical aspects. This ability also helps in bridging the gap between technical teams and other stakeholders, fostering alignment and mutual understanding.

Technical Knowledge as an Enabler: Your primary role is to define the product's vision, articulate its requirements, and highlight its value to customers. While technical knowledge is a valuable tool, it should complement, not overlook, the strategic and user-focused aspects of your role. Participate in technical discussions, but always with an eye on your primary goals as a Product Manager.

Balancing Involvement: Having technical acumen might tempt you to get heavily involved in the nitty-gritty of software development. However, it's crucial to distinguish when to step back and trust your development team to handle the technicalities, allowing you to focus on broader strategic and managerial responsibilities.

Valuing Developer Expertise: Acknowledge and respect the development team's technical expertise. Their hands-on experience with the technology can provide invaluable insights that enrich the product. Foster a culture of open communication where their technical input is actively required and factored into decision-making.

Maintaining Team Efficiency: Place trust in your developers' expertise, offering support and guidance without micromanaging their technical tasks. Be mindful not to influence on areas that could lead to inefficiencies or disrupt team dynamics.

Leveraging Technical knowledge: Aim to use your technical understanding to enhance product management and foster team collaboration. Your ability to interpret and translate technical concepts for non-technical stakeholders, and vice versa, is a valuable skill that contributes significantly to the product development process and helps in forming a more holistic vision of the product in your roadmap.

By finding the optimal balance between technical knowledge and your managerial duties, you can lead your team more effectively, ensuring that product development is aligned with customer needs and business goals. This balance allows you to use your technical insights to enrich the project while maintaining the strategic and user-centric focus of your role as a Product Manager in sharp relief.

A Technical Product Manager: A Niche Expertise in Action

As this chapter wraps up, we turn our focus to the specialized role of a Technical Product Manager (TPM), a distinct branch within the realm of product management. TPMs differentiate themselves by bringing a deep well of technical knowledge to their roles, which may encompass expertise in programming, system architecture, or sophisticated database management.

The significance of a TPM excels in environments where the product's core is deeply technical. Here, their expertise isn't just an advantage; it's essential for steering the product's direction and ensuring its technical strategies are in coherence with business goals. TPMs excel at demystifying complex technological concepts, making them accessible to non-technical team members, thereby fostering a unified approach among all parties involved in the product lifecycle.

Imagine a scenario where a company is developing a cutting-edge AI-driven analytics platform. A TPM with a robust foundation in artificial intelligence and machine learning would be invaluable, offering insights into selecting appropriate AI frameworks, decoding the complexities of model training, and aligning technical capabilities with the company's strategic ambitions.

The decision to appoint a TPM hinges on the product's technical depth and the specific requirements it entails. For technically intensive products, a TPM is equipped to navigate complex technical landscapes, adding a layer of expertise that complements the skill set of a conventional Product Manager. This ensures that the product's technical dimensions harmonize with its market strategy and user experience objectives.

Conversely, for products where technical complexity is not as pronounced, a general Product Manager, skilled in market analysis, user experience design, and strategic foresight, would suffice. Such individuals are adept at aligning the product with market demands and user expectations without delving deeply into technicalities.

Ultimately, whether to engage a TPM or a general Product Manager should be guided by the specific technical demands of your product and the overarching goals of your organization. Successful product management balances technical proficiency with a keen sense of market dynamics and user needs, tailored to the technological intricacy at hand.

Chapter Conclusion and Reflection

As we conclude this chapter, we've deepened our understanding of the integral role technical skills play in product management. Our exploration ranged from the foundational technical knowledge that strengthens communication and decision-making to the specialized competencies that define a Technical Product Manager (TPM). This journey highlights how technical acumen can foster stronger collaboration with engineering teams, underpin informed strategic choices, and refine product planning processes.

However, it's vital to remember that technical know-how should enhance, not overshadow, the diverse array of skills pivotal for successful product management. A skilled Product Manager seamlessly integrates technical understanding with strategic insight, market analysis, user-centric design, and effective communication. It's this comprehensive skill set that enables you to smoothly navigate your product's lifecycle, whether you're in a generalist or a technically focused role.

The required level of technical knowledge varies, tailored to the unique demands of your product and its market context. Some products may necessitate a deep technical dive, whereas others might prioritize market positioning or user experience more heavily.

Moving forward, our next chapter, "Launching and Scaling Your Product," will pivot from the foundational to the actionable, focusing on how to successfully introduce and grow your product. We'll tackle effective launch strategies, the details of release planning, and the nuances of scaling, providing you with strategies to penetrate new markets, overcome growth-related challenges, and sustain success in a competitive landscape.

Embark on this next phase with us, as we arm you with the knowledge and strategies to not only launch your product but also elevate it to greater heights in the market.

CHAPTER 6 LAUNCHING AND SCALING YOUR PRODUCT

Welcome to a critical stage in your product management journey! You've now reached a key milestone where the focus shifts from product development to the exciting tasks of launching and scaling your product. This chapter is a celebration of your hard work, marking the transition of your product from an idea to a workable entity.

In this phase, we'll dive deep into the art of product launch, often referred to as "shipping the product." This is a pivotal moment when your product, shaped by your dedication and expertise, is introduced to its intended users. We'll explore the details of release planning and deployment strategies, laying the groundwork for your product's launch in the market.

A Product Manager's role doesn't stop at launch. The subsequent phase of scaling is equally dynamic and challenging, focusing on extending your product's reach, solidifying its market position, and maximizing its impact. Your strategic involvement is crucial in scaling efforts, and this chapter will guide you through the necessary actions and strategies for this growth phase.

We'll go through two fundamental concepts vital to effective product scaling. First, we'll explore "Product-Led Growth" (PLG), a cutting-edge strategy that has become increasingly influential in product management. You'll learn about the foundational principles and tactics of PLG, highlighting its importance in modern scaling principles.

Next, we'll explore the "Crossing the Chasm" framework, a well-known model that offers valuable insights into navigating the various stages of user adoption throughout your product's lifecycle. This model is an indispensable tool for Product Managers, providing a strategic perspective on engaging with different user segments.

While this chapter primarily focuses on scaling from a product management viewpoint, it's worth noting that related areas such as marketing strategies and growth campaigns are outside our current scope. Our goal is to equip you with the targeted strategies and tools necessary to adeptly manage the scaling process.

Now, let's start this exciting phase, learning how to drive your product to greater heights and broader success!

Shipping Your Product

The launch phase for your product, whether it's unveiling a new offering, introducing an innovative feature, rolling out a significant update, or implementing minor enhancements, is a pivotal stage in product management. This stage requires careful planning, stakeholder alignment, strategic orchestration, in-depth quality assurance, and transparent communication.

Release Planning Essentials

Mastering the art of release management is fundamental in product management, and practices can vary widely between organizations. Consider the contrast between Apple's strict, scheduled release dates and Facebook's more fluid, readiness-oriented feature rollouts. While the engineering team typically leads the release process, some companies designate this critical function to a specialized release manager. As a Product Manager, you play an essential role in ensuring each release aligns with the product's broader strategy and objectives, guaranteeing that every update offers tangible value to your users.

Initiating the release process involves defining two key elements: the scope and the release date. Scope determination requires identifying the specific features, enhancements, or bug fixes to include in the upcoming release. Collaborating closely with the engineering team, you'll assess the technical viability and the effort needed for each item, guiding the decision on which features are ready for launch and which need more refinement.

Your key role is to synchronize the engineering team with other stakeholders. Leveraging your skills in communication and collaboration is vital throughout the release journey. Regular interactions, such as release planning meetings, daily stand-ups, and progress reviews, are essential for keeping all parties aligned with the release's goals, requirements, and timeline. These continuous engagements ensure that the team remains informed and adaptable, ready to address any unexpected difficulties that may arise.

Quality Assurance and Testing

Quality Assurance and rigorous testing are indispensable before any product release. Collaborating with engineering teams to create a detailed testing strategy is essential. This phase requires setting explicit testing protocols, and swift resolution of any discovered bugs or issues.

Quality Assurance (QA) is fundamental in product development, involving diverse testing types and stages to ensure the product's seamless operation, adherence to quality standards, and fulfillment of user expectations. For a Product Manager, understanding these aspects is vital to effectively oversee the development process. Let's explore these key testing components:

Functional Testing: This initial testing is conducted post-feature development within each development squad, typically during the sprint process and before the sprint review. It checks the software's individual functions against the specified requirements and design documents.

Integration Testing: After functional testing, integration testing evaluates how newly developed features interact with each other and existing features. This ensures seamless integration and confirms that new additions don't adversely affect the overall software functionality.

User Acceptance Testing (UAT): Involving end-users or the business team, UAT mimics real-world usage scenarios to validate that the software fulfills the intended needs and specifications.

Performance Testing: This testing assesses how the system performs under specific conditions like surge in traffic. It identifies performance bottlenecks and evaluates various performance metrics like response times and resource utilization to ensure they align with the established performance benchmarks.

Security Testing: Especially crucial in our digital era, security testing probes for system vulnerabilities, ensuring robust data protection and network security.

Regression Testing: A continuous process conducted with every code change to confirm that new changes haven't adversely affected existing functionalities.

Smoke Testing: Performed after a new software build, smoke testing verifies that the software's key functionalities operate correctly.

Sanity Testing: This targeted form of regression testing focuses on particular functionalities, typically unscripted, to detect any missing functionalities that were expected to be included.

By understanding and actively participating in these testing stages, you ensure that the product not only meets the technical requirements but also delivers a user experience that aligns with the highest quality standards.

The Role of the Product Manager in QA Process

While Quality Assurance (QA) is traditionally seen as an engineering task within development or release rituals, your engagement as a Product Manager in guiding the QA process is crucial. Let's delve into your key roles:

Defining Requirements: Your collaboration with QA teams and developers is essential in defining clear testing requirements and expectations. Ensuring that the QA team has developed comprehensive test cases that cover all scenarios is fundamental to guaranteeing they fully understanding the product's requirements.

Prioritization: Not every test can be conducted for each release due to time and resource constraints. You'll need to work closely with QA leads to prioritize tests, focusing on those most critical for the product's current stage, and outline a testing strategy for each release.

Risk Assessment: An important part of your role involves evaluating the potential risks at each testing stage. Post-testing, organize reviews with the QA team to triage any issues and determine the associated risks. Your objective and intuitive judgment will highlight whether the product is ready for the next phase, requires additional testing, or needs further development.

Quality Checks: Although the QA team conducts the tests, as a Product Manager, you should review the outcomes to ensure they meet the product's goals and uphold quality standards. Adopting a practice of personally testing key features before they go live and sharing your insights with the QA team can provide an added layer of quality assurance.

Your involvement in the QA and testing process is dynamic and essential. By setting clear objectives, developing a detailed testing strategy, actively participating in User Acceptance Testing (UAT), monitoring defect management, and analyzing performance metrics, you significantly influence the product's journey to market success. Your proactive involvement ensures that the final product not only meets technical specifications but also delivers the intended value to users, aligning with the overarching product strategy.

Deployment Strategies

Transitioning from testing to deployment is a landmark phase in your product's lifecycle. The deployment strategy you choose plays a critical role in ensuring a smooth transition and a successful product launch. Let's explore various deployment strategies and their optimal applications:

Big Bang Deployment: This strategy involves launching the entire product or a significant update to all users at once. It's most appropriate for products that have been thoroughly tested and where the likelihood of deployment-related issues is low. While this approach allows for a unified user experience, it requires careful preparation and risk management.

Rolling Deployment: Also known as incremental deployment, this method introduces the product or update to users gradually. For instance, you might start with 5% of your user base and gradually expand. This phased approach lets you monitor performance and user feedback, providing an opportunity to pause or adjust the deployment based on real-time insights.

Canary Release: Similar to "the canary in a coal mine", this strategy targets a small, specific user group or infrastructure subset at first. It acts as a live test, offering valuable data on the product's performance in a controlled, real-world setting. This strategy allows for early issue detection and resolution, reducing overall risk before a wider release.

Feature Flags: With this technique, new features are deployed in a dormant state and are not visible to users until you activate them. This allows for segmented, controlled testing and phased releases, enabling you to gather targeted feedback and refine the feature before a full-scale launch.

Hotfixes: These quick deployments address urgent issues that arise post-launch. While hotfixes may occasionally skip some standard testing protocols due to their urgency, they are crucial for rapid problem resolution, although with a slightly higher risk factor.

Selecting the right deployment strategy exceeds technical considerations—it's a strategic decision that profoundly affects user experience and market reception. By thoroughly assessing the advantages and risks of each method and aligning your choice with your product's objectives, you can navigate this pivotal stage effectively, paving the way for a successful product introduction to the market.

Strategic Considerations for Effective Deployment

Achieving successful deployment exceeds technical implementation; it's a strategic endeavor that requires careful planning and collaboration across various departments. To ensure a seamless deployment process, consider these essential strategies:

Preparing for Major Releases: For substantial updates or releases concurring with peak usage periods (like Black Friday), it's vital to synchronize with your operations and infrastructure teams. Verify that the production environment is equipped to handle potential surges in user activity. Collaborate with your marketing team to project the anticipated Daily Active Users (DAU) and communicate these projections to your engineering and infrastructure teams to prevent system overload and guarantee a smooth user experience during high-demand periods.

Developing Instant Rollback Strategies: Unanticipated issues can arise post-deployment, possibly requiring a return to an earlier version of the product. Collaborate with your engineering and operations teams to formulate a quick and efficient rollback strategy. This preparation is essential for minimizing downtime and protective user confidence if deployment challenges occur.

Streamlining Communication Across Teams: Clear and consistent communication is essential for deployment success. Publish comprehensive deployment plans and schedules to all relevant stakeholders, including customer support, marketing, and sales teams. Transparent communication prepares these teams for the upcoming deployment, enabling them to address any subsequent customer inquiries effectively and fostering a unified, informed approach across your organization.

By emphasizing these strategic considerations, you enhance your product's deployment prospects, minimizing risks and ensuring your team's readiness. The effectiveness of your deployment strategy deeply impacts your product's initial market reception and lays the groundwork for its ongoing success and growth.

Release Documentation and Training

Comprehensive documentation is an integral part of the product management lifecycle, crucial from the initial stages of defining product requirements to the final steps of launching your product. A well-structured documentation strategy ensures all stakeholders are informed and aligned, facilitating a seamless product launch. Let's delve into the key aspects of release documentation:

Crafting Effective Release Notes

Release notes are vital documents that accompany each new version of your product, detailing changes, new features, and important notices for stakeholders. To create impactful release notes, consider the following components:

Version Number: Clearly display the version number to aid in tracking developments and addressing issues.

Introduction: Offer a brief summary of the key updates or features in the release, providing readers with a snapshot of what to expect.

New Features: Describe new functionalities in clear, user-friendly language, ensuring that all users, regardless of their technical background, can grasp the changes.

Enhancements: Explain any improvements made to existing features, highlighting aspects like performance boosts, user interface refinements, or additional functionalities.

Resolved Bugs: List bugs that have been addressed in this release, particularly those previously reported by users, to demonstrate responsiveness to feedback.

Breaking Changes: Alert users to any modifications that might impact their use of existing features, offering guidance on how to adapt.

Deprecations: Notify users about features or elements that are being phased out, setting expectations for future updates.

Known Issues: Be transparent about any unresolved issues, helping users manage their expectations and prepare for potential workarounds.

Upgrade Instructions: Provide clear instructions if the release requires user action, such as updating software or modifying settings.

Acknowledgments: Recognize the efforts of team members or acknowledge community feedback that has contributed to the release.

Contact Information: Include details for stakeholders to reach out with questions, feedback, or to report issues.

Well-crafted release notes are a multifaceted tool; they not only inform but also engage your audience, equipping users with necessary information, empowering sales, and marketing teams to highlight new features, and enabling customer support to offer precise assistance.

The User Guide

A User Guide serves as an essential resource, providing end-users with the knowledge they need to effectively operate a product or software application. Distinct from release notes, which detail specific updates, the User Guide offers a comprehensive overview of the product's features, optimal usage practices, and solutions for common issues. It's crucial to update the User Guide with each new release to reflect any changes or additions. Key elements of a well-structured User Guide include:

Introduction: Craft an inviting introduction that explains the product's purpose, capabilities, and target audience, setting the stage for the information that follows.

Table of Contents: Ensure the guide has a detailed and well-organized contents section, with hyperlinks if possible, allowing users to quickly find the information they need.

Getting Started: Provide essential information on initial setup, such as installation, initial login, and basic configuration, guiding users through their first interactions with the product.

Feature Exploration: Offer comprehensive descriptions of the product's features, organized logically, perhaps by sections or chapters, to facilitate easy understanding and reference.

Step-by-Step Tutorials: Deliver in-depth, user-friendly instructions for common tasks or feature utilizations, empowering users to make the most of the product.

FAQs: A section dedicated to frequently asked questions can address common user queries, providing quick and accessible answers.

Troubleshooting Tips: Include advice for resolving common problems, helping users to independently troubleshoot issues they may encounter.

Glossary: Clarify technical terms, abbreviations, and industry-specific language used within the guide to ensure it's comprehensible to all users.

Appendices: Utilize appendices for additional information like technical specs, compliance details, or advanced configurations, catering to users who seek deeper understanding or specific data.

Contact Details: List information for reaching customer support or technical assistance, ensuring users know where to turn for help beyond the guide.

Beyond the User Guide, consider leveraging other educational touchpoints like platform FAQs, which can address more immediate or feature-specific inquiries from users.

In B2B technology contexts, the depth of technical documentation is even more critical, encompassing details on APIs, SDKs, and other technical aspects, providing developers and technical users with the in-depth knowledge required for comprehensive product integration and use.

In summary, launching a product is a complex process that encompasses careful planning, rigorous testing, thoughtful deployment, and detailed documentation. As we transition from launch to scaling, our next focus will be on magnifying your product's reach and impact. We'll explore effective strategies, proven methodologies, and key considerations crucial for scaling your product successfully. Join us as we continue this journey, learning how to broaden your product's influence and achieve new levels of success.

Scaling Your Product

Launching a product is a significant achievement for Product Managers, yet it's just the starting point of a crucial ongoing journey - scaling your product. While the launch sets the initial path, introducing your product to the market and creating interest, the true test of success lies in its ability to grow, evolve, and capture a larger share of the market.

After your product goes live, the emphasis transitions to closely monitoring its performance. Using advanced analytics tools becomes essential, as they enable you to analyze user interactions, track key performance metrics like traffic, conversion rates, and engagement levels, and, if applicable, monitor customer sign-ups. This critical data defines the foundations of your strategy for scaling, shedding light on what resonates with your audience and identifying opportunities for enhancement.

Scaling exceeds technical barriers; it represents a holistic strategy to strengthen your product's reach, user engagement, and revenue generation while upholding quality and user satisfaction. It involves exploring new markets, refining user experiences to cater to varied customer segments, and continually innovating to stay aligned with or ahead of competitors.

In this growth phase, your role as a Product Manager is dynamic. Scaling demands a combination of technical knowledge, strategic insight, and operational expertise. You're tasked with ensuring the product operates seamlessly, customizing experiences for different users, and fostering innovation to meet evolving market needs.

Collaboration is essential during this phase. By working in alignment with teams across engineering, marketing, sales, and customer support, you drive the product along its growth path. The collective goal is to not only fulfill but surpass user expectations, ensuring that the product's expansion is in harmony with the broader objectives of your company. This section aims to arm you with the strategies and insights needed to successfully navigate the challenging yet rewarding journey of scaling your product.

The Three Pillars of Effective Product Scaling

Scaling a product is more than team expansion or augmenting platform capacity; it's a complicated, comprehensive strategy that integrates various facets of your product, development lifecycle, and organizational framework. Effective scaling is characterized by coordinated efforts that span infrastructure enhancement, process refinement, and strategic consistency across different teams. It involves developing a multi-faceted strategy that aligns the product's growth path with its foundational vision and market needs.

In the domain of product scaling, three critical pillars stand out: Customer Experience, Business Viability, and Technical Feasibility.

Customer Experience: Central to product scalability is the customer experience, a pivotal element that drives product evolution. A deep understanding of your customers—their needs, obstacles, and aspirations—is essential. Utilizing these insights to refine your product not only boosts user satisfaction but also cultivates loyalty and forces broader adoption. Integrating continuous customer feedback into your product roadmap ensures your product's evolution is adapted to user expectations.

Business Viability: This aspect concentrates on aligning every product enhancement or new feature with your primary business objectives. It necessitates a careful evaluation of growth sustainability and strategic fit with your broader product vision. Selecting growth opportunities that support a solid, scalable business model is key. When thinking over new features or enhancements, critical questions should be addressed: Does this align with our long-term objectives? What is the anticipated return on investment? How does this integrate with our overall mission?

Technical Feasibility: From a technical standpoint, scaling involves assessing whether your current technology infrastructure and stack are equipped to support your expansion goals. It's an in-depth review of your system's scalability, security, performance, and integration capabilities. Ensuring your product can accommodate increasing user numbers, data volume, and new feature integrations without sacrificing stability or performance is vital.

Mastering the art of scaling involves a delicate balance of enhancing user experience, aligning with business objectives, and ensuring technical robustness. While product scaling covers a wide range of topics, from financial strategy to external partnerships, our focus will be on the role of the Product Manager in this expansive domain. Next, we'll explore an emerging, critical concept for Product Managers: Product-Led Growth (PLG), an approach that's reshaping how products are scaled in today's market.

Product-Led Growth: A Paradigm Shift

In the traditional business growth model, emphasis is often placed on aggressive sales tactics, significant marketing spend, and intense focus on lead generation. Yet, the digital age has shaped itself with a significant shift towards Product-Led Growth (PLG), a methodology that's rapidly gaining traction, especially in the tech industry.

In today's informed market, consumers show a clear preference for products that allow them to perceive inherent value before any financial commitment. They are leaning more towards genuine product value rather than being influenced by forceful sales tactics or elaborate marketing campaigns.

PLG is a transformative approach for growth strategies, positioning the product itself as the primary driver of customer acquisition, retention, and expansion. This model leverages the product's inherent value and superior user experience as the main catalysts for organic growth, offering a scalable and cost-efficient route to expand the user base. It aligns with today's consumer preferences, who are more inclined to value direct product interactions over traditional marketing messages.

The success story of Slack is a testament to PLG's potential. By sidestepping conventional sales strategies and focusing on crafting an intuitive, user-centric platform, Slack naturally attracts users. Its freemium model allowed individuals and teams to explore the product's value firsthand, fostering organic growth that transitioned smoothly into paid subscriptions.

Slacks' journey highlights how prioritizing product excellence and user-driven growth can lead to significant market success.

At its core, PLG redefines the growth strategy narrative, promoting the creation of products that are so compelling that they virtually market and sell themselves. This approach is not just a tactic but a mindset shift, resonating deeply with the values of the modern digital landscape where product experience and tangible value are vital in driving business success.

Why Should Companies Transition to PLG?

Transitioning to Product-Led Growth (PLG) represents a fundamental shift, not just in tactics but in the strategic orientation of an organization. It demands a holistic commitment across all levels, from leadership to operational teams. Opting for PLG goes beyond following a market trend; it's a deliberate choice of strategy aimed at unlocking numerous benefits:

Customer-Centricity at the Core: PLG is built on delivering value-driven user experiences, placing customers at the heart of the growth strategy. This approach boosts user engagement, driving increased adoption, longer retention, and natural growth through user satisfaction.

Cost-Effective Customer Acquisition: By leveraging the product itself as the main channel for growth, PLG can significantly lower Customer Acquisition Costs (CAC), offering a cost-efficient alternative to conventional sales-centric models.

Elevated Product Excellence: A product-led approach inspires a culture of continuous enhancement, fueled by ongoing user feedback. This results in a product that not only meets but exceeds user expectations, ensuring competitive market positioning.

The Power of Viral Advocacy: When users are delighted by the product, they're likely to become advocates, promoting it through word-of-mouth. This organic advocacy is a potent driver of sustainable and viral growth.

Insightful, Data-Driven Decisions: PLG facilitates the collection of rich user interaction data, offering critical insights that influence product optimization and user experience personalization.

Inherent Scalability: PLG inherently supports scalable growth. As the user base expands and the product evolves in response to user feedback, its growth mechanisms become more refined and potent, creating a virtuous cycle of enhancement and expansion.

Adopting PLG is a strategic pivot that requires a shift towards product-centricity and a deep commitment to delivering value to users. It's about cultivating a growth model that is sustainable, data driven, and closely aligned with user needs, setting a strong foundation for long-term success.

Zoom Case Study: A Testament to Product-Led Growth

Zoom's domination in the competitive video conferencing market underscores the impact of Product-Led Growth (PLG). Despite launching in 2011 amidst established players like Cisco, Google, and Microsoft, Zoom's commitment to product excellence and user experience drove it from a growing startup to a market leader, representing the core principles of PLG.

Founded by Eric Yuan, who was motivated by his own frustrations with existing conferencing tools, Zoom differentiated itself through its user-friendly design and reliable performance. This focus on creating an intuitive and effective product quickly gained a dedicated user base, boosting Zoom from 3 million users in 2013 to 100 million by 2015, and leading to a successful IPO in 2019 with the company valued near $16 billion.

Central to Zoom's growth story was its freemium model, which offered free 40-minute conference calls. This approach lowered the entry barrier, attracting a broad spectrum of users and enabling viral growth as satisfied customers became brand advocates, inviting others to join. The high-quality and reliability of the product motivated many to upgrade to premium plans for extended features.

Moreover, Zoom's growth was fueled by a solid commitment to enhancement and responsiveness to customer feedback, ensuring the product not only met but exceeded user expectations. Strategic partnerships and integrations, such as with Slack, further embedded Zoom into users' daily workflows.

Zoom's journey exemplifies the power of a PLG strategy, showcasing how a focus on product quality, user satisfaction, and a clever freemium model can drive organic growth and disrupt the market.

This model isn't unique to Zoom. Other enterprises, including Atlassian and Figma in the B2B realm and Pinterest and Expensify in the B2C sector, have successfully harnessed PLG to attract their target audiences and fuel rapid expansion. These cases confirm PLG's capacity to transform market dynamics and catalyze significant business achievements, offering valuable lessons for any company aspiring to harness the potential of product-led strategies.

Mastering the Art of PLG Strategy

Adopting a Product-Led Growth (PLG) strategy isn't just a series of steps but a comprehensive shift in approach, embedding the product's value at the core of growth from acquisition to retention. Here's how to quickly integrate PLG into your product's essence:

Prioritize User Onboarding: Onboarding refers to your user's introduction to the product's capabilities. Build an experience that not only welcomes but educates users about achieving their objectives with your product. Ensure onboarding is dynamic, evolving with new feature releases to continually engage and educate your user base.

Adopting Freemium or Free Trial Models: Ensure every interaction delivers tangible value. A free version should address the user's primary need, while paid tiers enhance this value. If a free version isn't viable, offer free trials to showcase the full product experience, inviting users to explore and eventually convert.

Leverage Product Analytics: Utilize advanced analytics to explore user behaviors and preferences, guiding product refinement and user journey optimization. This data-driven approach allows you to customize experiences, like tailoring onboarding to highlight features that maximize satisfaction and encourage upgrades.

Promote Self-Service and Accessibility: Design your product for intuitive use, reducing reliance on customer support. Empower users to discover and leverage your product independently, strengthened by clear documentation and accessible resources, enhancing the overall user experience.

Integrating into Daily Routines: Aim for your product to become indispensable in users' daily activities. Successful products embed themselves into daily workflows, becoming tools users can't envision their routine without. For example, Trello and Evernote have excelled by providing essential, time-saving functionalities that effortlessly integrate into daily workflows for its users.

Encouraging Organic Sharing: Embed features that naturally prompt users to share your product, be it through referral incentives, social sharing options, or collaborative functionalities that not only improve the user experience but also widen your reach.

Utilize In-Product Messaging: Employ in-product messages to guide users, unveil new features, or prompt actions that deepen engagement or conversion, keeping users engaged with your product's evolution.

Establish Customer Feedback Loops: Create effective channels for gathering and acting on user feedback. This not only informs product enhancement but also cultivates a community, enhancing user loyalty and retention.

Introduce these elements into every phase of your product's lifecycle. Regularly question how each feature or update aligns with PLG objectives, such as improving onboarding or enhancing user value. By ensuring these principles are integral to your product strategy, you position PLG not just as a facet of your approach but as its driving force.

Next, we'll delve into Grammarly's PLG journey, extracting key insights and strategies from their successful PLG implementation.

Grammarly Case Study: A Paradigm of Product-Led Growth

Grammarly, well-known for its advanced writing assistance tools, demonstrates an excellent implementation of Product-Led Growth (PLG). Central to its success is a well-structured Freemium model, an effective onboarding process, and the strategic application of data analytics to enhance user experience.

Freemium Model as a Growth Lever: Grammarly's Freemium model introduces users to its core offerings, providing essential grammar checks and writing suggestions at no cost. This approach not only allows users to witness the tool's immediate benefits in their daily writing tasks but also serves as a gateway to the broader functionalities of the full version, inviting users towards potential upgrade paths.

Onboarding Excellence: Grammarly's onboarding process is designed to seamlessly integrate users into the ecosystem, whether through browser extensions or desktop apps. This detailed onboarding ensures users can effortlessly incorporate Grammarly into their writing routines, fostering consistent engagement and a solid foundation for long-term use.

Data-Driven Personalization: Grammarly stands out for its AI-powered analytics, which tailor the user experience by identifying individual writing styles, recurring errors, and preferences. This personalization not only enhances user value but also wonderfully demonstrates Grammarly's advanced capabilities, encouraging users to explore further into its premium features.

Interactive User Interface: The platform's interface is intuitive, offering real-time suggestions and detailed explanations, which go beyond mere grammar checks to include style, tone, and structure enhancements. These interactions not only help users in improving their writing but also highlight the advanced benefits of Grammarly's premium service.

Premium Offering Differentiation: Exclusive features like plagiarism detection and genre-specific writing style recommendations are reserved for Grammarly Premium users, creating a distinct appeal for the paid version. The outlining between free and premium features is strategically crafted to sustain user engagement with the free version while presenting clear, compelling reasons to upgrade.

Grammarly's strategy highlights the effectiveness of a user-focused product approach. By consistently delivering value and enhancing the user experience with intelligent analytics and an engaging interface, Grammarly has not only attracted a vast user base but has also successfully converted a significant portion into premium subscribers. This narrative serves as a powerful illustration of how a sophisticated PLG strategy can catalyze growth and secure a challenging position in a competitive market.

Transition to Product-Led Growth

Shifting to a Product-Led Growth (PLG) model is a comprehensive organizational change, extending beyond the product team to influence the entire company's philosophy and strategy. This transition redefines the growth paradigm, placing the product at the core of customer acquisition, retention, and expansion initiatives. It's vital to assess the extent to which a product-centric philosophy influences your organization: Is your product just a solution, or is it the driving force for growth and customer engagement?

Successful adoption of PLG requires cross-functional teamwork and consistency across the organization. Various teams must unite to gather customer insights, study user behavior, and link this intelligence into continuous product enhancement and innovation. This continuous cycle of learning and adaptation is crucial for staying ahead in a dynamic market environment.

In a genuinely product-led organization, this approach impacts every party:

Marketing Transformation: Marketing in a product-led organization shifts to emphasize the product's inherent value and features, transitioning from traditional lead generation to highlighting the product as the main attraction for prospective customers. Marketing efforts are crafted to reveal the product's benefits and user success stories, attracting users based on the product's merits.

Sales Team Evolution: In a PLG model, sales strategies change to leverage the product as a cornerstone for building customer relationships. The sales approach focuses on illustrating the product's value and aligning it with customer needs, often leveraging product demos or trials as key tools in the sales process.

Engineering and Product Development: Engineering teams in a PLG-focused organization prioritize features and enhancements that boost user experience, ease of use, and flawless functionality. This alignment ensures the product doesn't just meet technical standards but actively facilitates user engagement and satisfaction, driving growth.

Implementation a PLG model involves reorienting every department's objective and strategy around the product, fostering a cohesive effort to push growth through user satisfaction and product excellence. This holistic approach not only enhances user acquisition and retention but also cultivates a company culture that's inherently aligned with delivering value through product innovation.

Facilitating a Smooth Transition To PLG

As a Product Manager, you play a pivotal role in steering your organization's shift toward Product-Led Growth (PLG). To successfully maneuver this striking transformation, it is imperative to interweave engineering, marketing, sales, customer support and business operations into a collective mindset with a mindful execution of your insights.

Here are key strategies to guide this transformation effectively:

Foster a Customer-Centric Mindset: Encourage an organizational culture where decisions and discussions are always customer-focused. Utilize your deep understanding of the product and its users to lead this cultural change.

Highlight how the product solves user problems or meets their needs, shifting the narrative from product features to customer benefits.

Data-Driven Insights: Utilize product analytics to inform and influence decision-making across departments. Share user behavior and engagement data to illustrate the direct impact of feature developments on customer satisfaction and product acceptance, fostering a unified, data-informed approach to product evolution.

Promote Collaborative Efforts: Ensure all teams are in sync with the PLG culture. As a Product Manager, you're tasked with fostering an environment where interdepartmental collaboration fuels a more potent and unified product strategy, aligning collective efforts toward shared objectives.

Lead Change Management: Addressing resistance to change is crucial in this transition. Communicate the advantages of the PLG model clearly and work to get support from all organizational levels, ensuring a unified move towards this new growth paradigm.

Embrace Continuous Learning: The PLG model succeeds on adaptability. Stay up-to-date with industry trends, shifts in user preferences, and technological innovations to continuously refine your PLG approach, ensuring your strategy remains dynamic and responsive.

Transitioning to a PLG framework presents its challenges, but the promise of sustainable, user-centric growth it offers makes it a worthwhile endeavor. A commitment to ongoing feedback, iterative development, and an unwavering focus on enhancing user experience is crucial for thriving in this new landscape.

Ultimately, shifting to a product-led framework is more than just a strategic adjustment; it's a continuous journey of learning, adapting, and growing. As a Product Manager, your leadership and vision are influential in ensuring this transition not only succeeds but also drives your organization toward new heights of innovation and customer engagement.

Frameworks for PLG Strategy

To excel in Product-Led Growth (PLG), leveraging established frameworks can provide a structured approach to crafting and executing your strategy. Let's dive into one such framework, understand its components, and explore how it can shape your PLG initiatives.

The Growth-Loop Framework

This framework encapsulates a comprehensive view of PLG, emphasizing a self-sustaining cycle of growth through three interconnected stages: Acquisition, Activation, and Retention/Engagement. Here's a breakdown of how to implement this framework effectively:

Acquisition Stage: This initial phase is all about attracting new users through various channels, such as organic search, social media, referrals, and targeted campaigns. As a Product Manager, collaborate with marketing, sales, and analytics teams to pinpoint and optimize the most effective channels, ensuring they lead potential users to discover your product.

Activation Stage: Activation is where users first encounter the real value of your product. It's crucial to streamline the onboarding process, helping users navigate and engage with your product's key features swiftly. Refine this stage by mapping user journeys, identifying critical activation metrics, and enhancing the onboarding experience based on user feedback and analytical insights.

Retention and Engagement Stage: The aim here is to transform initial users into committed, active customers. Creating an engaging product experience that goes beyond meeting user expectations can nurture loyalty and promote advocacy. Implement strategies like personalization, continuous feature updates, community engagement, and proactive customer support. Apply user interaction data and feedback to pinpoint areas for enhancement and to uncover opportunities for new features that elevate the user experience.

The cyclic essence of the Growth-Loop Framework is its most significant advantage, with each stage feeding into and reinforcing the next, creating a dynamic growth cycle. Your role as a Product Manager is to refine these loops, drawing on data and user insights to optimize the processes of user acquisition, activation, and retention.

Mastering this framework equips you to tackle the complexities of PLG, enabling you to optimize each component and foster a powerful, self-reinforcing growth mechanism for your product.

The SurveyMonkey Example

SurveyMonkey's clever use of the Growth-Loop Framework demonstrates a well-orchestrated Product-Led Growth (PLG) strategy, illuminating how each phase can be optimized for long-term success.

Acquisition Phase: SurveyMonkey capitalizes on its free tier to attract a wide user demographic, positioning its simple and efficient survey creation tools as a compelling entry point. This initial offering is key, attracting users to the platform and laying the groundwork for their journey through the subsequent growth stages.

Activation Phase: At this stage, SurveyMonkey excels in offering a seamless onboarding experience. New users are welcomed with a user-friendly interface, complemented by interactive guides and concise tooltips, which facilitate the creation of their first survey. This seamless onboarding is critical for converting sign-ups into engaged users, showcasing the platform's value and encouraging further exploration of its functionalities.

Retention/Engagement Phase: With the user's initial value recognition in place, SurveyMonkey shifts focus toward enhancing user engagement and fostering lasting retention. It achieves this by nudging users toward advanced features, collaboration tools, and deeper interaction with the platform, which solidifies user loyalty and increases the tendency for free users to upgrade to premium plans.

Expansion Strategy: SurveyMonkey cleverly turns every distributed survey into a new user acquisition channel. Survey recipients are prompted to create their surveys at the end of their participation, leveraging a moment of high engagement to potentially convert them into new platform users, showcasing a seamless transition that embodies a core aspect of SurveyMonkey's growth strategy.

Closing the Loop: The brilliance of SurveyMonkey's strategy lies in its self-reinforcing growth engine. Each survey distributed not only serves its intended purpose but also acts as a channel for lead generation. New users signing up post-survey participation help to expand the user base, effectively closing and reinitiating the growth loop.

SurveyMonkey's methodical approach across the Growth-Loop Framework's stages demonstrates how wise management of user acquisition, activation, and retention can foster a sustainable cycle of growth. Their story highlights the significance of an accurately planned PLG strategy that resonates with the product's core strengths and user expectations, driving continuous, organic expansion.

The Hook Model for Habit-Forming Products

Nir Eyal's Hook Model, detailed in his book 'Hooked,' provides a strategic framework for designing products that naturally engage and retain users, aligning seamlessly with Product-Led Growth (PLG) strategies. It's helpful in creating products that not only attract users but also fosters a habitual pattern/behavior. The model's four interconnected stages—Trigger, Action, Variable Reward, and Investment—work collectively to intensify the user's product integration and engagement.

Trigger: Triggers are the initial prompts that encourage product usage. They can be external, such as notifications or advertisements, nudging the user towards the product, or internal, rooted in emotional states or needs. Identifying and leveraging the right triggers can effectively initiate user engagement. For example, Facebook's notifications serve as external triggers, while the internal need for social connection draws users back to the platform.

Action: This step focuses on the user's response to a trigger, emphasizing ease of action and clear user benefit. The action, whether a simple click or a more involved interaction, should be intuitively designed to reduce user effort. Applying principles of behavioral psychology, like scarcity or social proof, can enhance user motivation to engage with the product.

Variable Reward: Rewards maintain user interest post-action, fulfilling their needs and promoting ongoing interaction. The key here is variability; unpredictable rewards keep users engaged and curious. Instagram, for instance, leverages variable rewards by offering a constantly refreshing content stream, keeping users engaged and eager for more. Rewards can range from gamified points and badges to personalized content recommendations.

Investment: This phase sees users investing time, data, or effort into the product, which not only enriches their experience but also boosts their commitment. User investments, such as building connections within a platform or content creation, increase the likelihood of continued product use and loyalty.

The Hook Model's cyclic design ensures a persistent loop of engagement, with each stage seamlessly leading to the next. As a Product Manager, your role is to orchestrate each phase, utilizing tools like data analytics, A/B testing, and user feedback to refine the process, ensuring sustained user interest and engagement.

By smoothly applying the Hook Model, you can transform your product into a habitual part of users' daily routines, fostering long-term engagement and delivering long-term value for both users and your business.

Duolingo and the Hook Model:

Duolingo stands out as a prime example of the Hook Model's effective application in creating engaging, habit-forming experiences. Through the strategic integration of the model's four phases—Trigger, Action, Variable Reward, and Investment—Duolingo has revolutionized language learning, making it an engaging and addictive pursuit.

Trigger: Duolingo skillfully uses a mix of internal and external triggers to prompt user engagement. Externally, it sends out timely notifications and reminders, nudging users to continue their lessons and sustain their learning habit. Internally, users are driven by personal goals, such as preparing for a trip, planning for a language exam, or simply the joy of learning a new language, which act as powerful motivators to regularly interact with the app.

Action: In this stage, users are invited to engage in lessons through Duolingo's accessible and enjoyable interface. The app breaks down the challenging task of language learning into bite-sized, interactive exercises, transforming the learning process into an enjoyable activity rather than an overwhelming routine.

Variable Reward: Duolingo's rewards system is perfectly designed to provide immediate, positive feedback. Users earn points and advance through levels with each lesson, experiencing a sense of accomplishment. The platform maintains user interest by introducing unexpected challenges and bonuses, offering a variety of rewards that keep the learning experience diverse and attractive.

Investment: User investment grows with each interaction, as time and effort spent on Duolingo enhances language proficiency and deepens their connection with the app. Advancing through levels, accessing new content, and maintaining traits make each subsequent app interaction more meaningful and rewarding.

By applying the Hook Model, Duolingo has transformed the often-difficult journey of language learning into an enjoyable and compelling experience. The platform continuously motivates users to engage, rewards their achievements, and fosters their commitment to learning, establishing a self-reinforcing cycle of user growth and engagement. This methodical approach not only enriches the user experience but also underpins Duolingo's sustained success and widespread appeal.

Additional PLG Frameworks

Exploring various frameworks enriches your toolbox for implementing a robust Product-Led Growth (PLG) strategy. These models offer unique lenses to examine and enhance user experience and product impact. Listed below are a few commonly used Frameworks:

AARRR Framework (Pirate Metrics): Dave McClure's **AARRR** framework is a holistic tool for tracking the customer lifecycle, including Acquisition, Activation, Retention, Revenue, and Referral. It empowers Product Managers to analyze and optimize each stage, crafting strategies that strengthen product engagement and success.

HEART Framework: Originating from Google, the HEART framework concentrates on Happiness, Engagement, Adoption, Retention, and Task Success. This user-centric approach assists teams in evaluating and refining user experiences, providing crucial insights into user satisfaction and the long-term value of products. It guides teams toward user-centric enhancements and breakthroughs.

Jobs-to-be-Done Framework (JTBD): JTBD delves into understanding the core needs and drivers behind customer behaviors. It's about pinpointing the 'jobs' customers expect the product to accomplish and ensuring the product's features align with these expectations. This framework assists Product Managers in sharpening their offerings to better resonate with user needs, boosting satisfaction and relevance.

While every framework offers distinct perspectives and methods, they can be interlinked or tailored to fit your organizational needs. Their successful application depends on a culture that values experimentation, leverages data-driven insights, and possesses a deep comprehension of user dynamics.

Integrating these diverse frameworks into your PLG strategy equips you with a comprehensive set of tools for driving growth. By utilizing these varied insights, you're better positioned to make informed decisions that steer your product and organization toward enduring growth and relevance in a user-centric marketplace marked with competition.

As we explore deeper into Product-Led Growth (PLG), we've recognized it as an integral strategy that places the product at the core of the business ecosystem. PLG exceeds the simple development of an exceptional product;

it requires aligning every aspect of your business—marketing, sales, engineering, customer service, and operations—around the intrinsic value of your product. This holistic integration ensures that your product not only fulfills market demands but is also ready for effective adaptation and scaling.

However, the journey of scaling your product is clearly connected with the broader dynamics of technology adoption and market openness. As your product matures, its integration into your customers' technology ecosystems becomes crucial, addressing their evolving needs and preferences. This pivotal evolution brings us to a critical milestone in a product's lifecycle: "Crossing the Chasm."

"Crossing the Chasm" refers to a key transition phase where your product moves from early adopters to a wider mainstream audience. This shift is burdened with unique challenges, demanding strategic insight and careful implementation. Mastering this leap is crucial for securing broad market adoption and ensuring sustained growth.

Crossing the Chasm: Mastering Technology Adoption Journey

In the dynamic world of digital innovation, the successful introduction and widespread adoption of new technology exceeds the product's inherent features. It demands a profound understanding of the technology adoption lifecycle, an essential element determining the fate of innovative offerings, whether in software, hardware, or digital services. Numerous promising startups have fallen not due to a lack of innovation but due to the complexities involved in this essential adoption phase and their inability to tackle these early on.

The journey typically initiates with innovators, the experimental who embrace new technologies. They are followed by early adopters, pragmatic yet receptive to innovation. The crucial test, however, is transitioning to the early majority—mainstream consumers who exhibit caution and a tendency to avoid risks. The goal extends to engaging even the late adopters, who are usually the most resistant to change.

The leap from early adopters to the early majority, or 'crossing the chasm,' represents a tough challenge. This phase demands a detailed understanding of market dynamics and consumer behavior, beyond just showcasing innovation. Having said that, let's try to understand what is exactly implicit in 'crossing the chasm', and how can one smoothly handle this decisive phase in the technology adoption journey?

This section explores the distinctions of the technology adoption lifecycle, with a keen focus on the 'chasm' that divides early adopters from the early majority. We aim to equip you with fresh insights and actionable tactics to effectively navigate this critical passage. By the end of this exploration, you will gain the expertise and strategies needed to steer your product through the complex process of technology adoption, setting the stage for widespread market acceptance and enduring success.

Navigating the Technology Adoption Life Cycle

A nuanced understanding of where your customers fall within the Technology Adoption Life Cycle is crucial for product management. Recognizing the different motivations and preferences of various user groups is quintessential as your product evolves. Geoffrey Moore's 'Crossing the Chasm' provides an insightful breakdown of these market segments:

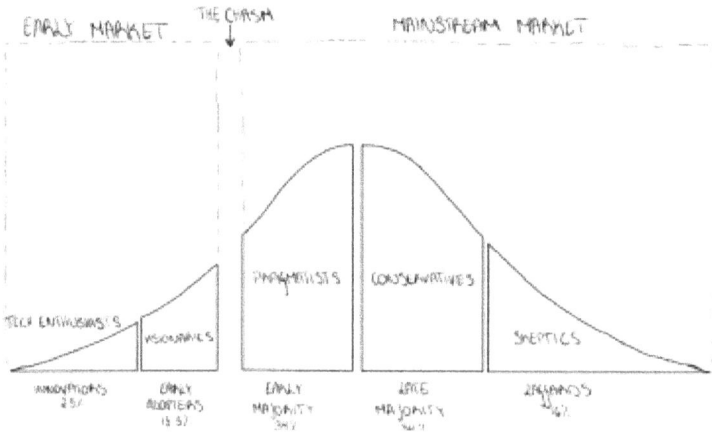

Innovators "Technology Enthusiasts": These early adopters, making up about 2.5% of the market, are eager to explore and experiment with emerging technologies, often overlooking initial limitations. Their appetite for risk and willingness to provide feedback are invaluable during the early stages of product development, offering critical insights and preliminary validation.

Early Adopters "Visionaries": Accounting for around 13.5% of the market, these individuals adopt technology to drive significant changes. They're choosy, socially conscious, and look for innovations that deliver major benefits. Although they're open to new ideas, their approach is more selective than that of Innovators, making their endorsement powerful for your product's direction.

Early Majority "Pragmatists": Representing about 34% of the market, Pragmatists are key to reaching a mainstream audience. They adopt new technologies cautiously, requiring clear evidence of utility and dependability.

Their acceptance is key for securing mass market approval and achieving essential market penetration.

Late Majority "Conservatives": Also representing around 34% of the market, this group is traditionally hesitant about new technologies, preferring to wait until they are broadly proven and adopted. Their eventual acceptance is typically influenced by practical benefits and societal validation, aligning with established norms.

Laggards "Skeptics": The final slice of the market, Skeptics are highly resistant to change, often adopting new technologies only when absolutely necessary or when their existing solutions become obsolete. They favor conventional methods, so winning them over requires demonstrating undeniable utility and compatibility with trusted systems.

The vital challenge in scaling your product lies in 'Crossing the Chasm' that separates Visionaries and Pragmatists. While Visionaries are fascinated by the prospective impact of your product, Pragmatists demand tangible, reliable solutions. Mastering this transition is critical for your product to secure a foothold in the mainstream market. In the next section, we will explore targeted strategies to effectively bridge this gap, guiding your product toward general adoption and success.

Case Study: Adobe's Transition to Creative Cloud

Adobe's strategic shift from offering standalone software packages to a cloud-based subscription service, Creative Cloud, provides a compelling case study in the transition from Visionaries to Pragmatists within the technology adoption life cycle.

Engaging Visionaries: Initially, Adobe captivated design professionals and creatives—typical Visionaries who seek the latest tools to enhance their work. Despite the steep costs of traditional software licenses, they valued Adobe's robust, feature-packed offerings. The transition to a cloud-based model presented attractive benefits: continuous updates, lower initial costs, and adaptable solutions. To engage these Visionaries, Adobe:

Granted early access to innovative features, appealing to their desire for the latest improvements.

Offered specialized customer support to help users maximize the utility of their software.

Fostered a user community to exchange success stories and best practices, reinforcing the value of their transition.

Crossing the Chasm: The leap to engage Pragmatists—known for their caution and demand for proven reliability—posed a significant challenge. Adobe's move to a subscription model required convincing these users of its tangible benefits. Adobe thus embarked on the below key steps.

Leveraged testimonials and case studies from Visionaries as social proof to reassure Pragmatists of the cloud service's value.

Ensured the cloud offerings matched or surpassed the reliability and robustness of their traditional software.

Provided free trials and money-back guarantees to mitigate perceived risks, making the transition more acceptable.

Introduced flexible pricing tiers to accommodate a broad range of users, from individual freelancers to large enterprises, making it an attractive option for diverse market segments.

Winning Over Pragmatists: Over time, Pragmatists recognized the advantages of Adobe Creative Cloud. The promise of constant updates provided access to the latest tools without additional investment. Varied subscription plans offered cost-effective, tailored solutions, meeting the needs of different user groups, and setting a new industry standard.

Adobe's journey from catering to Visionaries to successfully engaging Pragmatists underlines their strategic foresight and adaptability. They not only managed to maintain their leadership in the creative software domain but also transformed their business model to thrive in a continuously evolving digital landscape.

Achieving the Transition: Strategic Execution for Product Managers

As a Product Manager, your role is fundamental in facilitating the journey across the chasm, transitioning from appealing to Visionaries to capturing the Pragmatist market segment. Here are strategic approaches to ensure a smoother transition:

In-Depth Market Understanding: Start with a comprehensive analysis of your target market. Dig into the Pragmatists' core values, pinpoint their significant concerns, and understand their uncertainty toward new solutions. Tailoring your product to align with their specific needs is essential.

Highlighting Practical Benefits: Pragmatists prioritize proven, reliable solutions. Emphasize the tangible benefits of your product, showcasing real-world success stories and case studies that underscore its efficacy and dependability.

Offering Comprehensive Solutions: Pragmatists look for holistic solutions. Strengthen your product with extensive support services and detailed user documentation, representing it as a complete answer to their challenges.

Seamless Workflow Integration: Ensure your product integrates effortlessly with existing workflows. The easier it is for Pragmatists to embed your product into their daily routines, the more likely they are to adopt it.

Strategic Partnerships: Forge partnerships with established entities to reinforce your product's credibility and expand its reach. Such alliances can be pivotal in convincing Pragmatists to give your product a chance.

Targeted Marketing Efforts: Customize your marketing strategies to resonate with Pragmatists, highlighting aspects like reliability, efficiency, and cost-effectiveness. Leverage user testimonials and reviews to build trust, credibility and authenticity.

Iterative Product Refinement: Continuously ask and incorporate user feedback to refine your product. Demonstrating a commitment to ongoing improvement and attention to customer needs is crucial in showcasing your dedication to delivering superior solutions.

Employing these strategies can greatly aid in traversing the gap between early adopters and the broader market. Reflecting on Adobe's transition to Creative Cloud provides valuable insights into navigating this critical phase. Next, we'll examine Slack's progression from a niche communication tool to a fundamental asset in modern business environments, offering another perspective on mastering this crucial transition.

Case Study: Slack's Strategic Mastery in Crossing the Chasm

Slack, the widely recognized cloud-based team collaboration tool, showcases an exemplary journey of transitioning from an innovative solution favored by Visionaries to a pragmatic tool embraced by the Early Majority.

Catering to Visionaries: Slack initially captivated Visionaries with its innovative approach to enhancing workplace communication. These early adopters were attracted by Slack's user-friendly interface, real-time messaging, and seamless integration with an array of productivity tools, viewing it as a platform set to revolutionize team dynamics.

Strategic Transition: The key challenge for Slack was to illustrate tangible, practical benefits for the Pragmatists, who prioritize reliability and proven efficacy over novelty. Slack tackled this by emphasizing its capacity to streamline team collaboration, organize communication, and reduce the overload of information—qualities that directly appealed to the pragmatic segment of the market.

Key Transition Strategies:

Seamless Integrations: Slack highlighted its compatibility with well-known tools such as Google Drive and Trello, ensuring users that it could easily blend into their existing workflows.

Robust Third-Party Ecosystem: Slack encouraged a dynamic marketplace of third-party integrations, allowing for a high degree of customization and versatility, which appealed to a broad spectrum of team needs.

Freemium Model: Implementing a freemium model played a strategic role, offering users a no-cost way to explore Slack's value, which significantly encouraged initial adoption.

Continuous Product Enhancement: Slack's dedication to evolving its features—such as introducing threaded conversations and advanced file-sharing options—underscored its commitment to addressing user feedback and enhancing its utility.

Marketing and Adoption Tactics: Slack's marketing efforts were cleverly designed to spotlight the platform's immediate impact on team efficiency and solidity. By providing a free basic version, Slack lowered entry barriers, allowing teams to witness its benefits directly.

The Outcome: Slack's well-rounded strategy successfully navigated the transition to the Early Majority, broadening its user base and solidifying its status as a leader in team collaboration solutions. The essence of Slack's success lay in its ability to demonstrate its transformative potential, deliver real-world benefits, integrate smoothly into user workflows, and adapt continually to user input and market trends.

Chapter Conclusion and Reflection

Embarking on the journey of launching and scaling a product stress on one of the most dynamic and fulfilling aspects of product management. It's a path full of challenges yet offers profound satisfaction through the positive impact on customers' lives. This chapter has guided you through the pivotal stages of introducing a product to the market and the complicated process of scaling it smoothly.

Launching with Precision: Our exploration began with an in-depth look at the vital components of a successful product launch. We dived into the strategic planning of releases, highlighted the pivotal role of quality assurance, and analyzed the details of effective deployment. We highlighted the significance of thorough documentation, from crafting insightful release notes to creating detailed user guides, as essential tools for aligning stakeholders with each iteration of your product.

Beyond the Launch: We established that a product's launch only marks the beginning of its lifecycle. The continual cycle of monitoring, refining, and enhancing your product is crucial for elevating the user experience and sustaining business growth. We examined the triad of product scaling—customer experience, business viability, and technical feasibility—unveiling the nuances of expanding your product's reach and impact.

Embracing Product-Led Growth: We shed light on the transformative concept of Product-Led Growth (PLG), offering strategies to position your product at the heart of user engagement and business growth. Through innovative frameworks like the Growth-Loop and the Hook Model, we provided new perspectives to inspire and catalyze product growth.

Mastering 'Crossing the Chasm': Digging into Geoffrey Moore's concept of 'Crossing the Chasm,' we explored the essential phase of technology adoption, guiding you through the spectrum of technology adopters from innovators to late majority. We shared targeted strategies to connect with Pragmatists, emphasizing the need to demonstrate tangible benefits, utilize social proof, and ensure seamless integration.

Strategic Frameworks for Scaling: We accentuated the importance of flexible strategies and the ongoing evolution of your product as key drivers for successful scaling, ensuring a transition from nascent stages to a substantial market presence.

In Conclusion: This chapter has equipped you with a holistic toolkit for effectively launching and scaling your product. Moving forward, our following chapter will cover the critical landscape of product analytics, unveiling how data serves as the cornerstone for strategic insights and informed decision-making, propelling data-driven growth in your product management journey.

CHAPTER 7
UNLEASHING THE POWER OF PRODUCT ANALYTICS

In the fast-paced world of product management, data exceeds its traditional role as plain numbers and statistics to become the cornerstone of your product's journey towards excellence. It explains crucial insights—showcasing user actions, highlighting feature engagements, and pinpointing obstacles encountered by users. Picture data as your compass, enlightening the route to a deep understanding of customer behavior and emerging trends.

Yet, it's not the data or numbers that hold value; it's the nuanced analytics that transform these figures into actionable insights. Product analytics stands as a fundamental tool in your resources, clarifying the 'why' behind user interactions and the 'how' to steer them towards favorable outcomes. Mastering analytics empowers you to explore different audience segments, outline user journeys, and predict future trends, leveraging past and present data. This predictive competency is invaluable, steering strategic choices throughout your product's lifespan.

For a Product Manager today, proficiency in product analytics is indispensable. It demands a profound understanding of how to study and interpret data, transitioning you from a manager who relies on hypothesis to one who makes decisions based on practical evidence. Mastering product analytics allows you to extract essential insights from the overflow of data at your disposal. These insights form the cornerstone of developing robust product strategies, refining features, and enriching user experiences.

In this chapter, we'll dive deep into the world of product analytics. We'll explore effective data collection methods, explore various analytical techniques, and introduce you to tools designed to enhance your analytical expertise. Let's embark on this journey to transform data into a powerful partner in your product management endeavors.

Choosing the Right Metrics

In an era overflowing with data, the challenge isn't just about collecting information but identifying which data points genuinely inform and drive your product's success. Among millions of potential data points, selecting the ones that align with your product's goals and your company's objectives is crucial for informed, strategic decision-making.

Introducing the North Star Metric (NSM)

The concept of a North Star Metric is becoming increasingly pivotal in data analytics, adopted widely across industries, including top firms in Silicon Valley. So, what is a North Star Metric, and why is it so vital?

The NSM serves as a sign, guiding your organization's growth and strategic direction. It exceeds short-term wins, focusing instead on sustainable, long-term successes. This metric encapsulates the core value your product offers to customers, resonating with the primary business objectives. It acts as a cohesive force, aligning various departments and initiatives toward a singular goal.

However, the NSM isn't universal; it's distinct for each organization or product, reflecting its unique value proposition and goals. It's the metric that best captures how your product addresses customer needs or resolves their issues. For example:

Facebook uses 'Daily Active Users (DAU)' as its NSM, underscoring user engagement and the platform's ability to maintain daily user interest.

Airbnb opts for 'Nights Booked' as its guiding metric, directly connected to its core mission of providing accommodation solutions.

Spotify focuses on 'Monthly Active Users (MAU)' to measure its success in engaging and retaining a broad user base.

In these cases, the chosen NSM offers a critical perspective on each company's achievements and strategic focus. By pinpointing and concentrating on the most relevant metric, you can steer your efforts toward activities that significantly propel your product's growth, transforming data from a mere collection of numbers into a strategic compass guiding your decisions.

Why NSM is Valuable for Product Managers?

As a Product Manager, whether you're building a new feature or developing an entirely new product, the North Star Metric (NSM) is essential for aligning with the overarching company goals. It serves as a guiding sign throughout your product's lifecycle. Here's an in-depth look at why the NSM is indispensable for Product Managers:

1. Clear Focus and Alignment: The NSM provides a clear direction, uniting the team's efforts towards a singular, impactful goal crucial for the product's growth and success. It helps prevent the distractions often caused by chasing multiple, less significant metrics, ensuring the team's energies are focused on what's most vital for the product.

2. Data-Driven Decision-Making: Far from being just another number, the NSM is the foundation of your strategic choices. It allows you to measure the effectiveness of every new feature or modification, ensuring they all contribute positively toward achieving the primary goal.

3. Solid Customer-Centricity: At its core, the NSM revolves around delivering superior value to your customers. This focus isn't just critical; it's a strategic move that enhances customer satisfaction, boosts loyalty, and ensures retention, driving sustainable growth.

4. Cultivating Long-Term Vision: By exceeding short-lived achievements, the NSM fosters a mindset geared towards lasting success. Aligning with this metric ensures your strategies aren't just chasing the next big thing but are building a robust foundation for the future.

5. Enhanced Cross-Functional Synergy: The NSM unifies various teams—engineering, marketing, sales, customer support—under a unified objective. This shared goal enhances interdepartmental collaboration, each unit understanding and contributing towards the same end, thus accelerating the product's forward momentum.

In summary, the North Star Metric is not just a directional tool; it's a cornerstone in effective product management. It offers clarity, supports evidence-based decisions, embeds a customer-first approach, promotes a vision for the long haul, and catalyzes organizational synergy, all of which are crucial for a Product Manager's success in steering the product journey.

How to Craft Your North Star Metric (NSM)

Creating a North Star Metric (NSM) is a strategic process that requires a deep understanding of your product, your customers, and your business goals. Here's a structured approach to help you craft an NSM that will serve as a powerful guide for your product's growth journey:

Understand Your Value Proposition: Start by outlining the core value your product offers to users. What problem does it solve? How does it enhance users' lives or workflows? Your NSM should directly reflect this value, embodying the essence of what makes your product indispensable to users.

Align with Business Objectives: Ensure your NSM is in harmony with the broader business goals. It should not only resonate with the product's value proposition but also contribute to the overarching objectives of the company, whether it's increasing revenue, enhancing customer satisfaction, or driving user engagement.

Involve Key Stakeholders: Crafting an NSM isn't a solo mission. Involve key stakeholders from various departments—product, marketing, sales, customer success—to gather diverse insights and ensure the metric resonates across the organization.

Identify Key User Actions: Pinpoint the user behaviors or actions that are critical indicators of your product's value delivery. These actions should have a clear correlation with user satisfaction and the perceived value of your product.

Ensure Measurability and Relevance: Your NSM should be quantifiable and directly linked to your product's health and success. Choose a metric that is not only measurable but also offers clear insight into progress toward your product and business goals.

Test and Iterate: Like any aspect of product management, crafting your NSM is an iterative process. Test the effectiveness of your chosen metric, gather feedback, and be prepared to refine it. An NSM may evolve as your product and market dynamics change, so stay adaptive and responsive to new insights.

Communicate and Educate: Once established, ensure that every team member understands the NSM and its significance. Educating your team about how their work contributes to this metric can foster alignment, motivation, and a cohesive drive towards common objectives.

While the North Star Metric (NSM) provides a broad, overarching goal, integrating the "One Metric That Matters" (OMTM) into your strategy adds a layer of precision, focusing on the most critical aspect of your product's current stage. Here's an in-depth look at how OMTM complements the NSM, providing a dynamic, focused lens for your product's growth strategy.

Understanding One Metric That Matters (OMTM)

The OMTM, a concept introduced by Alistair Croll in "Lean Analytics," is the single most impactful metric aligning with your product's immediate objectives. It's about determining the crucial performance aspect that demands attention now.

The Importance of OMTM:

Focused Prioritization: The OMTM enables you to focus on one significant metric at a time, ensuring that your efforts are concentrated and impactful.

Adaptive Focus: As your product evolves, so does your OMTM, ensuring that your focal point is always timely and relevant.

Simplified Decision-Making: By centering on one key metric, your strategic planning becomes more streamlined, enabling clearer progress tracking and decision-making.

Tailoring OMTM to Your Product's Lifecycle:

Inception and Early Growth: In the early days, metrics like daily active users or sign-up rates might serve as your OMTM, providing insight into user acquisition and initial engagement.

Expansion and Scaling: During growth phases, financial metrics like Monthly Recurring Revenue (MRR) could take precedence, especially for SaaS products, reflecting financial health and customer commitment.

Established Maturity: As your product matures, focus may shift to retention and satisfaction metrics, such as Net Promoter Score (NPS) or Customer Lifetime Value (CLV), indicating user satisfaction and long-term value.

Applying OMTM in Different Contexts:

In different contexts, the application of the One Metric That Matters (OMTM) can significantly shape a company's strategic focus. For a SaaS enterprise, Monthly Recurring Revenue (MRR) often stands as the key OMTM, with targeted strategies aimed at strengthening customer acquisition, enhancing retention, and driving overall revenue growth. In contrast, for an e-commerce platform, the initial OMTM may focus on the conversion rate. Here, the primary efforts would be on optimizing the website interface, streamlining the purchasing process, and refining marketing tactics to boost this specific metric.

By carefully selecting and focusing on your OMTM, while simultaneously keeping the North Star Metric (NSM) in perspective, you ensure that your strategic initiatives are precisely adjusted to address the most immediate needs of your product at any given stage. This methodical approach provides you, as a Product Manager, with the clarity and focus needed to steer your product's lifecycle. It empowers you to make informed, data-driven decisions that propel your product toward success, aligning daily operations with long-term strategic goals.

Clarifying the Roles of NSM and OMTM in Product Strategy

Understanding the different roles and applications of the North Star Metric (NSM) and the One Metric That Matters (OMTM) is crucial for navigating the complexities of product growth and strategy. While both metrics are vital, they serve different purposes and offer unique perspectives on the product's journey.

North Star Metric (NSM): The Strategic Inspiration

Long-term Vision: The NSM represents the overarching goal that reflects the core value your product delivers to customers, aligning with the company's long-term vision.

Stability: Unlike the OMTM, the NSM remains consistent over time, providing a steady aim that guides the organization's collective efforts and strategic decisions.

Unifying Influence: As a constant metric, the NSM ensures that different departments and initiatives contribute cohesively towards the same end goal, fostering organizational alignment.

One Metric That Matters (OMTM): The Tactical Navigator

Short-term Focus: The OMTM zeroes in on specific, short-term goals, responding swiftly to immediate business needs and challenges within a particular segment or process.

Dynamic Nature: It's a fluid metric that can change with each phase of the product's lifecycle, allowing teams to adapt strategies based on current objectives or market feedback.

Tactical Application: Ideal for quick pivots and strategy adjustments, the OMTM helps in fine-tuning aspects of the product or user experience based on timely insights.

The Interplay Between NSM and OMTM:

Complementary Functions: While the OMTM adapts to immediate needs, the NSM maintains a steady path, ensuring that short-term successes contribute to long-term objectives.

Balanced Approach: Employing both metrics provides a comprehensive strategy framework, where immediate actions are informed by the OMTM, and overarching progress is measured by the NSM.

In Practice: Successful product management relies on a harmonious balance between these metrics. The OMTM allows you to focus and make quick, informed decisions in response to the product's immediate needs or market trends. In contrast, the NSM ensures that these decisions are aligned with the broader vision, keeping the product's journey on a path that delivers enduring value to customers.

In summary, while the OMTM provides the agility to respond to short-term challenges and opportunities, the NSM offers a consistent, long-term direction. Together, they equip Product Managers with a dynamic, two-pronged approach to driving growth and ensuring that every strategic move is both timely and aligned with the ultimate mission of the product.

Strategizing and Executing OMTM for Targeted Impact

Selecting and implementing your One Metric That Matters (OMTM) is a strategic step, crucial for steering your product's immediate direction. It should resonate with your current business priorities and offer actionable insights. Here's a refined approach to identifying, monitoring, and adapting your OMTM:

Business Model and Product Stage Consideration: Tailor your OMTM to your business model and the product's lifecycle stage. For B2C, engagement metrics like Daily Active Users may be key, whereas B2B might prioritize metrics like Customer Acquisition Cost or Lead Conversion Rate. Align the metric with the nature of your product (digital or physical) and the competitive landscape it operates in.

Complementary to North Star Metric: Ensure your OMTM aligns and synergizes with your NSM, offering a granular focus that contributes to your overarching goals. This alignment ensures consistency in your strategic approach across various levels of decision-making.

Actionable Insights: Select a metric that not only reflects critical aspects of your business but also drives actionable strategies. For instance, a decline in user retention might prompt a deeper dive into product features or user experience enhancements.

Measurement Precision: Confirm the availability of tools and methodologies to accurately track your OMTM. Reliable data is foundational for effective analysis and informed strategic decisions.

Cross-functional Buy-in: Engage various stakeholders in choosing the OMTM to ensure its reflective of and relevant to different facets of your organization, fostering a cohesive strategy.

Adaptability and Evolution: Your OMTM should be agile, capable of evolving with your business and market dynamics. Regularly review and adjust your OMTM to stay aligned with your product's growth phase and market conditions.

Competitive Benchmarking: Understand how your OMTM compares to industry standards or direct competitors. This context can illuminate your product's relative performance and uncover areas for strategic enhancement.

By accurately selecting and integrating your OMTM into your operational strategy, you equip your team with a focused lens to drive immediate and impactful actions. As we progress, we'll explore the mechanisms for tracking and leveraging analytics to maximize the utility of these crucial metrics in your product management journey.

Unlocking the Power of Product Analytics

Product analytics is a cornerstone in data-driven decision-making, serving as an essential tool for every Product Manager. It offers a transparent, objective lens into your product's performance, uncovering key trends, behaviors, and insights. These insights are not just data points; they are inspirations that guide your decisions and frame the strategic path for your product's journey.

To harness the power of product analytics effectively, you need to comprehend its fundamental aspects. This involves understanding the data collection process, utilizing a variety of analytical tools to set up robust tracking for essential metrics, and enhancing the skill of data interpretation.

Product analytics is a structured yet flexible process. The complexity of analytics initiatives can vary significantly. For some, leveraging analytics software that streamlines much of the process may be sufficient. In more complex scenarios, substantial engagement with data engineering teams might be necessary.

In this section, we'll explore every facet of this process, providing you with the knowledge to collect and analyze data smoothly.

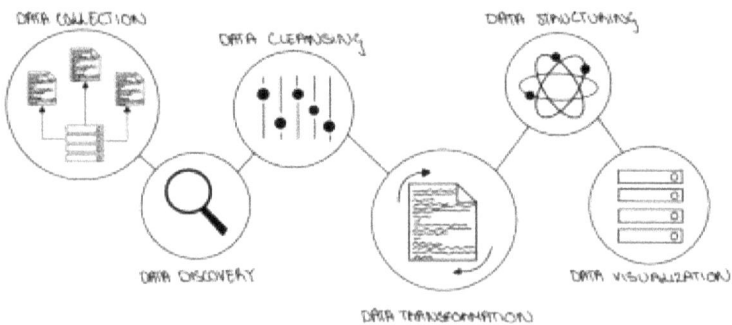

Data Collection in Product Analytics

Data collection marks the vital first step in the process of product analytics, laying the foundation for all the insightful analysis that come next. This pivotal phase is all about capturing a wide array of data points related to how users interact with your product. Remember, the depth and precision of this data directly impact the insights you'll be able to derive later on.

In the area of digital products, data collection typically centers around integrating tracking mechanisms or "events." These events are triggered through specific user actions within your product, such as - clicks, form submissions, purchases, or browsing patterns. The aim? To precisely record every possible user interaction, capturing a detailed picture of their journey through your product.

But there's more to data collection than just logging events. Each event should gather an array of additional data points or "dimensions" to enrich your understanding. These dimensions add layers to your event data, offering distinct insights into user behaviors.

Take an e-Commerce app as an example. You can track the user journey at every pivotal moment: from browsing products and adding items to the cart, to initiating the checkout process and completing a purchase. Each step is a separate event, infused with additional parameters that capture the essence of user actions—think product details like name, category, brand, price, or delivery terms. Such a rich dataset allows for a detailed analysis of user behaviors and preferences.

Leveraging specialized analytics tools simplifies this complicated data collection task. Once these tools are part of your product's structure, they collect, store, and structure event data, enriching each event with contextual details like timestamps, user locations, device types, and more. This complete set of data is crucial in understanding the complexities of user interactions, empowering you to refine and elevate the user experience in your product.

Data processing for Effective Analysis

Data processing is an essential bridge between the initial data collection and the insightful analysis that follows. This stage is all about refining and structuring the massive volumes of data you've gathered, preparing it for the deep dive analysis. While your role as a Product Manager is primarily oversight and providing guidance, understanding the fundamental of this process can greatly enhance your strategic contribution.

Data Cleaning: Think of this as the data hygiene phase. Here, you're ensuring the data's cleanliness by eliminating duplicates, rectifying inaccuracies, and addressing any missing values. The goal is to establish a solid foundation because the strength of your insights is directly tied to the data's integrity. For example, in an e-commerce setting, this might involve removing duplicate user records.

Data Transformation: Once your data is clean, it's time to convert it into a form that's ready for analysis. This could involve categorizing data, creating new computed fields, or standardizing data formats for uniformity. An everyday task might be normalizing different date formats into a single, consistent format.

Data Structuring: This phase is about organizing your data in a manner that's intuitive and accessible, preparing for efficient analysis. This could involve creating structured data tables or developing comprehensive data models. The aim is to ensure the data is not just clean, but also logically arranged for easy access and analysis. For an e-commerce app, this might mean categorizing user actions into distinct segments (search funnel, or purchases funnel) and arranging them cohesively.

Data processing is a crucial step that enhances the quality and usability of your data. It's the careful preparation needed before you dive into the analytics phase, where you transform raw data into compelling, actionable insights. This groundwork is essential for unlocking the strategic potential hidden within your data, setting the stage for the analytics that drive your product's evolution.

Data Visualization for Meaningful Insights

The journey through data collection and processing concludes in the critical stage of data visualization in product analytics. This step is where your structured and cleaned data comes to life, transforming into visually engaging and insightful representations that guide decision-making.

Data visualization tools are the cornerstone in this phase, converting complex datasets into digestible graphical formats like charts, graphs, and maps. These tools shed light on hidden patterns, reveal correlations, and highlight trends that are elusive in raw datasets. By employing visual analytics, you empower stakeholders to swiftly decode complex data narratives, streamlining analysis and comprehension.

The core of data visualization is its storytelling ability. It goes beyond mere aesthetic representation to infuse data with meaning and context. This visualization process makes complex insights accessible and appealing, enabling you and your colleagues to grasp critical data nuances swiftly. Whether it's identifying growth opportunities, interpreting user behavior, or monitoring progress toward goals, effective data visualization turns numbers into a strategic asset for informed decision-making and agile action.

Consider, for instance, the task of monitoring user engagement on a digital platform. With data visualization, you can instantly visualize which features users engage most with, understand peak activity times, and map user journeys across the platform. These insights, when presented visually, aren't just easier to interpret; they prompt faster, more informed decision-making, ensuring that your strategies and initiatives are emphasized by robust, visually articulated data insights.

Mastering the Art of Data Interpretation

Data interpretation stands as the critical stage in your analytical journey, transforming raw data into strategic decisions that shape the future of your product. This stage exceeds basic statistical analysis, digging deep into the extraction of actionable insights that drive your product's evolution and strategic direction.

At the core of data interpretation lies the detailed examination of your analytical outcomes. You're not just observing numbers but interpreting what they signify for your product's performance and user engagement. For instance, an increase in user registrations might seem promising at first glance. Yet, if this rise doesn't align with enhanced engagement or revenue growth, its true value demands a deeper investigation. By placing your data within the broader context of business objectives and user behaviors, you unlock the stories behind the statistics.

Here's a breakdown of key methodologies to enrich your data interpretation:

Trend Analysis: Deep-dive into trends to unlock more than just surface insights. When you analyze trends over time, you clarify patterns like seasonal behaviors, measure the impact of new features, and understand shifts in the market. For instance, identifying monthly sales trends might reveal consistent spikes during certain months, guiding inventory decisions. Spotting product category seasonality can direct your supply chain strategies. By analyzing these trends and other patterns across key metrics, you clarify the efficacy of your strategies—whether they're hitting the mark, holding steady, or signaling a need for recalibration.

Cohort Analysis: Recognize the diversity within your user base by using cohort analysis, which categorizes users based on shared attributes such as acquisition channels or demographic details. For example, you might uncover that customers from SEM channels show higher initial purchase values, but lower retention rates compared to those from email marketing, or discover that the 26-35 age group, particularly women, shows higher repeat purchase rates, signaling strong brand loyalty within this cohort. This method reveals complex user-product interactions, providing insights to refine user experiences and enhance engagement.

Funnel Analysis: This powerful method focuses on the various stages a user or customer goes through in their journey with your product. By analyzing each step of the conversion funnel, you can identify where potential users drop off and why they may not be converting into paying customers or continuing to the next stage. For example, in an e-commerce setting, you might track a user from homepage visit, to viewing product details, adding items to the cart, initiating checkout, and finally making a purchase. Funnel analysis allows you to pinpoint stages with high abandonment rates, offering insights into possible issues such as unclear product information, bulky checkout processes, or unexpected costs. Addressing these points can significantly improve user flow and conversion rates, directly enhancing overall business performance.

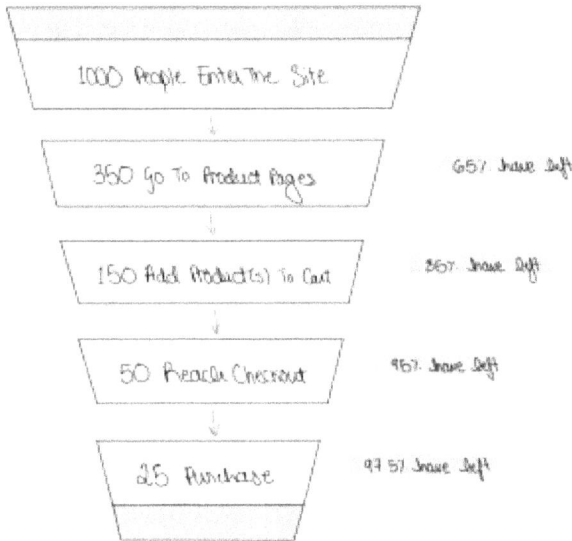

Correlation Vs. Causation: Navigate the thin line between correlation and causation with care. When examining metric relationships, differentiate whether the changes genuinely affect one another or just occur simultaneously. For instance, an e-commerce platform may observe a parallel rise in website traffic and sales. However, this correlation doesn't confirm that increased traffic directly boosts sales, which could also be influenced by concurrent factors like marketing campaigns or seasonal promotions. Conversely, if an e-commerce site revamps its checkout process resulting in a noticeable and sustained increase in conversion rates, this suggests a causative relationship, where the specific enhancement in the checkout experience directly contributes to improved conversions. Through such analysis, you can establish a more accurate and actionable understanding of your product's performance and user behaviors.

Investigating Outliers: Pay keen attention to exceptional data points, or outliers, which can be indicators of potential issues or untapped opportunities. For instance, a surge in return rates during a particular month could be attributed to defects in a new product batch, or an unexpected sales increase in an older product might trace back to its recent feature in a popular influencer's video. Analyzing these irregularities can uncover critical insights that may influence strategic adjustments or pinpoint areas for improvement.

Inquisitive Analysis: Embrace a curious approach when analyzing data trends. Don't settle for surface-level observations; dig deeper to understand the underlying causes of observed changes. For instance, if there's an unanticipated jump in order volume, investigate further: Was there a new marketing campaign launched? Did a particular promotion or product feature resonate exceptionally well with customers on that day? Such probing inquiries can unveil the dynamics driving your data, providing a richer context for informed decision-making.

Insights Validation: After your initial analysis, ensure the robustness of your findings by validating them. Complex patterns or surprising trends should not be taken at face value. Develop hypothesis based on your initial insights and put them to the test through further analysis, seeking user feedback, or conducting controlled experiments. This step is vital to confirm that your derived insights are reliable and reflective of genuine user behaviors or product performance dynamics, thereby guiding your product strategy with confidence and precision.

Action is the ultimate output of data interpretation. If your insights suggest that an enhanced onboarding experience boosts user retention, prioritizing and refining this aspect becomes imperative.

In essence, data interpretation in product analytics is an insightful journey into your data, aiming not just to analyze but to uncover strategic insights that inform impactful decisions. By using these multifaceted methodologies, you empower yourself to transform data into a strategic compass, guiding your product's trajectory towards success.

What Makes a Metric Valuable?

Choosing the right metrics in product analytics is as essential as the analysis itself. Among the extensive data available, prioritize metrics that are meaningful and directly relevant to your product's objectives, steering clear of the charm of vanity metrics. These are figures that may look impressive but offer little practical insight into your core business goals, potentially painting an inaccurate picture of your product's health and user engagement.

Take, for instance, a high number of app downloads. While initially promising, this metric doesn't inherently mean sustained user engagement or value delivery. Similarly, an extensive social media following, or high page views might not associate to meaningful user interaction or conversions, especially if your revenue model isn't ad-centric.

When assessing a metric's worth consider these critical attributes:

Business Goal Alignment: The most insightful metrics are those that directly mirror your progress toward business goals, offering tangible indicators of success or areas for improvement.

Measurability: A valuable metric must be consistently quantifiable, providing a reliable basis for ongoing analysis and comparison.

Actionability: Opt for metrics that clarify your decision-making, directing your product development strategies and initiative prioritization.

Ratio/Rate Format: Metrics expressed as ratios or rates often provide deeper insights, enabling easier comparisons over varied periods and a more nuanced understanding of trends or shifts.

Comparability: Being able to compare metrics across different time frames or user segments is essential for spotting trends and evaluating the effectiveness of product strategies.

Consistent Measurement: Ensure your metrics are gathered and calculated uniformly over time, securing their reliability, and aiding in accurate trend analysis.

Predictive Value: Metrics that can forecast future trends or user behaviors based on past data are particularly invaluable, enabling proactive adjustments in your strategy.

In essence, the true utility of metrics lies in their quality, not quantity. A few well-selected, impactful metrics can offer more strategic value than a vast array of non-strategic data points, guiding you towards informed, data-driven decisions for your product's growth.

Key Metrics to Measure Your Product Performance

Understanding your product's performance depends on tracking key metrics that rationalize various aspects of the user journey and business impact. While some metrics are universally applicable, others might need tailoring to align with your product's specific dynamics:

Product-Qualified Leads (PQLs): PQLs show potential customers who've engaged with your product significantly, showing behaviors that predict a higher likelihood of conversion to paying users. Monitoring PQLs offers insights into lead quality and conversion prospects.

Feature Adoption Rate: This metric reveals the percentage of users interacting with a specific feature, providing valuable feedback on the feature's acceptance and value among your user base.

Daily Active Users (DAU): DAU tracks the number of unique users who interact with your product daily, serving as a vital barometer of user engagement and your product's appeal.

Conversion Rate: This key performance indicator measures the percentage of users completing a desired action, be it a purchase or subscription. It's essential for evaluating how effectively your product moves users through the conversion funnel.

Customer Retention Rate: This metric shows the proportion of customers who continue to engage with your product over time, offering insights into customer satisfaction, loyalty, and the success of your retention strategies.

Customer Churn Rate: Churn rate calculates the percentage of users who stop using your product or service within a certain period, essential for understanding customer attrition and pinpointing underlying causes.

Average Revenue Per User (ARPU): ARPU determines the average revenue generated from each user, crucial for gauging the financial contribution of your user base, particularly for products relying on subscription models or in-app purchases.

Customer Lifetime Value (CLV): CLV estimates the total revenue a business can expect from a customer throughout their relationship, guiding strategic decisions about customer acquisition and retention investments.

Customer Acquisition Cost (CAC): CAC measures the cost associated with acquiring a new customer, providing clarity on the efficiency of your marketing strategies and the value derived from each new user.

These metrics collectively offer a holistic view of your product's performance, from user engagement and feature adoption to customer retention and churn. Regularly monitoring and analyzing these metrics enables you to make informed decisions, tailor your strategies, and enhance overall product effectiveness.

By carefully tracking and analyzing these key metrics, you establish a detailed understanding of your product's performance, spanning user engagement, financial outcomes, and market position. This depth of insight is indispensable for fine-tuning your strategies, enhancing your product features, and ultimately, boosting your product's market success. Remember, it's also essential to identify and monitor additional metrics that are uniquely tied to your business objectives or specific product functionalities. Consider the entire customer journey and identify crucial touchpoints. Determine which metrics will provide insightful analysis to optimize this journey for enhanced outcomes. For instance, if your product heavily relies on an internal search feature contributing significantly to your sales funnel, monitoring the search Click-Through Rate (CTR) becomes essential to assess the efficacy of your search algorithm and its alignment with user needs.

Essential Data Analytics Tools

In the era of data-driven decision-making, a Product Manager's skill with analytics tools is indispensable. These tools are critical not just for collecting and storing data but also for converting this massive array of information into actionable insights through sophisticated analytics and visualization techniques. Let's explore the mechanics of these analytics tools and their integral role in product management.

How Do Analytics Tools Work?

Analytics platforms, such as Google Analytics, Mixpanel, and Adobe Analytics, initiate their process with data collection, which is fundamental for understanding user behavior. For websites, this typically involves embedding a JavaScript tracking code, like the one provided by Google Analytics, into your site's pages. For native applications, analytics platforms offer SDKs (Software Development Kits) that integrate directly into your app's code, capturing user interactions without disrupting the user experience.

Once set up, these tools start tracking user activities. Every button click or link interaction, every page or screen view, and additional metrics like session duration, device type, and operating system are accurately logged.

This data is then sent to servers for storage, where it's organized for later access. The choice of storage solution varies based on the data volume and the speed of access required, ranging from SQL databases for basic needs to more advanced systems like Google BigQuery for extensive datasets.

The following stage is data processing and aggregation, where raw data undergoes transformation into comprehensive insights. This process converts the accumulated data into understandable metrics, such as total session counts or average session durations, providing a base for deeper analysis.

The final and most informative phase is data visualization, where tools like Tableau, Looker, and Power BI come into play. These tools transform complex datasets into intelligible, visually engaging formats, enabling Product Managers to identify trends, patterns, and outliers that might be unclear in raw data.

In the upcoming sections, we'll dive into the utilization of these tools for robust data analysis and how you can apply these insights effectively in product management, ensuring that your decisions are consistently informed by solid data evidence.

Google Analytics: A Comprehensive Tool for Product Managers

Since its foundation in 2005, Google Analytics has stood as a cornerstone in the landscape of digital marketing and product management, continuously evolving to deliver vital insights into user behavior and acquisition pathways. The launch of Google Analytics 4 (GA4) in 2020 ushered in a new era, shifting focus towards a more customer-centric analysis, facilitating a comprehensive overview of user interactions across various devices and platforms.

GA4 is particularly champion at offering a unified view of customer interactions, a feature that proves invaluable for Product Managers aiming to understand the whole of the customer journey, from acquisition through to retention. This comprehensive data landscape enables the identification of user behavior trends, highlights potential friction points in the user journey, and aids in refining the user experience.

One of Google Analytics' standout features is its seamless integration with other Google services, such as Google Ads, which allows for precise measurement of the impact of marketing campaigns and facilitates the optimization of advertising expenditures. By harnessing detailed user insights from Google Analytics, Product Managers can fine-tune targeted conversion strategies, ensuring a more efficient allocation of marketing resources.

Operating on a freemium model, Google Analytics offers a robust free version that caters well to the analytics needs of small to medium-sized businesses, providing a wealth of features at no cost. It supports key metric tracking, user demographic analysis, and performance assessment of websites or applications, offering a solid foundation for data-driven decision-making.

For larger enterprises with more complicated data needs, Google Analytics 360 presents an enhanced solution. This premium offering supports larger data volumes, broader data collection, more detailed reporting, and provides comprehensive access to Big Query for deep-dive data analysis. Additionally, it offers dedicated support, including account management and customized training, to ensure businesses maximize their analytics investment.

Choosing whether to upgrade to Google Analytics 360 should depends on your specific requirements, such as the need for handling extensive traffic volumes, sophisticated data analysis, or more granular reporting. Nonetheless, for many Product Managers, the standard version of Google Analytics offers a detailed collection of analytical tools essential for informed strategy development, user engagement optimization, and overall product improvement.

Mixpanel: The tool to effectively Deep Dive into User Engagement Analytics

Mixpanel has established a niche for itself as a sophisticated analytics platform, giving Product Managers an in-depth look into user behavior and product interaction. Its intuitive design welcomes Product Managers across all levels of expertise, providing a user-friendly interface for complex data analysis.

What sets Mixpanel apart is its emphasis on event-based tracking, offering a nuanced perspective on user interactions. Unlike the traditional pageview-centric analysis, Mixpanel's event tracking dives deeper into the user's journey, capturing their interactions across diverse touchpoints and platforms. This detailed insight enables Product Managers to chart a comprehensive map of the user journey, gaining an understanding of how users interact with various product features in different settings.

The platform's advanced user segmentation capabilities stand out, allowing Product Managers to segment user data based on various attributes such as demographics, behaviors, and acquisition sources. This segmentation empowers teams to craft strategies and features that resonate with different user groups, fostering a personalized product experience.

Mixpanel's real-time analytics is another notable feature. It provides Product Managers with immediate insights into product performance and user engagement, enabling them to swiftly detect and act on trends or issues as they arise. This agility is critical in adapting to user needs, optimizing the product experience, and staying ahead in a dynamic market.

In essence, Mixpanel offers a robust suite of tools for Product Managers aiming to investigate into detailed user behavior analysis. Its focus on event tracking, combined with powerful segmentation and real-time data, renders Mixpanel an indispensable ally in the quest to understand user interactions and drive data-informed product decisions.

Adobe Analytics: Comprehensive Insights for Advanced User Engagement

Adobe Analytics emerges as a heavyweight in the analytics arena, celebrated for its comprehensive analysis of user engagement and complex user behavior patterns. Particularly suited for expansive enterprises, it delivers an array of sophisticated functionalities designed to extract deep insights into user interactions and product dynamics.

The platform's competency in analyzing extensive datasets stands out, enabling the revealing of complex user behavior patterns. This granularity is invaluable for large-scale entities where subtle user interactions can significantly apprise product strategies and pivotal decisions.

A hallmark of Adobe Analytics is its bespoke reporting feature. Product Managers can craft custom reports that resonate with distinct business goals, offering insights tailored to specific strategic needs. This customization spans across data segmentation, funnel analysis, and cohort studies, providing a versatile toolkit for varied analytical requirements.

Being a key component of Adobe's Marketing Cloud, Adobe Analytics offers seamless integration with an array of Adobe products, facilitating a multidimensional analysis by merging data from diverse sources such as digital marketing, advertising, and CRM systems. For organizations already embedded in Adobe's ecosystem, this integration ensures a unified and efficient analytical workflow.

Beyond processing raw data, Adobe Analytics harnesses machine learning and predictive analytics to anticipate future user behaviors and market trends. This forward-looking analysis is enriched with advanced segmentation tools, empowering Product Managers to pinpoint and engage high-value user segments effectively.

Real-time data analysis is another cornerstone of Adobe Analytics, offering immediate insights into user activities. This immediacy is complemented by dynamic visualizations, transforming complex data into digestible, actionable intelligence.

In essence, Adobe Analytics stands as a comprehensive suite for rigorous data analysis, equipped with a broad spectrum of tools for detailed user behavior scrutiny. Its capabilities in advanced segmentation, predictive modeling, real-time insights, and integration with the Adobe suite render it an exemplary choice for large organizations poised to leverage data for strategic excellence and product innovation.

Amplitude: Navigating User Behavior for Strategic Product Management

Amplitude distinguishes itself as a leading analytics platform, highly valued for its user-centric perspective and in-depth exploration of user behavior and product strategy. Its appeal to Product Managers lies in its user-friendly interface and the actionable insights it delivers, essential for informed strategic decision-making.

At the heart of Amplitude's offerings is its exhaustive analysis of user behavior. The platform tracks user interactions across your product, capturing each nuance of the user journey. This level of detail equips Product Managers with the insights needed to pinpoint user engagement trends and identify opportunities for product enhancement or innovation.

Segmentation and cohort analysis stand out as one of Amplitude's key features, allowing managers to classify users based on various attributes such as behavior, demographics, or acquisition channels. This ability to segment users is crucial for customizing product and marketing strategies, ensuring they resonate with the intended audience segments and drive desired outcomes.

With Amplitude's real-time analytics, Product Managers gain the ability to observe user behavior changes instantaneously. This capability is invaluable for agile, data-informed decision-making, enabling rapid response to user engagement shifts or product issues.

The platform's customizable dashboards and reports empower Product Managers to tailor their analytics focus, highlighting the metrics and KPIs most relevant to their strategic goals. This personalization ensures vital data remains at the forefront, streamlining analysis and enhancing data-driven storytelling.

Amplitude's compatibility with a range of tools and platforms further amplifies its utility, facilitating a seamless flow of data across the tech stack. This interoperability ensures a holistic view of user interactions and product performance, integrating diverse data sources for a unified analytical perspective.

Leveraging machine learning, Amplitude offers predictive insights, equipping Product Managers with forward-looking analysis to anticipate user trends and market shifts. These predictive capabilities are fundamental for strategic planning, enabling product teams to stay ahead in a dynamic market landscape.

In essence, Amplitude serves as an invaluable resource for Product Managers focused on user behavior analysis and strategic product development. Its proficiency in real-time analytics, user segmentation, custom reporting, and predictive insights renders it an essential tool for those committed to elevating their product's user experience and market performance.

Data Visualization Tools: Transforming Data into Insights

In the dynamic world of product management, data visualization tools are indispensable. They transform complex data sets into accessible, actionable insights, allowing Product Managers to uncover trends, patterns, and correlations with clarity. This section explores three leading visualization tools—Looker, Power BI and Tableau—highlighting their distinct features and how they cater to different data visualization needs.

Looker: Comprehensive Data Exploration and Visualization

Looker, a cloud-based platform by Google, excels in data exploration and business intelligence. It's designed to be scalable, accommodating the growth and complexity of your data needs. Its integration with various data sources ensures a smooth transition of data into actionable insights.

Key Features:

Look ML: Looker's unique modeling language, Look ML, lets users define dimensions, aggregates, and calculations. This feature democratizes data access, allowing even non-technical users to generate reports and visualizations without deep SQL knowledge.

Looker Studio: An intuitive extension for building interactive dashboards and reports, Looker Studio (formerly Data Studio) emphasizes collaboration, enabling users to share and iterate on data models and visualizations.

Power BI: Intuitive Data Visualization by Microsoft

Power BI stands out for its user-centric design and robust analytical capabilities. It supports an array of data sources, making it a versatile tool for various data visualization needs.

Key Features:

User-Friendly Interface: Known for its intuitive drag-and-drop functionality, Power BI simplifies the process of creating detailed reports and dashboards.

Natural Language Queries: Power BI's ability to understand and process natural language queries allows users to ask questions and receive visual data responses, enhancing its interactivity and accessibility.

Tableau: Interactive and User-Friendly Data Visualization

Tableau is well-known for its powerful visualization capabilities, offering a wide range of options to represent data in a user-friendly manner. It's adaptable to various data sources, providing flexibility in data analysis.

Key Features:

Interactivity: Tableau's interactive dashboard allows users to explore data intuitively, uncovering deeper insights through direct interaction with visual elements.

Advanced Data Modeling: Beyond its visualization strengths, Tableau provides comprehensive data modeling tools, enabling customized data structures tailored to specific visualization needs.

Each of these tools—Looker, Power BI, and Tableau—brings unique strengths to the table. Whether it's Looker's data modeling language, Power BI's natural language processing, or Tableau's interactive visualizations, they empower Product Managers to distill complex data into clear, insightful narratives, facilitating informed decision-making and strategic product development.

Chapter Conclusion and Reflection

As we wrap up, let's reflect on the integral role of product analytics in the era of product management. This journey has highlighted that product analytics exceeds being just a tool—it's a strategic guide that navigates the complex pathways of product development and market positioning.

Our exploration began with the essentials of choosing the right metrics, emphasizing the distinction between the North Star Metric (NSM) and the One Metric That Matters (OMTM). These metrics, we discovered, are not just numbers but signs that guide our product strategy and operational focus.

Delving into the mechanics of product analytics, we uncovered the consecutive stages of data collection, processing, visualization, and interpretation. Each stage is pivotal, transforming raw data into a narrative of insights that drive informed and strategic decisions.

We then navigated through the landscape of analytics tools, exploring leaders like Google Analytics, Mixpanel, Looker, and Power BI. These tools don't just offer analytical competency; they unlock the hidden potential within our data, offering a gateway to transformative insights.

The essence of this chapter is the transformative potential of product analytics. It's about leveraging insights to make informed decisions, refine product offerings, and ultimately deliver unparalleled value to users.

In closing, let's commit to harnessing the full spectrum of product analytics. It's our channel to becoming more insightful, agile, and customer-centric. By aligning our strategies with data-driven insights, we ensure our products not only meet but exceed market expectations and user desires.

Final Thoughts

As we close this chapter on product analytics, it's vital to recognize its integral role in the shaping of product management. To fully leverage the power of product analytics, establishing a routine for consistent data analysis is crucial. Dedicating time each day to dive into your data not only uncovers patterns and dynamics but also deepens your understanding of how users interact with your product.

Remember, the value of analytics extends beyond just tracking conversions or user funnels. Adopting a holistic view of the customer journey, from initial engagement to long-term retention, is essential. This comprehensive approach allows you to identify trends, address potential issues, and harness opportunities for innovation, adding a competitive advantage to stay ahead of market changes.

Integrating data analysis into your product development cycle is fundamental. By including data tasks in your backlog and prioritizing them alongside development tasks, you ensure that data-driven insights remain central to your decision-making. This integration fosters a data-centric culture within your team, emphasizing the significance of analytics in shaping your product's evolution.

However, it's crucial to acknowledge analytics' limitations. Data provides invaluable insights but cannot fully capture the sensitivities of human emotion and behavior. Therefore, complementing quantitative analysis with qualitative feedback, user research, and an intuitive grasp of user needs is vital. Exercise caution to avoid data misinterpretation, ensuring that your conclusions are grounded in sound statistical methods and aligned with your product objectives.

Looking forward, we'll delve into the era of Big Data and AI and Digital Health—two sectors full of challenges and opportunities. These upcoming chapters will explore how product management navigates these evolving landscapes, highlighting the unique considerations and strategies pertinent to these dynamic fields.

CHAPTER 8
PRODUCT MANAGEMENT IN THE
BIG DATA, AI, AND ML ERA

The landscape of product management is undergoing a profound transformation, fueled by rapid advancements in technology. Staying up-to-date of these changes isn't just advantageous—it's vital for those looking to excel in the field. This chapter, and the one following it, explore two key areas redefining our profession: the integration of Big Data, Artificial Intelligence (AI), and Machine Learning (ML) in product management, and the growing sector of Digital Health.

Big Data has revolutionized our ability to understand and engage with customers, offering unprecedented insights and opening doors to innovative product solutions. But it's the synergy of Big Data with AI and ML that truly augments our capabilities, enabling the creation of products that adapt, learn, and personalize experiences in ways previously unimaginable.

In this new era, the role of the Product Manager becomes even more vital. They are the key player, combining complex technological capabilities with strategic business goals. While the fundamental mission to meet customer needs persists, the toolkit has expanded. Mastery of Big Data, AI, and ML isn't just preferred; it's becoming a necessity. Product Managers must now navigate the complex interaction between these technologies and traditional product strategy, collaborating closely with data scientists and engineers to harness their full potential.

This chapter aims to discover the complexities at the intersection of product management with Big Data, AI, and ML. We'll explore the essential components, tackle the inherent challenges, and highlight the massive possibilities these technologies unveil. From ethical considerations in data handling to enhancing user experiences through AI-driven personalization, we'll highlight the imperative of building products that are not only technologically advanced but also deeply resonant with users' needs and values.

By aligning with the advancements in Big Data, AI, and ML, Product Managers are positioned to lead innovation, building products that are not only transformative but also adapted to the evolving landscape of technology and user expectations.

Understanding The 'Big Data'

In our digitally driven world, 'big data' exceeds its buzzword of early stages, emerging as a critical resource across diverse sectors. It represents the vast pools of data collected from countless sources: user interactions, transactions, social media, Internet of Things (IoT) devices, and countless sensors.

The essence of Big Data lies in the 'Three Vs': Volume, Velocity, and Variety. 'Volume' highlights the massive amount of data being produced, reaching petabytes or exabytes, demanding sophisticated storage and processing solutions. 'Velocity' refers to the rapid rate at which this data is generated and must be analyzed, often in real-time, to deliver actionable insights straightaway. 'Variety' includes the broad spectrum of data types, from structured numbers to unstructured text, images, and videos, each presenting unique analysis challenges.

For Product Managers, engaging with Big Data is not simply about gathering extensive datasets. It's about leveraging advanced analytics to extract profound insights, discover hidden patterns, predict trends, and shape the development of groundbreaking features and solutions. Pairing Big Data with AI and ML paves the way for advanced product functionalities and more personalized user experiences.

Exploring Big Data's Impact Across Industries:

Healthcare: Big Data is revolutionizing patient care, enhancing medical research, and optimizing operations. It enables real-time monitoring, predictive risk assessments, and personalized treatment plans through data from wearables and health apps. It also streamlines healthcare operations, reducing wait times and hospital stays while boosting research through predictive models and cohort studies.

Retail: In retail, Big Data drives supply chain optimization, customer service enhancement, and consumer behavior prediction. Retailers leverage data from sales, social interactions, and web traffic to tailor recommendations, refine inventory, and create marketing strategies.

Finance: The finance industry utilizes Big Data for detailed risk assessments, fraud detection, and customized banking services. Investment firms and hedge funds use real-time market data for high-frequency trading, informed by Big Data analytics.

Energy: Big Data informs predictive maintenance, energy optimization, and outage prediction in the energy sector. Analytical insights enable power plants to minimize downtime and enhance efficiency.

Transportation: Companies like Uber and Lyft harness Big Data to set dynamic pricing, optimize routes, and anticipate demand patterns, boosting both efficiency and customer satisfaction.

Big Data's transformative impact across these sectors highlights its essential role in current business strategy. Next, we'll discover Artificial Intelligence (AI) and Machine Learning (ML), exploring how they redefine technological innovation and operational excellence.

Artificial Intelligence, Machine Learning, and Generative AI

Artificial Intelligence (AI) and Machine Learning (ML), standing at the frontline of technological evolution, are reshaping the world of product management. These interlinked disciplines, along with the growing field of Generative AI, are pivotal in shaping how products interact, engage, and provide value to users in today's digital landscape.

AI's broad spectrum covers tasks ranging from simple automation to complex decision-making, mimicking human intelligence in machines. ML dives deeper, refining pattern recognition and informed decision-making through data learning, allowing systems to adapt and evolve. Generative AI, the latest breakthrough, is revolutionizing content creation, offering new opportunities for product innovation and user experience enhancement.

Artificial Intelligence (AI):

AI in product management exceeds traditional boundaries, enabling machines to undertake tasks once solely tethered to human horizon. From understanding natural language, voice assistance to recommendation engines, AI's impact is universal, enriching user interactions and backend processes.

Narrow AI: Focused on specific tasks, Narrow AI excels within its designated domain, powering applications like voice recognition and autonomous vehicles without generalizing its intelligence across unrelated tasks.

General AI: Aiming for a broader intelligence scale, General AI hopes to perform any cognitive task a human can. While it's a fascinating area of research, its practical application remains within the realm of future possibilities.

Machine Learning (ML):

ML stands as a dynamic branch of AI, where systems evolve by learning from data, fostering the ability to make decisions or predictions with minimal human intervention.

Supervised Learning: This method involves training algorithms on a labeled dataset, where each input is paired with the correct output. The objective is to construct a model that, when presented with new, unseen data, can accurately predict the corresponding output. Consider a spam email classifier trained with a dataset labeled as 'spam' or 'non-spam.' Once trained, this model can efficiently classify whether new incoming emails are spam.

Unsupervised Learning: Unlike its supervised counterpart, unsupervised learning algorithms examine through data without predefined labels, aiming to uncover inherent patterns or structures. An example includes using clustering algorithms to segment customers into groups based on purchasing behaviors, unveiling potential market segments or customer preferences without prior categorization.

Reinforcement Learning: In this paradigm, an agent learns to make decisions by interacting with an environment. It's about trial, error, and adaptation, where actions lead to rewards or penalties, guiding the agent toward the most beneficial behaviors. Imagine a robotic agent in a maze; through exploration, it learns which pathways lead to rewards (exiting the maze), refining its strategy over time to optimize success.

Generative AI:

Exploring beyond the realms of AI and ML, Generative AI stands as an innovative force, revolutionizing how we conceive and interact with digital content. This branch of machine learning is dedicated to generating new, unique content—from text and images to music and code—that mirrors the complexity of human creations.

At the heart of Generative AI are advanced models like Generative Adversarial Networks (GANs) and Transformers. These models, trained on extensive datasets, are capable of producing inventive and original content. The implications for product development are insightful, offering possibilities to create distinctive and engaging user experiences.

Consider the potential applications: an e-Commerce platform employing Generative AI to automatically generate compelling product descriptions, an educational app crafting customized learning material, or a design application producing sophisticated graphics based on simple text prompts. The objective is to harness Generative AI not just for its innovation but to thoughtfully embed it within products, addressing genuine user needs, elevating experiences, and delivering exceptional value.

Product Managers, in this technologically enriched landscape, are the architects, skillfully integrating AI, ML, and Generative AI into the fabric of product development. Understanding the synergies between AI's analytical prowess, ML's predictive insights, and Generative AI's creative abilities is fundamental. It enables Product Managers to drive through technological complexities, crafting products that aren't just technologically sophisticated but are also intimately aligned with user expectations and aspirations.

Ultimately, the integration of Generative AI is about exceeding conventional boundaries, envisioning and crafting digital experiences that are not only intelligent but also inherently human-centric and enriching. For Product Managers, it's an invitation to pioneer, to frame technology in ways that resonate deeply with users, fostering products that are not only functional but also genuinely inspiring and transformative.

Case Study: Optimizing User Experience at Netflix

Netflix, famous for its vast content library, leverages machine learning to refine user experiences and provide highly personalized content recommendations. Let's explore how Netflix innovatively integrates machine learning to elevate its service:

Personalized Recommendations: At the heart of Netflix's user engagement strategy are its sophisticated machine learning algorithms, which analyze users' viewing habits, ratings, and preferences. This data-driven approach enables Netflix to offer individualized movie and TV show recommendations, enhancing user satisfaction and engagement.

Dynamic Artwork Personalization: Beyond recommendations, Netflix uses machine learning to tailor the artwork associated with its titles to individual user preferences. This dynamic customization not only makes the interface more visually appealing but also aids users in discovering content that resonates with them, boosting interaction rates.

Predictive Analytics for User Preferences: Netflix's machine learning competency extends to predictive analytics, allowing it to forecast user preferences with impressive accuracy. This anticipatory approach ensures that Netflix stays a step ahead, curating content offerings that align closely with viewer interests, thereby enhancing user retention.

Content Categorization and Engagement Prediction: Machine learning also empowers Netflix to categorize its extensive library into nuanced genres and themes, facilitating more targeted recommendations. Furthermore, the platform assesses the potential popularity of titles, prioritizing those likely to attract and engage audiences.

In essence, machine learning is central to Netflix's user-centric strategy. It's not just about tailoring content recommendations; it's about creating a holistic and engaging viewing experience. Through continuous learning and adaptation, Netflix ensures that its platform remains responsive and adaptive to user preferences, setting a benchmark in personalization and user engagement in the streaming industry.

AI in Product Management: Strategies for Success

Incorporating Artificial Intelligence (AI) and Machine Learning (ML) into product management requires a thoughtful approach that balances strategic insight with an understanding of technology. Here are essential strategies for Product Managers engaging in AI and ML initiatives:

1. Deepening Technological Understanding

Understanding the fundamental principles of AI and ML is critical for Product Managers in this field. While you don't need to dive deep into the details kept for data scientists, a robust understanding of data management, machine learning models, and the impact of different data types is necessary. This knowledge enables you to navigate customer data issues, security concerns, and set realistic project expectations. Aim to leverage AI and ML as strategic enhancers of your product's value, ensuring they're in line with business objectives and user benefits.

2. Problem Definition and Solution Design

The effectiveness of an AI/ML project largely depends on accurately defining the problem and designing a suitable solution. During the product discovery phase, deeply understand the users' needs and pain points. Transitioning to solution design requires translating these needs into technical requirements and envisioning how AI/ML can provide meaningful solutions. Work closely with your technical team to define project specifications, assess feasibility, and align the solution with AI/ML capabilities, ensuring the technology serves a clear purpose and adds value to the user experience.

3. Data Management

Data is the lifeblood of any ML project. Start by determining the necessary data types and volumes, bearing in mind that broader and more varied datasets typically yield better model performance. However, data collection must be ethical, prioritizing user privacy and adhering to standards like

GDPR. Ensure data consistency and standardization to prevent biases that could skew your model's results. The data collected should be directly relevant to the problem at hand, avoiding the inclusion of unnecessary information that could lead to model inaccuracies.

4. Model Development and Validation

Developing a machine learning model involves a structured series of steps, each crucial to ensuring the model aligns with your strategic goals. The process begins with the selection of an appropriate model type. For example, a regression model could be used to forecast future sales, while a classification model might be better suited for segmenting customer data based on specific characteristics.

After selecting the model type, the next step is the training phase. Here, the model is exposed to a subset of your data, learning from historical examples to understand patterns and behaviors. This phase is foundational, as it equips the model with the necessary knowledge to perform its designated tasks.

Following training, fine-tuning the model is essential to optimize its performance. This step may involve adjusting parameters to refine the learning process or modifying the data features used to improve how the model interprets the input data. Fine-tuning ensures that the model operates efficiently and accurately within its intended application.

Once the model is trained and fine-tuned, it proceeds to the validation phase. This involves testing the model against a new, unseen dataset to evaluate its ability to generalize from its training. This step is critical to confirm that the model does not only memorize the training data but can apply its learned insights accurately to new data. Performance metrics such as accuracy or error rates are utilized to assess the model's effectiveness and reliability.

Post-deployment, continuous evaluation of the model in a real-world environment is imperative. Regular monitoring helps to track the model's performance and utility, identifying any areas where it may not perform as expected. Based on real-world usage and feedback, the model may require periodic retraining, additional data inputs, or further fine-tuning to adapt to new conditions or to improve accuracy.

For Product Managers, having a comprehensive understanding of this machine learning model development process is essential. While the technical details may be handled by data scientists, your role as a Product Manager is to ensure that the model's development stays in line with the product's primary vision and meets user needs effectively. Being knowledgeable in the area of model development and validation empowers you to guide the project smoothly, making informed decisions that ensure the model not only meets but exceeds performance expectations and aligns seamlessly with your product objectives.

5. Fostering Collaboration with Data Teams:

In AI and ML projects, building a strong alliance with data scientists, engineers, and technical specialists is vital for effective product management. Your pivotal role as a Product Manager involves bridging the gap between the product vision and the technical execution. Ensure clear communication and mutual understanding of the product's data requirements and objectives among all team members. By maintaining close collaboration with technical teams, you can swiftly tackle data-related challenges, ensuring the data strategy aligns with your product's goals. Your responsibility extends to clarifying complex technical concepts for non-technical stakeholders, promoting a unified comprehension of the project's objectives and desired outcomes.

6. Navigating Ethical Considerations

The integration of AI in product development introduces critical ethical and legal considerations, especially concerning sensitive customer data. Engage proactively with legal and compliance teams to ensure your product adheres to applicable regulations and ethical standards. Prioritizing data privacy is essential—implement data anonymization and encryption techniques to safeguard user information. Additionally, vigilance against biases in AI/ML models is crucial to guarantee fairness and transparency in your product's outcomes.

In summary, understanding the complexities of AI/ML models — how they process data and the parameters influencing their outcomes — is vital. This knowledge should be made accessible to all stakeholders to promote transparency and ethical compliance.

Case Study: Building a Personalized Recommendation Engine

Laila, a dynamic Product Manager at a growing e-commerce company, pinpointed an ideal opportunity to enhance the customer shopping experience: Introducing a personalized recommendation engine. Inspired by the success stories from leading e-commerce giants, she recognized the potential of machine learning to tailor user experiences by analyzing individual behaviors and preferences.

Laila started with a deep dive into machine learning's landscape, focusing on understanding various algorithms and their applicability to personalized recommendations, rather than immersing herself in the technical details. This strategic understanding enabled her to strongly pitch the idea of a personalized recommendation engine to the company's executives.

With the project greenlit, Laila led a collaborative effort with a team of data scientists, engineers, and UX designers to bring the recommendation engine to life. She was active in identifying the critical data types needed for the engine, such as user purchase history, browsing behavior, product preferences, and reviews, ensuring these data points were accessible for analysis.

Throughout the prototype's development, Laila was actively involved, liaising with the data science team to select the most suitable algorithms, overseeing the training process, and contributing insights to enhance the model's precision. She also coordinated with the marketing team and other departments, preparing them for the feature's introduction.

To validate the engine's effectiveness, Laila organized a pilot program with a select user group, gathering invaluable feedback to refine the engine further. She remained cautious about user privacy and ethics, ensuring the engine's compliance with data protection regulations and addressing potential biases within the system.

Upon deployment, the recommendation engine transformed the e-commerce platform, offering users a personalized shopping journey and dynamically adapting to their unique tastes. However, Laila's involvement didn't stop with the launch. She continued to monitor the engine's impact, integrating user feedback and adapting to evolving market dynamics to maintain the system's relevance and efficacy.

Laila's journey emphasizes the critical role Product Managers play in merging technological innovation with strategic business objectives. Her initiative, strategic foresight, ethical commitment, and collaborative spirit were key to integrating a game-changing feature into the e-commerce platform, setting a new standard for customer engagement.

Addressing the Challenges of Machine Learning in Product Management

Integrating AI and ML into product management isn't just about using cutting-edge technology; it's about navigating a maze of unique challenges with skill and foresight. Here's how you can tackle these obstacles head-on to ensure the successful deployment of AI/ML-driven solutions:

Data Management Challenges: Managing vast datasets is a challenging task. It's not just about storage and processing; it's about maintaining data privacy, ensuring compliance with legal standards, and protecting personal user information. Strive to ensure this is understood by all stakeholders and collaborators involved.

Emphasizing Data Quality: The backbone of any successful machine learning model is high-quality training data. Ensuring the data's consistency, completeness, and neutrality is crucial. Remember, a model trained on faulty or biased data will yield unreliable results, undermining the importance of data integrity.

Enhancing Model Transparency: Clarifying complex machine learning models is vital for gaining stakeholder and user trust. Try to make the decision-making processes of these models transparent, especially with deep learning networks that can often seem like 'black boxes.'

Vigilant Performance Monitoring: Keep a constant eye on your model's performance. Monitor key metrics such as accuracy, precision, and recall to promptly identify and address any performance dips or anomalies.

Guiding Continuous Model Evolution: Machine learning models aren't set-and-forget tools; they need continual updates with fresh data to stay relevant and accurate. Managing this ongoing evolution, while ensuring uninterrupted service, is a critical and challenging responsibility.

Cultivating Trust and Ensuring Compliance: In an era of AI skepticism, building trust is vital. This involves transparent communication, securing user consent, and clarifying data and algorithmic processes to make them understandable and relatable.

Steering Through Project Complexity: AI and ML projects are complex, often masked in uncertainty. These projects demand iterative testing and may not always follow a linear path to success. As a Product Manager, you'll need to steer through this uncertainty, managing complexity, setting realistic expectations, and being agile enough to adapt to new findings and directions.

By adeptly addressing these challenges, you'll not only navigate the AI and ML landscape more effectively but also pave the way for these technologies to drive innovation and create substantial value in your products.

Enhancing User Experience in AI/ML-Driven Products

User experience (UX) in AI/ML-driven products exceeds traditional design—it's the cornerstone of product success. Excellence in UX demands more than just technological expertise; it requires steering AI/ML innovation towards delivering real user value, ensuring that groundbreaking technologies are not just impressive but are also meaningful and user-friendly.

User-Centric Development: Initiate AI/ML solution development with a deep dive into user understanding. Utilize user personas, empathy maps, and journey mapping to gather comprehensive insights into user needs and challenges. This foundational understanding should clarify how AI/ML can elevate user experiences, ensuring solutions are crafted with the user's perspective as a guiding star.

Achieving Strategic Balance: Strive for a harmonious balance where user needs, technological possibilities, and business objectives interconnect. This balance ensures AI/ML solutions are not just technologically advanced but also relevant and business-aligned. Engage with a broad range of stakeholders, from end-users to tech teams to business executives, to foster solutions that resonate across the board.

Clarity and Intuitiveness in Design: The details of AI/ML should be seamless for the end-user. Aim for designs that are intuitive, reducing the learning curve for users. For instance, in products with recommendation engines, clarity about why certain recommendations are presented can foster user trust and comprehension. Articulate the functionalities and benefits of AI/ML elements in straightforward, user-friendly language, making them relatable and beneficial.

Dedication to Evolution: The landscape of AI/ML is continually advancing, and your product should mirror this progress. Establish a robust feedback loop that captures user behaviors, preferences, and challenges, leveraging these insights to refine your AI/ML offerings constantly. Update your product regularly, responding to user feedback and leveraging the latest in AI/ML, to maintain technological relevance and user satisfaction.

Integrating these strategies into your product management approach ensures that your AI/ML-driven solutions aren't just cutting-edge; they're also profoundly user-centric and practical. The aim is to build products that aren't just functional and smart but are also intuitive, ethical, and engaging, delivering an unparalleled user experience in today's digital era.

Assessing Performance in AI and ML Projects

Integrating AI and ML into business processes necessitates the development of distinct Key Performance Indicators (KPIs) to evaluate their unique contributions and effectiveness. These KPIs combine traditional performance metrics with new ones, offering a holistic view of the AI/ML implementations' success. Here's an overview of critical KPIs for AI and ML projects:

Model Accuracy: These primary metric measures the model's correctness percentage, offering a straightforward assessment of its effectiveness.

Precision: Precision evaluates the ratio of correct positive predictions to total positive predictions made by the model. High precision indicates minimal false positives, which is essential in contexts where the outcomes of false positives are significant.

Recall (Sensitivity): Recall measures the model's capability to identify all actual positives correctly, crucial in scenarios where missing a positive case could lead to severe outcomes.

F1 Score: This metric provides a harmonized measure of the model's precision and recall. F1 score provides a single metric that conveys the overall accuracy of the model particularly beneficial when the consequences of false positives and negatives are similar.

Model Inference Time: Vital for real-time applications, this KPI assesses how quickly a model processes data and renders predictions, influencing user experience and operational efficiency.

ROI (Return on Investment): This KPI assesses the economic impact of AI/ML projects, comparing the derived benefits to the incurred costs, thus clarifying the projects' financial viability.

User Engagement and Satisfaction: Focusing on the user's interaction and perception of AI-enhanced functionalities, this KPI is key to understanding whether AI/ML features meet user expectations and foster engagement.

Selecting appropriate KPIs for AI and ML projects is a strategic endeavor, aimed not just at measuring success but at providing actionable insights to steer these projects. The correct set of KPIs can shed light on the efficacy of AI and ML initiatives, guiding their continuous improvement and optimizing their contributions to the business.

Final Thought

The overpowering impact of Artificial Intelligence (AI) and Machine Learning (ML) in product management can be appropriately summarized by the saying, "With great power comes great responsibility." As Product Managers, you are at the center of integrating these potent technologies into your products, not just as short-lived trends but as substantial tools that can elevate your product's value and market position.

Incorporating AI and ML demands flexibility and adaptability. The journey is full of unpredictability, presenting a series of challenges and learning curves. It's crucial to adopt an experimental mindset, viewing each obstacle as an opportunity for growth and every iteration as a vital step forward.

The exploration of AI and ML should not be an isolated endeavor. The landscape is rich with specialized firms and startups packed with cutting-edge AI and ML solutions. Engaging with these experts can inject innovative perspectives and robust solutions into your product, enriching its AI and ML features without having to start from scratch.

Consider starting partnerships with startups well-known for their AI competency. Such alliances can accelerate your product's journey into advanced AI and ML world, enabling you to bypass extensive development timelines. Assess how their specialized knowledge aligns with your product's vision and consider the synergies that such collaborations can foster. Strategic partnerships not only reinforce your product's AI and ML foundation but also equip you to navigate the complexities of these technologies more smoothly.

In closing, the shift towards AI and ML in product management calls for agility, openness to collaboration, and a commitment to on-going learning. By incorporating these tenets, you can harness the full potential of AI and ML, transforming technological challenges into channels for innovation and strategic growth.

Chapter Conclusion and Reflection

As we wrap up this chapter, it's evident that Big Data, Artificial Intelligence (AI), Machine Learning (ML), and Generative AI are more than just contemporary tech jargons; they are transformative forces reshaping product management. These technologies are revolutionizing industries, offering unparalleled advantages. For today's Product Managers, understanding and leveraging Big Data, AI, and ML isn't a luxury—it's a necessity.

Our exploration of Big Data revealed its potential not just in its vastness but in its capacity to yield actionable insights. We've seen how it serves as a compass, guiding strategic decisions and offering a deeper understanding of customer behaviors for feature enhancements.

In the world of AI and ML, we've transitioned from viewing machines as plain tools to recognizing them as intelligent entities capable of learning, adapting, and enhancing decision-making processes. The example of Netflix's recommendation engine illuminated how AI and ML could significantly improve user experiences and drive business success.

For Product Managers, embedding AI and ML into products comes with distinct challenges, from ensuring data accuracy to managing model performance. Yet, as demonstrated through Laila's journey in developing a personalized recommendation engine, these challenges can be effectively navigated with thoughtful planning and execution.

A key insight from this chapter is the criticality of a user-centered approach. Among the complexities of AI and ML, maintaining a laser focus on user needs ensures that technological advancements translate into meaningful and engaging user experiences.

We also explored the importance of data-driven decision-making, discussing key KPIs and metrics essential for evaluating AI/ML initiatives. These metrics aren't just numbers; they're navigational tools that steer progress, validate strategies, and drive ongoing enhancement.

In closing, the Big Data, AI, and ML era brings a blend of thrilling opportunities and tough challenges for Product Managers. To succeed, one must commit to continuous learning, flexibility, and an unwavering dedication to meeting user needs. As Product Managers steering through this era, you're at the frontline of technological evolution, charting a course rich with challenges but even richer in opportunities for growth and innovation.

CHAPTER 9
PRODUCT MANAGEMENT IN
DIGITAL HEALTH

After exploring big data, artificial intelligence (AI), and machine learning (ML) in the previous chapter, we now turn to the dynamic field of Digital Health. This sector represents a significant shift from conventional healthcare practices, navigating towards a future where technology not only empowers patients but also revolutionizes the way healthcare is delivered.

Previously, healthcare systems focused mainly on healthcare providers, giving patients limited access to their health data and little involvement in care-related decisions. Digital health, however, is shifting this narrative by enhancing patient empowerment and involvement. Modern technologies now enable patients to access their health records, understand their treatment options, and engage in their healthcare decisions through digital platforms and patient portals, transforming them from passive recipients to active participants in their health journey.

The rapid increase in financial investments highlights the growing importance of digital health. Funding for digital health startups jumped to $21.6 billion in 2020 from $2.8 billion in 2011. Projections indicate the market could grow to over $639.4 billion by 2026, driven by technological innovations, greater demand for remote monitoring after COVID-19, and a rising interest in personalized healthcare.

In this technology-driven healthcare setting, Product Managers are crucial as innovators and change-makers. They develop products that improve patient outcomes and raise healthcare standards, challenging traditional healthcare delivery methods. However, this role comes with challenges like navigating complex regulatory frameworks, protecting sensitive patient data, and integrating new technologies into existing healthcare systems.

This chapter explores the facets of product management within digital health. We will explore key components of developing digital health products, present case studies, and offer strategies to overcome specific industry challenges. Special attention will be given to understanding healthcare regulations, fostering collaboration across multidisciplinary teams, and emphasizing patient-centric design principles. Our goal is to arm Product Managers with the essential insights and tools required to lead digital health innovations in an era where technology is swiftly reshaping healthcare experiences and delivery.

Exploring the Digital Health Landscape

Digital health merges technology with healthcare, offering a visionary approach to personalized and precise health management. This field is a transformative force that is reshaping healthcare engagement, delivery, and personal well-being in the digital era.

Let's explore some fundamental elements that define the digital health landscape:

Telemedicine: A cornerstone of digital health, telemedicine eliminates geographical barriers, facilitating remote consultations and care. This innovation not only expands healthcare access to remote and underserved regions but also introduces a new dimension of convenience and continuity in patient care, emphasizing the shift towards a more accessible healthcare model.

Wearable Devices and Health Applications: The rise of wearable technology and health applications endorse an era of empowered self-health-management. From fitness bands monitoring physical activity to apps that offer medical insights at a tap, this trend highlights a significant move towards personal health autonomy, enabling individuals to monitor and manage their health proactively.

Remote Patient Monitoring (RPM) Systems: RPM technologies extend the boundaries of healthcare, facilitating at-home monitoring of critical health metrics. These systems represent a harmonious blend of patient self-governance and continuous healthcare supervision ensuring that care extends beyond the hospital or clinic, integrating seamlessly into daily life.

The essence of digital health innovation lies in coupling AI, ML, and big data to drive a new era of healthcare that is predictive, personalized, and preventive. These technologies analyze massive health datasets to uncover insights, forecast health trends, and tailor healthcare to individual needs, marking a paradigm shift from a one-size-fits-all approach to a tailored healthcare journey.

In summary, digital health exceeds being just a suite of technological tools; it represents a transformative culture, redefining healthcare to be more connected, informed, and centered around the patient's needs. Digital health links technology with healthcare, creating a more responsive and personalized system for each patient's health journey.

Revolutionizing Healthcare with Digital Health Innovations

Digital health stands at the forefront of healthcare transformation, enhancing patient care through technology-driven solutions and data insights. Let's explore some key initiatives that underscore the impact of digital health:

Advanced Diagnostics and Therapeutics: Leveraging AI and ML, healthcare professionals now access deeper insights from complex health data, leading to early disease detection and timely interventions. This not only elevates patient care but also reduces healthcare expenditures by preventing disease progression.

Tailored Patient Care: A standout achievement in digital health is the personalization of medical care. Analyzing diverse data points like genetics, lifestyle, and medical history, healthcare providers now offer treatments uniquely suited to each patient. This approach of precision medicine ensures more effective interventions, fostering faster recoveries and minimizing adverse reactions.

Preventative Health Insights: Through continuous data analysis, digital health tools proactively identify health risks, assisting in early intervention or prevention of severe conditions. This shift from reactive to preventive care transforms patient health significantly.

Seamless Care Coordination: Digital health solutions facilitate the integrated exchange of patient information among healthcare providers. This cohesive data sharing ensures a comprehensive approach to patient care, enhancing treatment effectiveness and patient satisfaction.

Efficient Resource Management: Digital health enables healthcare organizations to streamline operations, optimize resource allocation, and enhance communication within the organization. These efficiencies lead to cost reductions and improved patient monitoring, elevating the standard of healthcare services.

Insights on Public Health: Utilizing data analytics, digital health provides essential insights into public health patterns and the effectiveness of treatments at a population level. These insights inform and refine healthcare strategies and policies, benefiting broader communities.

Empowering Patients: Digital health empowers individuals to take an active role in their health management. With tools for monitoring health metrics, understanding treatment options, and engaging with providers, patients are equipped to make informed decisions, enhancing their involvement and outcomes in the healthcare process.

Digital health exceeds the digitalization of healthcare services; it is a profound reimagining of how healthcare is delivered and experienced. By integrating technology, data, and patient connectivity, digital health not only improves health outcomes but also democratizes access to healthcare, focusing on patient needs. As this field evolves, it offers expansive opportunities for Product Managers to drive innovation and significantly impact healthcare quality and patient experiences.

Overcoming Key Challenges in Digital Health

The expansion of digital health introduces a set of challenges that Product Managers must smoothly overcome. These challenges include regulatory compliance, data privacy, rapid technological evolution, and the essential of delivering a seamless user experience. Addressing these challenges is vital for crafting digital health solutions that are not only innovative and effective but also trusted and compliant.

In this section, we'll explore these key challenges one by one, reviewing the strategies and approaches necessary for Product Managers to effectively address them in the dynamic landscape of digital health.

Regulatory and Compliance Challenges in Digital Health

In digital health, navigating the regulatory landscape is crucial. Product Managers must comply with strict standards and use them to guide safe, effective, and trustworthy product development.

Comprehensive Understanding of Regulatory Frameworks: A nuanced understanding of the regulatory environment is indispensable. In the U.S., HIPAA safeguards patient health information, while the EU's GDPR dictates strict personal data handling rules. The FDA's vigilance on medical devices impacts digital health tools, necessitating rigorous testing and validation. Familiarity with these frameworks is essential for shaping product design and ensuring compliance.

Promoting User Trust through Compliance: Adhering to compliance standards from the start of product design is crucial for building user trust and ensuring that privacy and security are integral to the product. Transparently communicating data usage policies to users reinforces trust and clarifies the product's commitment to privacy.

Collaboration with Legal and Compliance Experts: Building strong partnerships with legal and compliance specialists is key to navigating the regulatory maze. These collaborations can significantly influence product trajectory, especially those concerning data handling practices.

Embracing Privacy by Design: Adopting Privacy by Design is crucial. This approach integrates privacy at every stage of the product lifecycle, ensuring it is a fundamental part of the product's architecture.

Conducting Privacy Impact Assessments: These assessments help proactively identify and mitigate privacy risks, enhancing compliance and product integrity.

Adapting to Regulatory Evolutions: The digital health domain is dynamic, with constantly evolving regulations, requiring updates to privacy policies, terms of service, and data protection measures to maintain compliance and meet shifting business demands.

Facing the complicated regulatory and compliance landscape in digital health is overwhelming yet essential. A proactive, informed, and collaborative strategy is crucial. By emphasizing regulatory adherence and prioritizing data privacy, Product Managers can develop digital health solutions that not only align with legal requirements but also secure the trust and confidence of users and stakeholders, thereby laying a solid foundation for success in the digital health ecosystem.

Enhancing Interoperability in Digital Health

Interoperability stands as a critical pillar in the digital health landscape, essential for advancing integrated, patient-centered care. It's the capacity of diverse healthcare information systems, devices, and apps to connect, exchange, interpret, and use data in a coordinated manner. Achieving effective interoperability is essential for delivering cohesive care, driving informed clinical decisions, and enhancing patient outcomes.

The challenge of interoperability comes from the various data formats used by different healthcare entities. These differences can block seamless data integration and complicate compliance with diverse privacy and security standards.

Addressing interoperability obstacles requires a comprehensive strategy:

Adoption of Standard Data Formats: Use established standards like Health Level Seven International (HL7) and Fast Healthcare Interoperability Resources (FHIR) to ensure consistent data exchange and system-wide compatibility.

Strategic Collaborative Integration: Developing an integrated approach requires collaboration among healthcare providers, data specialists, and IT professionals. This collaboration should focus on critical elements such as data mapping, transformation, and the creation of secure data channels to facilitate efficient and secure data integration.

Strict Data Governance: Establishing a robust data governance model is vital for protection data integrity and safeguarding privacy and security. This model should clearly outline policies for data access, utilization, and sharing, reinforced by vigilant monitoring and auditing to ensure policy adherence.

Leveraging Emerging Technologies: Employing machine learning and AI can significantly streamline the data integration process. These technologies assist in cleaning, reconciling, and standardizing different data sets, thereby simplifying data analysis, and enhancing integration efficiency.

Navigating interoperability in digital health is more than a technical challenge; it is crucial for unlocking digital healthcare's transformative potential. Ensuring fluid data interconnectivity and collaborative integration allows digital health solutions to revolutionize patient care, paving the way for more integrated and personalized healthcare experiences.

User Adoption and Acceptance in Digital Health

In digital health, where innovation involves intimate personal data, securing user adoption and acceptance is essential. Despite their potential to revolutionize healthcare, digital health technologies often face adoption barriers. Here's how to address them:

Addressing Privacy and Security Concerns: Trust is the core of digital health adoption. Users' fears about data breaches and privacy violations can significantly discourage technology uptake. Emphasize robust data protection measures, ensuring users are fully informed about how their information is protected. Transparent communication about security protocols not only builds trust but reassures users about their data's safety.

Navigating Liability and Ethical Dilemmas: The digital health domain is full of potential legal and ethical complexities, such as the accuracy of AI-driven diagnoses. Engaging with legal experts to understand and navigate these risks is essential. Clear user agreements, comprehensive risk mitigation strategies, and strict compliance with regulations and standards can address these concerns, fostering a secure and ethical digital health environment.

Overcoming Resistance to Digital Transition: Moving from traditional to digital healthcare can overwhelm users used to in-person care. However, designing user-friendly and accessible digital health solutions can ease this transition, especially among less tech-savvy users. Offering robust support and clear, accessible guidance can facilitate this digital shift.

Educating and Engaging Users: User education is crucial in revealing the benefits of digital health technologies. Clear, accessible information about how these tools enhance healthcare experiences can motivate users to embrace them. Engagement doesn't stop at education; asking user feedback and incorporating it into product development ensures that solutions are attuned to actual user needs and preferences.

Fostering Continuous Engagement and Feedback: Active user involvement in the development process, coupled with ongoing feedback collection, is helpful in building user-centered digital health products. This engagement supports in understanding user preferences, refining product offerings, and ultimately, driving higher adoption rates.

The variety of challenges in digital health presents unique opportunities for innovation and the creation of transformative healthcare solutions. Addressing these challenges directly is crucial for Product Managers stepping into this sector, guiding them in developing digital health products that not only meet regulatory and user standards but also make a meaningful impact on healthcare delivery and outcomes. As we explore further into the evolving role of Product Managers in digital health, we'll explore the strategies, skills, and insights essential for success in this dynamic and impactful field.

The Role of Product Managers in Digital Health

The digital health sector is rapidly transforming, shifting from traditional healthcare models to a digital-first, patient-centric approach. This transformation significantly broadens and deepens the role of Product Managers in the healthcare industry. In this dynamic environment, Product Managers must continually evolve, striking a balance between innovative digital solutions and the complicated requirements of healthcare delivery. Here are essential aspects of success for Product Managers in digital health:

Navigating Healthcare System Complexities: Product Managers in healthcare need to be expert at developing strategies for products that impact patient health and align with the multifaceted healthcare ecosystem, including patients, providers, insurers, and regulators. Balancing the diverse needs and expectations of these stakeholders requires a comprehensive understanding of their perspectives and the ability to combine these into unified product solutions that serve the broader ecosystem.

Bridging Technology and Healthcare: Technical expertise alone is insufficient in digital health. Product Managers must be well-versed in healthcare systems, medical terminology, and clinical workflows, acting as a bridge between innovative technology and healthcare's practical realities. This role demands effective communication and collaboration across various stakeholders, including developers, healthcare professionals, and regulatory bodies, and requires proficiency with emerging technologies such as AI, ML, telemedicine, and wearable tech.

Empathy and Patient-Centric Focus: Central to this role is a deep empathy for patients and a solid commitment to understanding their needs. Product Managers must prioritize patient experience, aiming to create products that not only fulfill medical requirements but also enhance patient engagement and outcomes. This involves engaging with patients, conducting thorough user research, and integrating patient feedback throughout the product development process. The goal is to deliver solutions that not only elevate the patient experience but also empower individuals in their healthcare journeys, leading to better health outcomes.

In conclusion, the role of a Product Manager in digital health is both demanding and rewarding, requiring a blend of technical expertise, healthcare knowledge, empathetic insight, and strategic acumen. As pivotal figures in digital health, Product Managers have the unique opportunity to drive meaningful improvements in healthcare outcomes and actively contribute to the sector's ongoing evolution.

Developing Patient-Centric Digital Health Solutions

In healthcare product management, the core principle is to adopt a patient-centric approach. This strategy is fundamental in ensuring that products not only meet the clinical needs but also resonate with the users, enhancing their health management journey. Here's a breakdown of essential steps in building patient-centric digital health solutions:

Identifying the Target Market: Understanding your target market is the first step in developing a product that addresses the specific needs and preferences of its intended users. The healthcare industry caters to a wide array of demographics, each with unique health conditions, lifestyles, and technological fluency. By pinpointing the exact demographic your product serves, whether it's young adults with chronic conditions, elderly individuals with mobility issues, or wellness enthusiasts, you can tailor your development, marketing, and distribution strategies accordingly.

Creating User Personas: Dive deeper into understanding your target audience by developing detailed user personas. These personas should reflect the users' healthcare challenges, their interactions with healthcare systems, technological comfort levels, and expectations from a digital health solution. Consider the broader healthcare ecosystem, including providers and insurers, to ensure a holistic view of the user experience.

User Research and Validation: Validate your market assumptions and personas through robust user research. Engaging with potential users early in the development process can unveil invaluable insights, guiding your product's design and ensuring it aligns with the users' real needs.

Simplifying UX/UI Design: In designing your digital health product, prioritize simplicity and intuitiveness. The complex nature of healthcare, coupled with the varying degrees of technological ability among users, demands an interface that simplifies navigation. Ensure that interacting with healthcare information through your product is clear and accessible for all users, regardless of their background or familiarity with technology.

Boosting Patient Engagement: Design your product to actively engage users, encouraging them to take proactive steps in managing their health. Incorporate interactive features like notifications, educational content, progress tracking, and personalized goal setting. Gamification can also play a key role in motivating users to adhere to health regimes and achieve their wellness objectives.

Emphasizing Personalization: Personalization is key to enhancing user engagement. Adapting the user experience to fit individual health profiles and preferences can transform your product from a generic tool to a personalized health companion, offering targeted advice, routines, and reminders that users find truly beneficial.

Prioritizing Accessibility: Accessibility is crucial in ensuring your product is usable by everyone, irrespective of age, disability, or tech adoption. Design features like voice navigation for the visually impaired or larger tap targets for the elderly can make a significant difference in user experience. Furthermore, adapt your content to cater to varying levels of health literacy, presenting information in a clear and understandable way.

Strategizing Information Hierarchy: Effective information hierarchy is vital in digital health apps to minimize cognitive load and streamline user navigation. This strategy involves organizing content to highlight essential health information, such as critical metrics or urgent notifications, at the forefront of the user interface. For instance, prioritize displaying vital stats like blood pressure readings or upcoming medication alerts upon app entry.

The aim is to create an intuitive user flow, allowing patients to effortlessly access and interact with their key health data without feeling overwhelmed.

Mastering Data Visualization: Transforming complicated health data into easy-to-understand visual formats is important in aiding patient comprehension and engagement. Utilize graphs, progress bars, and color-coded indicators to show health metrics visually. For instance, illustrating a patient's cholesterol level trends over time can provide more immediate insight than a list of numbers. Effective data visualization not only enhances user understanding but also empowers patients and healthcare providers to make more informed decisions regarding care plans, lifestyle changes, and treatment adjustments.

By following these guidelines, you'll be well on your way to building digital health solutions that are technologically advanced and deeply accommodated to the needs and preferences of the users, enhancing their health outcomes and overall experience with the product.

Case Study: Onduo Virtual Diabetes Clinic by Verily

Onduo is a virtual clinic established by Verily, a subsidiary of Alphabet Inc., that specializes in the management of type 2 diabetes. The platform creatively integrates wearable sensors, software applications, and direct access to healthcare professionals to deliver tailored and responsive patient care.

Central to Onduo's technological suite are continuous glucose monitors (CGM) that capture blood sugar levels in real time. This crucial data is transmitted to a mobile application where advanced machine learning algorithms assess trends and fluctuations to offer immediate feedback and actionable recommendations to users. Further enhancing its user-centric approach, the application includes features for dietary guidance and medication management, crafting a personalized care plan for each user based on their unique health data.

The efficacy of Onduo's method has been marked by substantial improvements in diabetes management outcomes. Users have experienced significant reductions in HbA1c levels, a key indicator of long-term blood glucose control essential for mitigating the risks of diabetes-related complications. Furthermore, the platform fosters an educational environment that promotes self-management, thereby empowering individuals to actively participate in their healthcare regimen. This empowerment has been associated with improved patient engagement and superior long-term health results, highlighting the success of Onduo's integrative and technology-driven approach to chronic disease management.

Clinical Validation: Building Trust in Healthcare Products

In the landscape of digital health, clinical validation is not just a technical step; it's the core that validates a product's effectiveness, safety, and reliability in real-world healthcare environments. It exceeds the boundaries of basic accuracy tests and regulatory compliance, diving deep into the impact of products on patient health outcomes and their practical value in diverse clinical settings.

Understanding Clinical Validation: At its core, clinical validation is about empirically verifying the claims of a digital health product. It's an in-depth evaluation that assesses the product's performance beyond controlled environments, focusing on its application in everyday patient care. Consider a digital tool designed for diabetes management that tracks blood glucose levels through innovative means. While initial tests may confirm its technical accuracy, clinical validation explores its effectiveness in patients' daily lives, its consistency across various settings, and its real contribution to better health outcomes, such as improved glycemic control or reduced hyperglycemic episodes.

Addressing Challenges with Emerging Technologies: The fast pace of innovation in healthcare technology brings unique challenges to clinical validation. New devices or software applications may lack established testing frameworks. This scenario necessitates a collaborative approach where Product Managers work alongside medical professionals, regulatory experts, and statisticians to develop tailored validation strategies that align with the technology's novel aspects.

Building Trust Beyond Compliance: Clinical validation goes beyond meeting regulatory requirements—it's a critical element in building user trust. In an industry where trust is principal, proving a product's efficacy and safety through rigorous validation is fundamental. It reassures patients, healthcare providers, and insurers of the product's value and dependability, fostering confidence in its adoption and use.

Executing Clinical Validation Effectively: The process should be detailed, with study designs that replicate real-world healthcare scenarios, ensuring participant diversity to reflect varied patient demographics. Following validation, transparently sharing the outcomes with stakeholders is essential. This openness enhances the product's credibility and provides valuable insights for ongoing enhancement, supported by actual usage data and patient experiences.

In essence, clinical validation is a critical endeavor in the digital health landscape, essential for affirming a product's real-world utility and efficacy. For Product Managers, it's a strategic priority that ensures their innovations are not only technologically advanced but also genuinely beneficial, trustworthy, and ready to make a meaningful impact on healthcare delivery and patient well-being.

Enhancing Digital Health with AI and Analytics

Integrating Artificial Intelligence (AI) and Machine Learning (ML) into digital health transforms healthcare. It offers unparalleled opportunities for innovation in diagnostics, patient care, and personalized medicine. To effectively incorporate these technologies, Product Managers must navigate the connection of healthcare and tech with insight and precision.

Leveraging AI and Analytics for Deeper Healthcare Insights: Healthcare generates vast data pools from patient interactions, offering a rich ground for AI and ML to extract actionable insights. These technologies are revolutionizing fields like epidemiology and radiology, enhancing patient care with predictive models and personalized treatment plans. Analytics, on the other hand, are helpful in refining clinical outcomes and promoting an evidence-based approach to medicine, driving healthcare into a new age of accuracy and efficiency.

Seamless Integration of AI into Healthcare Products: The effectiveness of AI in digital health depends on its seamless integration, where AI tools not only complement but elevate the product's core features, enhancing user experience. This requires a strategic approach, from building custom ML models to integrating efficient data exchange APIs or connecting third-party AI solutions. For instance, an AI-enhanced feature in a chronic disease management app could analyze patient data in real-time, offering personalized health insights and recommendations.

Addressing AI Integration Challenges: Integrating AI into healthcare comes with its set of challenges, with data integrity at the forefront. Inaccurate data can lead to incorrect AI predictions, potentially impacting patient health. Algorithmic transparency is another critical aspect; understanding and interpreting AI-driven decisions is vital in healthcare, where outcomes can significantly affect patient well-being. Moreover, aligning with strict healthcare regulations such as HIPAA and GDPR adds another layer of complexity to AI integration.

Role of Product Managers in AI-Driven Digital Health: Product Managers play a key role in weaving AI and analytics into digital health products. Beyond technical integration, their responsibilities include addressing ethical considerations, ensuring regulatory compliance, and maintaining a user-centric focus. By prioritizing patient needs, ensuring data quality and transparency, and staying up-to-date of regulatory standards, Product Managers can effectively leverage AI and analytics to not only innovate but also personalize and elevate patient care, setting a new standard in digital health.

For example, Babylon Health, a UK-based healthcare service provider, has developed an innovative digital health application that leverages artificial intelligence (AI) to offer remote medical consultations and health services. This app enables users to engage in virtual consultations with doctors and healthcare professionals through text and video messaging. A standout feature of the app is its AI-powered symptom checker, which interacts with patients by asking targeted questions about their symptoms. Based on the user's responses, the AI provides preliminary medical advice and assists doctors with the initial triaging of cases, ultimately allowing healthcare professionals more time to focus on patient care.

In summary, the successful incorporation of AI and analytics into digital health products demands a balanced approach that considers technical expertise, ethical standards, regulatory compliance, and, most importantly, patient-centricity. As Product Managers navigate this complex landscape, their strategic and thoughtful integration of AI can significantly enhance the value and impact of digital health solutions, ushering in a new era of personalized and efficient healthcare.

Ethical Considerations in Digital Health Product Management

In the era of digital health, where innovations directly impact human lives, the significance of ethical considerations cannot be overstated. As Product Managers, there is a profound responsibility to ensure that the development and deployment of digital health solutions are guided by strict ethical standards. Here's a deeper exploration into the ethical dimensions that are essential for Product Managers in this sector:

Bias and Fairness: The integrity of digital health solutions depends on their ability to provide rightful care across diverse patient populations. It is crucial to examine AI algorithms and data collection methodologies to prevent the embedding of biases which could lead to disparate healthcare outcomes. Awareness in this area safeguards the fairness and reliability of healthcare services, fostering inclusivity and trust.

Informed Consent: The cornerstone of ethical medical practice, informed consent, takes on added complexity in the digital landscape. It is essential to establish transparent, understandable, and patient-centric processes for obtaining consent. This entails ensuring that patients are fully aware of how their data is being utilized, the benefits of data sharing, and any potential risks involved. Clarity and transparency in consent processes empower patients, allowing them to make well-informed decisions about their healthcare data.

Digital Divide: The promise of digital health must be inclusive, exceeding barriers of socio-economic status, geography, or digital literacy. Product Managers must be watchful of the digital divide – the gap between those who have access to digital technologies and those who do not. Efforts should be directed toward creating digital health solutions that are universally accessible, providing equitable healthcare benefits to all individuals, irrespective of their background or technological proficiency.

By placing a strong emphasis on these ethical considerations, Product Managers in digital health can navigate the complex landscape of healthcare innovation responsibly. It's about building solutions that are ethically sound, ensuring that digital health advancements contribute positively to patient care and healthcare equity.

Chapter Conclusion & Reflection

As we wrap up this chapter, we reflect on the dynamic and impactful role of Product Managers in the ever-evolving digital health sector. This journey has simplified the vast challenges and opportunities inherent in digital health, showcasing the central role product management plays in this growing field.

Digital health exceeds its technological components, serving as a bridge connecting innovative technology with genuine human needs. It paves the way for enhanced patient outcomes, improved healthcare experiences, and more streamlined healthcare systems. Product Managers in this domain rise as visionaries, merging technological competency with deep healthcare insights to build solutions that truly make a difference.

Central to their mission is a patient-centered approach, the guiding principle for every phase of product development, from conceptualization to clinical validation. This patient-first perspective ensures that solutions not only meet but exceed user needs and expectations, laying the groundwork for genuinely impactful digital health products.

Mastering the complicated regulatory landscape of healthcare is crucial for Product Managers. Their creations must align with strict regulations, maintaining the utmost data integrity and prioritizing patient privacy. Moreover, tackling challenges like interoperability and data integration demands innovative strategies and solid technical know-how.

Exploring the world of AI and analytics, we've seen their transformative potential in healthcare. From revolutionizing diagnostics to tailoring patient care, these technologies offer a frontier for groundbreaking product innovation.

In conclusion, Product Managers are central to guiding digital health's trajectory. Their expertise in user-centric design, stakeholder collaboration, regulatory compliance, and technological innovation positions them to lead the digital transformation in healthcare. They are not just innovators but also key agents in enhancing healthcare experiences.

As this chapter closes, it's clear that as a digital health Product Manager, you stand at the frontline of a healthcare revolution. You hold the capability to shape healthcare's future, creating truly life-enhancing solutions. Embrace this role with enthusiasm and dedication, and you will play a crucial part in advancing healthcare in the digital age.

CHAPTER 10
ENJOY THE JOURNEY

As we navigate to the closing chapter of our exploration, it's time to pause and reflect on the journey you've undertaken in the world of product management. This chapter, rightly titled 'Enjoy the Journey,' encourages you to enjoy the path you have crossed, celebrate the milestones, and appreciate the wealth of experiences that have shaped your journey. In product management, success isn't solely quantified by product launches or performance metrics; it's also found in the depth of experiences, the learnings acquired, and the personal growth achieved along the way.

Being a product manager in the rapidly evolving tech landscape brings an exciting blend of challenges and rewards. It's a role that continuously invites your curiosity, creativity, and passion for innovation to come to the forefront. Each product you develop tells a story of the challenges you tackle, the questions you explore, and the innovative solutions you bring to life. A limitless desire for knowledge and growth marks your journey, steering your teams and influencing your organization's direction.

Yet, the essence of product management exceeds achieving targets or driving organizational success. It involves finding meaning and joy in your work and recognizing that every facet of product development—from ideation to execution and strategic planning—can impact meaningful change. Whether it's simplifying user experiences, addressing complex challenges, or inspiring shifts within the industry, your contributions extend beyond product creation; they shape experiences, unlock new possibilities, and even transform lives.

This concluding chapter is not just a recap of essential skills and strategies; it's an epic story summing the passion, commitment, and satisfaction that make product management a uniquely fulfilling profession. Product management is more than a career—it's a journey loaded with impactful achievements and great personal development. Each step on this path enriches your professional story, adding layers of depth and meaning.

Continuous Learning and Growth in Product Management

In product management, your journey involves more than just completing tasks or achieving goals. It is about evolving, gaining new perspectives, and becoming a more skillful and insightful professional. Central to this journey is adopting a growth mindset, which involves believing in your potential to grow your abilities and intellect over time.

Accepting this mindset means understanding that learning and self-improvement are continuous. Every day brings new concepts to learn, skills to acquire, and challenges to overcome. Approach these opportunities with enthusiasm and see them as chances for growth.

One fundamental way to maintain this growth-oriented attitude is to actively seek and embrace feedback. Regular interactions with your team, stakeholders, and mentors can provide invaluable insights into your performance. View feedback not as a criticism but as a compass guiding your growth, where each piece of advice is a step towards your development as a product manager.

Regularly challenge yourself by stepping out of your comfort zone. Try new tools, technologies, or lead a project in a new area. These challenges will push your limits and enhance both personal and professional growth.

Adopting a growth mindset benefits not just you but also your team. Foster a team culture that encourages risk-taking, experimenting, and learning from failures. Create an environment where taking risks, experimenting, and learning from failures are encouraged. Share your learning journey, celebrate successes, and reflect openly on setbacks, motivating your team to embrace a similar path of continuous learning.

Remember, in product management, growth and learning never stop. There are always new challenges, obstacles, and skills to refine. Embrace this continuous journey, which will enhance your abilities as a product manager and enrich your professional life, filling it with continuous discovery and infinite potential for development.

Curiosity and Exploration: The Core of Product Management

In the dynamic world of product management, curiosity is not just a trait; it's the catalyst that drives innovation, initiates problem-solving, and drives the continuous search for knowledge. As a product manager, nurturing a deep-seated curiosity is essential, urging you to constantly question the status quo and explore the realms of 'why,' 'how,' and 'what if.'

To introduce this culture of inquiry in your journey, treat every question as a gateway to new insights, no matter how straightforward or complex it may appear. Encourage your team to adopt this questioning spirit. Whether in brainstorming sessions, meetings, or casual discussions, promote an environment where every question is valued, and every perspective is welcomed.

Challenge existing assumptions relentlessly. Your role as a product manager is to question conventional practices, reevaluate existing methods, and bravely innovate beyond the familiar. Broaden your perspectives by immersing yourself in diverse fields of knowledge, engaging with a variety of individuals, and seeking to understand different viewpoints. The wider your spectrum of exploration, the richer your source of creativity.

Couple your curiosity with a strong commitment to experimentation. Cultivate a team culture where testing, learning, and refining are foundational principles, highlighting the essence of exploring new ideas and learning from their outcomes. Create a supportive environment where experimentation is encouraged, and failure is seen as a valuable learning experience, not a setback.

Ground your experimental ventures in data and user insights. Use these insights as compasses to guide your hypotheses, design experiments, and interpret results. Recognize that achieving perfection on the first attempt is a myth; instead, focus on the gradual enhancement of your product, ensuring it resonates with users and aligns with strategic goals. Embrace the iterative nature of product development, acknowledging that the evolution of an idea into a successful product is an ongoing process of refinement and improvement.

In your role as a product manager, you stand at the crossroads of curiosity and exploration. By fostering a culture that celebrates inquiry and champions experimentation, you not only fuel your own growth but also pave the way for your product's success. Every question asked, every test conducted, and every adjustment made is a step forward in the journey of innovation and excellence.

Finding Meaning and Impact in Product Management

The role of a product manager exceeds conventional job responsibilities, offering a unique platform to significantly affect user experiences and societal standards. It's in the potential of your product to address key issues, enhance daily life, and promote positive change through which you discover the deeper meaning and purpose of your work.

Consider the broader influence of your product. How does it redefine user experiences or tackle significant challenges they face? This perspective elevates your role from routine tasks to a mission-centric journey. Think a digital education platform, for instance. In developing this tool, you extend your work beyond product development by actively contributing to educational accessibility and empowering learners worldwide.

To fulfil your role with greater meaning, strive for alignment between your personal values and the mission of the products you build. This harmony enriches your job with a sense of purpose that exceeds conventional rewards, driving you with intrinsic motivation and a commitment to the broader impact of your work. Your role is not just about developing a product but about actualizing a vision that can transform lives.

At the core of this mission-centric approach is a deep commitment to understanding and prioritizing the user. Engage deeply with their experiences, empathize with their challenges, and imagine how your product can mitigate their difficulties or enhance their well-being. This user-focused perspective is essential for building products that are not just commercially successful but are truly beneficial to the end user.

Moreover, it's crucial to maintain a balance between fulfilling user needs and achieving your company's strategic objectives. This balancing, while challenging, is a key to ensuring that your product is impactful and aligns with broader business goals, fostering a sustainable and rewarding sense of achievement in your work.

In essence, finding meaning and purpose as a product manager involves recognizing and leveraging the transformative potential of your product. It's about connecting with its mission, understanding its impact on users, and aligning your efforts with this greater purpose. By doing so, you're not just advancing in your career; you're contributing to something larger and more rewarding, enriching both your professional journey and the lives of those your product touches.

Embracing Successes and Navigating Challenges

In the dynamic world of product management, your journey will be marked by both achievements and difficulties. Embracing your victories and extracting insights from obstacles is fundamental to your growth and the evolution of your team. Celebrating successes, regardless of their scale, not only acknowledges hard work but also reinforces commitment, innovation, and perseverance.

It's vital to honor the collective achievements of your team as well as individual milestones. The journey from a promising idea to a fully-realized product is a testament to the synergy and diverse expertise of your team members. Recognizing these achievements nurtures a culture of appreciation and motivation, boosting team morale and driving further innovation.

Celebrations might highlight various milestones—whether it's exceeding user engagement targets, successfully overcoming product barriers, or launching innovative features. Promoting a culture that recognizes these accomplishments highlights the positive outcomes of your team's dedication and hard work.

On the flip side, confronting setbacks is an integral part of the product management landscape. Viewing these challenges as lessons rather than failures is essential for personal and team growth. Each obstacle presents a chance to refine your strategies, enhance problem-solving skills, and deepen your understanding of what drives success.

Adopt a structured approach to analyzing setbacks, employing techniques like post-mortem analyses or retrospectives. This methodical evaluation allows you to extract valuable lessons from challenges, applying these insights to enhance future endeavors. It fosters a culture where obstacles are viewed as catalysts for learning and innovation, encouraging a forward-thinking and resilient mindset.

Encouraging resilience and adaptability within your team is vital. Encourage a philosophy where challenges are seen as a step for improvement and learning. The objective is not to avoid difficulties but to learn from them, adapt strategies, and advance. Introducing this perspective helps build a team that's not just equipped to handle setbacks but is also well-informed for growth and continuous improvement.

In conclusion, as a product manager, celebrating successes and transforming challenges into learning opportunities are pivotal components of your role. By valuing victories and embracing difficulties as pathways to growth, you nurture a culture of positivity, resilience, and constant evolution, setting the stage for sustained success and innovation in your product management journey.

Empowering Leadership and Influential Collaboration

In the expansive role of a product manager, your impact extends far beyond managing tasks and timelines. Your true value excels through in your ability to lead with vision and collaborate with influence. As a key player within cross-functional teams, your role surpasses routine supervisory duties. You are tasked with uniting diverse talents and perspectives towards a shared objective, transforming individual efforts into a unified and purpose-driven force.

Leadership in product management is a naturally evolving phenomenon and dynamic in nature. It's about fostering a culture where open communication, inclusivity, and mutual respect are the norm. Polish your communication skills to articulate your vision and expectations with clarity and persuasion. Adopt a decision-making approach that is well-informed and inclusive, valuing a multitude of viewpoints while staying true to your strategic objectives. When conflicts arise, your role as a mediator is crucial—facilitating solutions that respect individual contributions while maintaining team harmony.

The power of your leadership is measured by your ability to inspire and motivate. Keep the vision of your product alive and compelling, engaging your team in a collective mission that fuels enthusiasm and dedication. Your genuine passion for the product's potential can inspire similar commitment within your team, driving them towards shared goals with an energized purpose.

Moreover, your leadership extends to influencing a broader range of stakeholders, from executives to engineers, designers to marketers. Effectively communicating the value and vision of your product is essential to securing their buy-in and collaboration.

Building robust relationships with these stakeholders is crucial. Invest time in understanding their perspectives, addressing their challenges, and demonstrating how your product aligns with their goals. This not only gathers essential support but also fosters a collaborative environment encouraging your product's growth.

Your negotiation skills are equally critical, especially when faced with diverse opinions and priorities. Your ability to mediate, finding common ground that aligns different interests, is key to managing the complicated relationship of stakeholder expectations and advancing your product's agenda.

In summary, as a product manager, your capacity for leadership and influence is vital to achieving success. By cultivating an environment of open communication, inspiring your team, and engaging stakeholders effectively, you maximize your role, guiding your product and team towards collective success and impactful outcomes.

Harmonizing Professional Excellence and Personal Fulfillment

In the demanding world of product management, balancing professional demands with personal well-being is essential. This balance is the cornerstone of sustained productivity, creativity, and overall job satisfaction, ensuring you remain engaged and effective over the long-term success in your career.

Effective time management is crucial for this balance. Identify your most productive hours for demanding tasks and learn to delegate. Trust your team's abilities and say no to tasks that don't match your key responsibilities.

Creating a supportive work environment is crucial. Encourage open discussions about work-life balance to foster mutual respect for personal boundaries, boosting both individual well-being and team morale.

Don't neglect self-care. Regularly engage in physical activity, hobbies, and allow time for relaxation. These activities are not just breaks; they are investments in your long-term productivity and mental health.

Your support network, both professional and personal, is invaluable. Build connections across various functions within your organization to gain diverse perspectives and foster interdepartmental collaboration. Outside work, nurture relationships that provide emotional support and enrich your life beyond the office.

Maintaining work-life balance is a continuous process that needs regular attention. While being a product manager is integral to your identity, remember that life offers more beyond professional achievements. Investing time in relationships, hobbies, and relaxation not only enriches your personal life but also reinvigorates your professional endeavors.

View your career journey in product management as a marathon, not a sprint. By prioritizing balance, you not only enhance your current job satisfaction but also pave the way for enduring success and fulfillment in your career. Embrace the challenge of balancing the scales, and you'll find both your professional and personal lives thriving in harmony.

Enriching the Product Management Community

As you progress in your product management career, your engagement with the wider professional community becomes integral to your growth and the collective advancement of the field. Your journey, loaded with successes and learning opportunities, offers invaluable insights that can illuminate the paths for others in this dynamic domain. Here's how you can contribute meaningfully to the product management ecosystem:

Share Your Expertise: Your experiences are a wealth of knowledge. Channel this wealth by writing articles, leading workshops, or speaking at industry events. Your insights can serve as inspirations for others, providing guidance and motivation to fellow professionals and those aspiring to join the field.

Mentorship: Embrace the role of a mentor. Your expertise can significantly impact the careers of emerging product managers, helping them navigate the complexities of the role and accelerate their professional development. Reflect on the mentorship you've received and pay it forward, shaping the next generation of product leaders.

Engage in Professional Gatherings: Actively participate in conferences, workshops, and meetups. These are platforms not just for sharing knowledge but also for sparking dialogue about the evolving landscape of product management. Each interaction is an opportunity to influence and foster community growth.

Digital Engagement: Utilize online platforms to extend your reach. Whether through LinkedIn posts, a professional blog, or podcast appearances, your digital presence can significantly contribute to the discourse in product management, offering perspectives that resonate across the global community.

Innovate Within the Field: Your contributions can extend to shaping the discipline itself. Whether by developing new frameworks, advocating for the strategic value of product management, or engaging in academic research, your efforts can help define the future contours of the profession.

Cultivate Community: Whether by founding a discussion group or actively participating in existing forums, fostering a sense of community among product managers is invaluable. These spaces are not just for knowledge exchange but also for support, offering a network that can be essential in navigating the challenges and triumphs of the profession.

Your role in the product management ecosystem extends far beyond your immediate responsibilities. By sharing your knowledge, mentoring, engaging in community dialogues, and innovating within the field, you contribute to a vibrant, evolving professional community. This mutual exchange not only drives the industry forward but also enriches your own career journey, filling it with a sense of purpose and fulfillment.

Conclusion & A Final Reflection

As I pen down these final words, it's a moment of honor and gratitude. The past three years have been a journey similar to building a product from its promising idea to its fruition in the market. This book, envisioned with the ambition to empower product managers with the knowledge and strategies to excel in their roles, has evolved through thorough research, iterative enhancements, and invaluable insights from seasoned professionals.

This guide is more than just a collection of chapters; it's a companion for your journey in product management, designed to offer insights, strategies, and inspiration at every turn of your career. Your role in the dynamic field of product management is not just about managing products but about being a catalyst for innovation, an advocate for users, and a visionary in the tech landscape.

As you navigate the complexities and triumphs of your career, remember that the principles of product management—user focus, problem-solving, and value creation—are your guiding stars. Embrace the continuous evolution of technology and market trends whilst anchoring your decisions and strategies in these timeless principles.

Your journey is also a narrative within the larger story of the product management community. Your experiences, insights, and contributions are invaluable to nurturing a vibrant, collaborative, and forward-thinking community. Share your knowledge, mentor emerging talent, and engage in dialogues that drive our profession forward.

I am deeply thankful for your engagement with this book and invite you to share your reflections, critiques, and stories of how these insights have influenced your journey. Your feedback is not just valuable for the evolution of this book but is an inspiration that illuminates the path for future editions and endeavors. Please feel free to connect with your thoughts at shady@productcoaching.me.

Your journey in product management is one of continuous learning, innovation, and impact. Embrace it with the passion and determination that defines great product managers. Thank you for allowing this book to be a part of your professional adventure.

As we close this chapter, I look forward to hearing about your successes, learning from your challenges, and celebrating the mark you make in the world of product management. Here's to the journey ahead, filled with opportunities, growth, and transformative experiences.

www.ingramcontent.com/pod-product-compliance
Lightning Source LLC
Chambersburg PA
CBHW071721200326
41519CB00021BC/6518